CLASSICAL
ANATOLIA

The name Hellene no longer suggests a race but an intelligence, and the title Hellene is applied rather to those who share our culture than to those who share our blood.

ISOCRATES

CLASSICAL ANATOLIA

■■■■■■■■■■

The Glory of Hellenism

Text and photographs by
HARRY BREWSTER

I.B. Tauris & Co Ltd
Publishers
London · New York

Published in 1993 by
I.B. Tauris & Co Ltd
45 Bloomsbury Square
London WC1A 2HY

175 Fifth Avenue
New York
NY 10010

In the United States of America
and Canada distributed by
St Martin's Press
175 Fifth Avenue
New York NY 10010

A full CIP record is available from the British Library

Library of Congress cataloging-in-publication card number: available
A full CIP record is available from the Library of Congress

ISBN 1-85043-773-4 hardback

The publication of this book has been made possible by the
contribution of the Leventis Foundation, for which the author and
publishers express appreciation and gratitude.

Designed by Barbara Mercer
Typeset by Cambridge Composing (UK) Ltd, Cambridge

CONTENTS

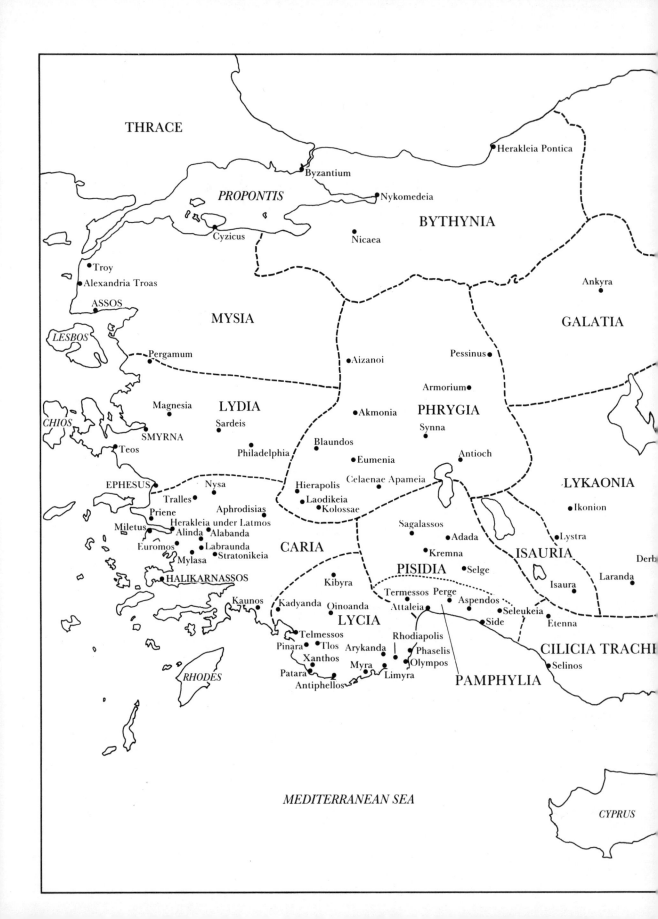

Sinope

EUXINE SEA

PAPHLAGONIA

Amaseia ● ● Kabeira

● Komana Pontica

Zela ●

PONTUS

● Tavium

ARMENIA

● Mazaka (Caesarea)

● Komana

CAPPADOCIA

● Tyana

Anazarba ● ● Kastabala

CILICIA PEDIAS

● Tarsus

Soli ●

MESOPOTAMIA

eukeia

SYRIA

| 0 | miles | 80 |

| 0 | km | 150 |

CLASSICAL ANATOLIA

INTRODUCTION

BY AN INTERPLAY OF GULFS AND ISLANDS ALONG THE EASTERN EDGES of Greece and the western coast of Turkey, the European continent comes in touch with Asia. They here finger each other, as it were, with the intimacy of an intercourse thousands of years old. This ancient closeness reached its apogee in the Hellenistic age. In dealing with the history of the Middle East of that period there is nowadays a tendency among scholars to regard the diffusion of Hellenism as a product of Macedonian colonialism and imperialism, which consisted in ruthless economic exploitation. As regards Greek mores and culture, it is claimed that the influence of Macedonian rule took effect only in the cities which were founded for political expansion.[1]

Whether such views are correct with reference to Egypt and Syria is a question which lies beyond the scope of this book. But as far as Asia Minor is concerned, if it is to be regarded as part of the Middle East, to assume that the diffusion of Hellenism in that region was merely the result of economic imperialism would amount not to a mere over-simplification but to an incorrect view of what actually took place.

It can be misleading to use terms such as 'colonialism' and 'imperialism', which have a vivid modern implication, in dealing with an age more than two thousand years ago when the ethos of people and the circumstances of life were totally different. Also misleading is the habit of lumping together different regions under the epithet of 'Middle East' because they were conquered by Alexander the Great and lie geographically between Europe and the Far East.

The expansion of Hellenism in Anatolia was of a unique kind. No doubt it gained momentum from Alexander's conquest and his widespread prestige. However, circumstances in that region were extremely different from those in Syria, Mesopotamia or Egypt. By far the greater number of the hundreds of city states that came into existence throughout Asia Minor consisted of indigenous centres of habitation which became thoroughly hellenized without ever being occupied by Macedonian or Greek colonists.

Beyond the sea and the Aegean islands there was no territory with which Greece had so deep a bond as with Asia Minor, a territory in which the native people, as in the rest of the Levant, were of non-Hellenic stock. Anatolia, the land of the east 'where the sun rises', was destined to share in the great wealth of Greek mythology and to contribute to it as no other land of the Middle East ever did to the same extent. This rapport had already begun in the days of Homer, centuries before the actual process of hellenization through the institution of the *polis*.

In the world of mythology Greeks and Anatolians were treading a ground that had no boundaries, a world in which they met and mingled. If Troy was the enemy city in the great Homeric saga, the Trojan heroes were Homeric heroes. Glaucus, the Lycian warrior who fell in battle smitten by Ajax, was the grandson of the Corinthian Bellerophon. Teucer was half-Greek and half-Anatolian, being the nephew of Priam himself. The priestly kings of Olba, far away in Cilicia, claimed descent from him and adopted his name. Tantalos, son of Zeus, was a Phrygian king who ruled over Lydia from Mount Sipylos. His punishment in the underworld for a crime he had committed is vividly described in the *Odyssey* (XI, 582). Pelops, his son, emigrated from Asia Minor to Greece where he prospered as a Greek hero after his victory in King Oinomaos' chariot race, whereby he won the hand of the king's daughter, Hippodamia. This event has come down to us immortalized in stone on the east pediment of the temple of Zeus at Olympia. There, it was said, Pelops had founded the Olympic games. His many descendants were no less eminent: Theseus, Agamemnon, Ajax among them. It is not surprising that the Peloponnesus should have derived its name from him.

Niobe, daughter of Tantalos and sister of Pelops, whose harrowing story about her daughters is first mentioned by Homer,[2] fled in distress to her father in Lydia where the gods turned her into stone on a cliff of Mount Sipylos.[3]

The story of Bellerophon also appears first in the *Iliad* (VI, 153ff.), where his exploits in Lycia are related by Glaucus. Not only did he kill the monster Chimaera, but he also fought the Amazons and eventually obtained in marriage the daughter of Iobates, King of Lycia, thereby founding the royal family of Lycia. While Bellerophon's offspring of Hellenic origin were integrated into the Lycian nation, the Chimaera of Hittite origin was absorbed into Greek mythology, giving rise to some of the most vivid Greek iconography.[4]

Another Anatolian monster, Typhon, whose den was in the Corycian cave of Cilicia, where he was born and reared, was destined to play an important part in Greek mythology. The fact that this monster, half-man and half-animal, father of the Chimaera and of the Hydra of Lerna, was the son of the earth-goddess Gaia and of Tantalus, did not make him any less Anatolian in origin. Ending up

10

crushed under Mount Aetna as punishment for having challenged Zeus, he figures prominently in mythology from Hesiod to Nonnos in the fifth century AD.

As for the Amazons, whom we again find mentioned by Homer,[5] there can be no doubt that they were Anatolian. These extraordinary women of a very warlike race had their home in remote Pontus,[6] but were destined none the less to play a major part in Greek mythology, giving rise to a most fruitful subject for treatment in the field of sculpture.[7]

As regards the major deities, Leto herself, mother of Apollo and Artemis, is believed to have been of Anatolian origin.[8]

Anatolian kings, nymphs and satyrs are not lacking in Greek mythology. Tmolos, a mythical king of Lydia, was a son of Ares. The great mountain overlooking Sardeis received its name from him. Glaucia, daughter of the Phrygian river god Skamandros, was taken to Greece by Heracles. Ilos, ancestor of Priam, Teucer, Telamon and Anchises, was the founder of Troy. Teuthras, king of Mysia, married Auge, daughter of Aleus, king of Tegea. She had been raped by Heracles and as a result gave birth to Telephos. Teuthras adopted Telephos and gave him his daughter in marriage. Marsyas, who dared challenge Apollo in a musical contest, was a Phrygian satyr. The famous contest was held at the Carian city of Nysa and the judges consisted of a panel of Nysaeans.[9] Midas, king of the Phrygians, disagreed with the verdict given by the judges in favour of Apollo and it was said that Apollo punished him by changing his ears into those of an ass. But the amusing stories told in Hellenistic times about the legendary Midas have of course little to do with the historical Midas, the last king of the Phrygians before the invasion of the Kimmerians.

It was in the Hellenistic age that several Graeco-Anatolian myths developed while others emerged perhaps for the first time. It is difficult to tell their age, the surviving written records being inadequate. One of these myths is the delightful story of Endymion, the handsome young shepherd of Mount Latmos in Caria, with whom Selene, the goddess of the moon, fell in love. According to one version of the myth she put him into perennial sleep after he had given her fifty daughters. Various versions of the tale developed in Hellenistic times, but the core of the story dates back to earlier days, since it is not only mentioned by Apollonius Rhodius in the third century BC but also by Plato in the preceding century.[10]

The abundance of the Graeco-Anatolian myths clearly shows that in this field of creative imagination there was a special relationship which sprung from the ethos of the people on both sides of the Aegean sea. This special relationship was indeed very ancient; but the actual hellenization of Anatolia, whereby people of non-Hellenic stock were transformed into Greeks, occurred some centuries later through the insitition of the *polis* and through its diffusion across most of Asia Minor.

No country in Europe, in the Mediterranean area and in the whole of the

Middle East can show so many splendid tokens of so many totally different successive civilizations as Turkey – Hittite, Urartian, Phrygian, Lydian, Lycian, Graeco-Roman, Armenian, Byzantine and Seljuk-Ottoman, each most distinctive, each of them following and virtually wiping one another out. Each was fundamentally different from the others in spirit, social customs, the arts, intellectual life generally and in practically every case religion and language. Greek pervaded the Graeco-Roman age and was also the language of the Byzantines, but a deep gulf separated the Christian from the pagan world, a gulf plainly manifest in virtually all branches of culture.

The most impressive ruins still standing in Asia Minor are not of the Byzantine age. They are remains of buildings erected in the course of many centuries before the Byzantine era during which the vast majority of the native people of Anatolia, whose ethnic origins were most varied, of their own free will were remoulded into citizens of the Greek *polis*. The impetus Alexander the Great gave to the expansion of Hellenism beyond the traditional confines of the Greek world was immense, but the spirit that made it possible was already in existence. It was Isocrates who towards the beginning of the fourth century was the first to put it into words: 'The name Hellene no longer suggests a race but an intelligence, and the title Hellene is applied rather to those who share our culture that to those who share our blood.'[11]

What follows is neither a guide book nor a travel book, though we are setting out on a voyage none the less. Our aim is to follow visually and historically, as well as geographically, the extraordinary penetration of Hellenism into the hinterland of Anatolia by examining the sites and architectural remains of the ancient cities that were originally *barbarian* centres of habitation, as well as the ruins of later Macedonian foundations, which survive as tokens of that development. Our attention will be drawn primarily to whatever still stands and strikes the eye in the landscape.

Even in the remoter parts of Anatolia, in Pisidia, Isauria and Rough Cilicia, where the inhabitants of antiquity were renowned for their wild habits and plundering propensities, the traveller will marvel at the sudden sight of the remains of a city, often most wonderfully situated – a Greek city with the characteristic features of Greek city life, the most civilized form of life in ancient times: a theatre, a council chamber, a music hall or odeion, an agora, a stoa, a gymnasium and a stadium as well as one or more temples. Only some of these buildings may still be standing in a fair or partial state of preservation, but traces of practically all can usually be seen. If you scratch the ground you may find a coin inscribed in Greek. How did it all happen, we may well ask?

The traveller familiar with Greece will have noticed there the paucity of sites, apart from the few famous ones, where cities stood, grew, flourished for many centuries and left remains that reflect this past. Even Pausanias, that indefatigable tourist of the second century AD, exclaimed:

Megalopolis, the foundation of which was carried out by the Arcadians with the utmost enthusiasm and viewed with the highest hopes by the Greeks, now lies in ruins, shorn of its beauty and ancient prosperity. I do not marvel at this, knowing that the daemonic power of heaven is always willing something new, and likewise that all things, strong and weak, increasing and decreasing, are being changed by Fortune who drives them with hard necessity according to her whim. Mycenae, which led the Greeks in the Trojan war, and Nineveh, where was the royal seat of the Assyrian kingdom, are utterly ruined and desolate, while Boeotian Thebes, once the chosen champion of Greece, has left its name to nothing but the fortified rock and a tiny population. Centres of overwhelming wealth in antiquity, like Egyptian Thebes and Minyan Orchomenos, are not so prosperous now in the power of riches as a single moderately wealthy individual, and Delos, the common marketing place of Greece, if you took away the sanctuary guards who come from Athens, would be utterly deserted as far as Delians are concerned. The sanctuary of Bel survives at Babylon, but of that Babylon which was once the greatest city the sun saw in its time, nothing remains but a fortress wall, such as it is with Tiryns in the Argolid. All these have been reduced by heaven to nothing, and Alexander's city in Egypt and the one of Seleukos on the Orontes were built yesterday and the day before, and have risen to such greatness and such prosperity because Fortune is favouring them.[12]

Megalopolis may have been one of the extreme cases of decay Pausanias came across, but the picture he gives us of the Greece he visited is of a country of little towns and villages thinly populated, not a country teeming with prosperity. The temples, public buildings and shrines, most of them still standing in his days and stocked with pieces of sculpture, betokened a prosperity of the past. Greece was in decline economically, demographically and culturally. Except in Athens very little was being built. There were no great cities and the famous ones of the past were shrinking and declining. Not so in Asia Minor. There, in addition to the thriving cities of the coast, the old Greek settlements such as Miletus, Ephesus and Smyrna, many scores of other Greek cities, large and small, studded the whole of Anatolia. They were still flourishing under the Roman principate and went on building on a lavish scale as well as maintaining and repairing the old buildings which from time to time suffered from earthquakes. Many are the remarkable ruins of these cities which reflect past prosperity. They began to be discovered and described by travellers at the end of the eighteenth century and in the nineteenth, by travellers such as Chandler, Leake and Fellows; but the ruins of some forgotten cities remain scarcely explored let alone excavated today.

Those cities, most of them inhabited by indigenous Anatolian people who at first spoke various native languages, became entirely Greek in the course of the three hundred years that preceded our era. The Greek colonies of the coast had been great cities of long standing for centuries before then, the cities of the Ionian league and the Aeolian cities further north. Their contribution to Greek civilization was immense in the fields of philosophy, literature and art. But even when they came under the sway of the kings of Lydia and subsequently of Persia, they tended to keep themselves aloof from the indigenous people of the hinterland. Doubtless there was considerable mutual influence in the cultural sphere between the Lydians and the neighbouring Greeks of the coastal settlements, but not until Alexander the Great and his successors did any Hellenic cities emerge from Lydian centres of habitation.

The first to establish close contact with the native inhabitants, with intermarriage ensuing, were the Dorian settlers on the coast of Caria, in particular the Halicarnassians who found that the Carians were akin to them in many respects. So in Caria the penetration of Greek culture had started by the fifth century BC. In the next century, under the influence of the Hekatomnid dynasts who fostered Hellenism and ruled the country as satraps virtually independent of the kings of Persia, Carian villages, such as Mylasa and Alabanda, became *poleis* – Greek cities with a Greek constitution and Hellenic buildings. Greek was adopted as the official language and coins with Greek legends were struck.

With Alexander's conquests the prestige of Hellenism became irresistible not only in Asia Minor. Every city of Anatolia and practically in the whole of the Middle East aspired to become, and to be regarded as, a Greek city. The policy of Alexander's successors, the Seleucid, Ptolemaic and Attalid kings, was to do everything to promote this process. New cities were founded and the transformation of old indigenous towns was accelerated, sometimes by an input of Macedonian settlers. In the third century BC Sardeis, which had been the capital of the Lydian kingdom and the centre of Lydian culture, was recognized by Delphi as a Greek city. By the first century BC the indigenous languages of Caria and Lycia were extinct, and so was Lydian in Lydia though it still survived in the outlying enclave of Kibyra.[13] Mysian was also extinct except in the extreme eastern area of the region, where the absence of cities had left the native people practically unaffected by Hellenism. In other parts of Anatolia wherever there were cities Greek was not only the official language but also the language spoken and written by all citizens, though they most likely knew also the language of the uneducated inhabitants wherever it survived. The indigenous languages spoken by the still barbarian people of the vast inland stretches of the country were more like patois, since they never assumed written form, not even to the extent Phrygian had done in the remote past. Education and literacy were entirely Greek.

The foundation of new cities and through them the diffusion of Hellenism by the Seleucid and Attalid kings in the wake of Alexander the Great constituted a policy which is in no way surprising – the policy of conquerors. Nor is it perhaps surprising that people whose level of culture and social development are comparatively low and whose ties with the past are tenuous, should be affected by conquerors who are ostensibly on a higher level of social organization and cultural achievement. But it is, to say the least, strange that nations possessing a notable ancient culture of their own, such as the Lydians, Phrygians or Lycians, should at a particular stage of their history give up their language, or lose the use of it, in favour of a different one and adopt a new way of life. This is what happened in Anatolia. In Egypt and Syria, where Hellenism flourished in the big cities, the indigenous people of the country as a whole remained attached to their roots; their language survived and so did their way of thinking which came to the fore again when Hellenism started to decline in the Middle East.

The conversion of the Anatolian people to Hellenism, whereby Asia Minor became a Greek world in which the indigenous cultural manifestations vanished, or survived only in a hellenized form, is an interesting anthropological event the causes of which are complex, varying from region to region. One important fact was simply that the ancient Anatolian civilizations which had preceded the advent of Hellenism, in particular the Phrygian and Lydian, were in a state of advanced decay – indeed moribund – by the time Alexander overran Asia Minor. Scarcely any elements of those ancient cultures, except to some extent in the field of religion, were surviving in the fourth and third centuries BC. The indigenous roots were by then not deep enough or strong enough to withstand the impact of Hellenism after two hundred years of Persian domination.[14] This, however, can hardly be said of the Lycians, whose culture and way of life had until then remained remarkably alive. And yet by the third century BC they had given up their language for Greek under no trace of duress and had wholeheartedly adopted the Greek *diaita* or way of life.

We must always bear in mind the irresistible prestige of Hellenism as the result of Alexander the Great's conquests which led to the formation of one world. For anyone not born a Greek who wished to make his way in life and achieve something, it was essential not only to know Greek fluently if not perfectly, but actually to become Greek, to absorb its culture, to follow its *diaita*. No one could claim to be Greek, no one could be active as such without being the citizen of a *polis*, whether he resided in it or lived elsewhere. Cultural participation was essential even if political activity was not possible.

At the beginning of our era hellenization had reached completion in so far as the cities were concerned. The contribution to civilization by the Ionian colonies of the coast has always been fully recognized; but it should be stressed that the contribution of the hellenized cities of Anatolia, most of whose citizens were of indigenous stock, was also very great. Pausanias, to whom we are indebted for his invaluable description of second-century AD Greece, was a Lydian. Strabo, the great geographer who will be our companion in much of the following exploration, was a native of Pontus. Epictetus, the famous ex-slave Stoic philosopher, was a Phrygian from Hierapolis. Dozens of the eminent personalites in the sphere of philosophy, literature, rhetoric, history, architecture and sculpture, throughout the Hellenistic and Graeco-Roman ages, came from hellenized Anatolia (see Appendix A).

What did it mean to be a Greek city; what did a barbarian centre of habitation have to achieve and establish to be able to regard itself, and be regarded, as a Greek city?

Of course the official language had to be Greek, but this was only one of several essential features. Whether subject to a tyrant, a satrap, a dynast or an imperial governor, and whether more or less self-governing, as in many cases the Anatolian city was, its administration and cultural structure had to be modelled on the basis of metropolitan cities like Athens. It had to take shape in keeping with what the *polis*, the Greek city state, implied. The constitution of the *polis*, reflected in the buildings it needed, was based on the institution of the *ekklesia*, or assembly of the citizen body, and on the *boule*, or council, which together ruled the city. The members of the council were originally elected by the assembly, but in course of time they ceased to be elected, their office becoming hereditary on the basis of wealth in the later Graeco-Roman age. So the constitution of the cities in Anatolia became progressively oligarchic, a process encouraged by Rome. At first the magistrates too were elected by the assembly, but as time went on they were appointed by the members of the council who proposed their nomination to the *ekklesia*, after choosing them from among themselves. The task of the assembly, from the second century onwards, amounted merely to approving any resolution submitted to it by the council. In fact little by little the assembly became no more than a confirmatory body. None the less, the *demos*, or people, of whom the *ekklesia* was the assembly, never ceased to be mentioned on inscriptions side by side with the *boule*, or council, for any enactment or public decision reached. This formality was maintained as long as the *polis* survived.

The principal magistrates, though their functions and names could vary from city to city, were the following:

The *strategoi*, who brought resolutions to the assembly for acceptance and were responsible for the general management of the community, including public finances. They also arrested those charged with banditry. In some cities they were called *probouli* since they were members of the council.

The *grammateos*, or clerk, who dealt with several bureaucratic details of administration.

The *gymnasiarch*, in charge of the gymnasium and education generally.

The *agoranomos*, controller of the market and responsible for establishing food prices.

The *astynomos*, whose duty was to see that houses and walls were kept in repair, and who was responsible also for water supply, drains and fountains. He could impose fines within his field of administration.

The *eirenarch*, taking charge of the maintenance of order, responsible for public order and morals. Under his command was a body of men called *diognitai*, who made actual arrests and captured bandits.

The *paraphylax*, with duties similar to those of the eirenarch, but mainly in charge of the city's rural territory.

An institution essential to the city state was the gymnasium for the training in athletics of the ephebes, youths from the age of about 17 to 19, and their preparation for citizenship. In Athens the training was mainly in athletics and of a military nature, but in the Ionian cities and in those of Anatolia generally the gymnasium was also educational in a general sense, grammar, literature and rhetoric being taught. For the purpose of giving the mind its Hellenistic stamp education was of course fundamental, and the gymnasium was the institution through which this hallmark was implanted.

In the bigger cities there was not only a gymnasium for the young but also one for adult citizens – a sort of club. At the head of the institution stood a gymnasiarch appointed by the council, a magistrate of considerable importance. He was usually a rich munificent citizen prepared to shoulder the responsibility of running an institution of cardinal position in the life the *polis* and to bestow lavish donations to enhance its importance – including, of course, his own prestige. So important was the institution that no city in Anatolia and the Middle East could claim to be a Greek *polis*, as most of them wished to be, unless it had a gymnasium.

In the smaller cities of Anatolia we often find only a palaestra to serve the essential physical exercises and educational tasks of the institution. For athletic pursuits that required an open space such as running and throwing the discus, which could not be practised in the gymnasium proper, a race course would be used.

A stadium would always have to be provided, a long open structure or running track flanked with rows of seats, for races in which all citizens competed with each other and took pride.

Of course in every city there stood a number of temples, often splendid edifices, colonnaded and built according to the classical Greek patterns, with columns usually fluted even in the Roman age, the order being Ionic or Corinthian more often than Doric and always in conformity with the well-established rules. The gods worshipped consisted of the Greek pantheon which could easily absorb local cults and alien deities of older civilizations or at any rate camouflage them; for instance, Cybele took on the garb of Artemis and Ishtar that of Aphrodite. Greek religion was always tolerant and eclectic.

From an architectural point of view the remains of such temples, whether impressive or inconsiderable, stand as tokens of the splendour of these Anatolian cities which never shrank from spending lavishly on their construction, thereby displaying their Hellenism. But apart from this aspect the temple did not stand for a specific or exclusive Greek institution, as for instance the gymnasium did or the bouleuterion or the theatre. No earlier civilization ever had a theatre, whereas they always had temples.

Perhaps the most characteristic feature of the city was indeed the theatre which reflected much that was essential in the Greek way of life. No self-respecting Anatolian city could afford not to have at least one theatre, often built on a large scale to accommodate most of the citizens. In addition to theatrical performances it was used by the assembly to congregate in, and also for various cultural activities. The theatrical presentations consisted mainly of dramatic works, especially comedies which were being written in great numbers and for which prizes were given throughout the Hellenistic period and in the first two centuries of our era. Unfortunately the texts of these plays have failed to come down to us. At the end of the second century they began to be supplanted by the mime which came to dominate the stage having become extremely fashionable, until Christianity put an end altogether to theatrical performances.

Wherever their remains are to be seen in Anatolia theatres and stadia consitute the most eloquent tokens of the Hellenic *diaita*, or way of life. They survive as emblems of much that is typical of our western civilization – theatrical performances, athletics and games. No preceding civilization ever built so extensively to serve the requirements of cultural activities and public recreation.

Musical performances also formed an important part of the cultural life of the *polis*, for which a specific building had to be provided – the odeion. Most cities aimed at possessing one. It consisted of a structure very similar to the bouleuterion, but was often furnished with a roof, probably for acoustic reasons, which was usually made of timber.

Of course the agora, featuring prominently at the heart of the city, stood for an essential element of *polis* life. Here, besides marketing, all kinds of activities took place such as assembly meetings. More often than not it was flanked by a stoa, another characteristic component of the *diaita*, which consisted of a long colonnaded edifice containing shops of various kinds.

In addition to these basic elements there were other architectural structures that reflected the city life of the Hellenistic and Graeco-Roman world such as city gates, fountains, libraries, granaries and buildings to house various administrative services.

It is important not to lose sight of the fact that the hellenization of Anatolia eastward, from the coastal regions already hellenized in the course of the three or four centuries preceding our era, was not hindered but furthered by the expansion of Roman rule. Where the Seleucid and Attalid kings had left incomplete the transformation of indigenous Anatolia into a Greek world, the Romans carried on the process with vigour. They came to realize that the most efficacious method of promoting prosperity and at the same time consolidating their dominion was to found cities wherever a core of Greek or hellenized settlers was available. This policy, which had been started by Pompey, was adopted by Augustus and energetically pursued by the succeeding emperors in the first and second centuries AD. The Roman emperors were wise enough to realize that much of the prosperity of the empire depended on the well-being and vitality of the cities. Therefore the policy of the principate was to favour their local economy and self-reliance, as long as they remained loyal, often conferring privileges and sponsoring the erection of spendid buildings. At the same time there was never any attempt to change the cities from being typically Greek, in other words to latinize them. Being appreciative of the eminence of Greek culture, Rome never tried to impose its language on those who spoke Greek. The constitution of the existing Hellenic cities would continue to be that of the *polis*, and so would that of the newly founded ones. The official language would be Greek, and a considerable degree of local autonomy would be afforded. Old tribal centres were transformed into *poleis* so that by the beginning of the third century AD there were more than three hundred cities in Anatolia. Even where no conspicuous ruins survive an inscription or two will be usually found recording the enactments of the council and the people – the *boule* and the *demos*.

Anatolia was honeycombed with cities which enjoyed not only considerable prosperity until the third century but also a good measure of administrative autonomy. Many were declared 'free' by successive Roman emperors, which meant not only that they could run their own administration but also that they were relieved of taxation. What they could not do was to wage war upon each other as the cities of Greece used to do. But rivalry and mutual emulation were expressed in the sphere of architectural achievements, games, theatrical performances and festivals.

Most of the ruins we see today belong to the age of the Roman principate, in particular those first two hundred years of our era during which money and generous benefactors were plentiful. Because of a real mania to build anew on a grand scale and because of frequent earthquakes which necessitated reconstruction or replacement, less has survived of the Hellenistic period, but enough to show that continuity in the style of architecture and in the method of building, of which ashlar masonry is such a striking element, was never interrupted and came to an end only with the Byzantines.

Although every city was a centre of Hellenism, beyond its territorial confines the rural Anatolian people, scarcely affected by the civilizing wave from the west, went on leading their tribal life and speaking their indigenous languages for a long time, especially in the vast uplands of the interior. They remained uncouth and often given to robbery in the mountainous regions even under Roman rule. As late as the third century AD there were parts of Galatia where the country people still spoke their Gallic language. But education, in which literacy would play a part, had to be Greek. As the Byzantine age set in, Greek as a language spread to the entire population through Christianity. But not Hellenism: by then the *polis* was dead.

In the second century of our era Tatian, who as a young man before his conversion to Christianity travelled from his native Syria to Rome, was deeply shocked by the particularism of the cities, each with its own laws. 'There should be one code of laws,' he protested, 'and one political organization.' This totalitarianism is what happened under the Byzantines, stifling the vitality of the cities.

It is a fallacy to think that the end of the city state came about as the result of Macedonian military expansion and the imperialism of Rome. In Anatolia the contrary happened. It was in the Hellenistic period and Roman age that most of the cities came into their own, very many of them of barbarian origin. Of course they had no political power, but most of them never had had any, and the fact that they could not wage war upon each other was to their economic benefit. So they became rich and flourished, retaining at the same time their sense of identity. Municipal autonomy was not ineffective or fruitless; it allowed sufficient scope for emulation, intellectual activities and the construction of buildings worthy of the constitution of a *polis* and all that this meant. Wealth entailed patronage, which the arts and intellectual activities required.

When and how did all this come to an end? How was it that these cities, the embodiment of Hellenism in Asia Minor, declined and died out after flourishing for more than six centuries? What brought about this extinction?

Intermittent incursions and raids, pillaging and depredations by Persians, Arabs and pirates from the end of the sixth century onwards were only a secondary cause. Decay in the cities, or more exactly decline in the city state, had started long before. The Eastern Roman Empire went on for a whole millennium with alternating periods of splendour and reverses, but the city state, the *polis*, was dead in Anatolia by the sixth century AD, though of course a few towns in their places, with a bishop presiding instead of a council, would carry on a dwindling existence for a number of centuries. Except for some churches, monasteries and fortifications nothing lasting was built and only defensive walls were sometimes repaired.

The main causes of decline and final extinction were various as well as complex. They can be examined, however, under four interconnected headings: the sinking away of the council as the governing body, the disappearance of the gymnasium as the educational institution, bureaucratic centralization, and Christianity.

First the assembly faded away as a basis of political and social influence. But decline in democracy did not mean decline in prosperity or in civic pride. The council, instead of being elected, became a hereditary body of rich citizens who could afford the financial burden involved. They were called decurions in the Roman age and sat for life. As time went by they had to have a substantial property qualification, usually meaning land which passed from father to son.

As long as the civic spirit lasted, and during the first two centuries of our era it was still very high, the decurions went on spending generously for the city's needs, especially, though not only, on municipal festivals, games and splendid buildings. Mainly at their expense the city's amenities were being constantly looked after and improved. The principal streets were kept paved, often sheltered by colonnades. The drainage system and public water supply had to be properly maintained, and likewise the public baths. The fuel for heating them had to be provided. All such services involved considerable expenditure, much of which was met by munificent decurions who took pride in their city. Indeed, as far as all this was concerned, there was a notable inter-city rivalry. But the palmy days did not go on indefinitely and there came a time when the normal expenditure the decurions would defray became so great that even wealthy citizens began to find the office a burden rather than an honour. So the notables would refrain from standing for office.

It was important for the empire that the cities should be kept alive and prosperous under efficient administration: the collection of revenue due to the central imperial authority was the responsibility of the decurions. Legislation was introduced by the emperors to rectify the situation by making the office of decurion compulsory on those whose property placed them under such obligation. But the rich were able to evade the new laws by obtaining immunities. Corruption became rife and the city spirit declined, to a great extent also as the result of Christianity. Having become progressively influential in the fourth century, the Church was able to obtain for the clergy immunity from service on the council,[15] and so more and more decurions opted to become members of the clergy. Then the attraction of the great capital, Constantinople, meant that senatorial rank was much sought after and obtained by the rich when the rank, which held the privilege of immunity from service on the council, was thrown open to all notables of the empire. Fewer and fewer would stand for the office of decurion. Generous benefactors for the city services and embellishments so plentiful in the first two centuries of our era, ceased to obtain in the fourth century and thereafter. Endowments and bequests went to the Church. Buildings began to be neglected and few edifices were erected after the fifth century apart from churches and monasteries embodying a spirit that turned away from city life proper. In the sixth century there were scarcely any councils left; Justinian bemoaned the fact in 536.[16] But even before they ceased to exist they had lost control of the city administration which from the fifth century onwards was taken over by the centralized imperial bureaucracy and by the bishops who appointed the magistrates. Bureaucracy had a crippling effect on the *polis* despite the efforts of the emperors to bring back life to it. City patriotism and pride, which until the end of the second century had been much alive, not merely faded but vanished.

Undoubtedly the disappearance of the gymnasium as the educational institution, which occurred in the fourth century, contributed a great deal to the decline in this city spirit. Decline in this institution is already noticeable when the huge Roman baths, the *thermae*, appear on the scene. Bathing became the chief pursuit, gradually displacing the gymnasia in which bathing was secondary to athletics and intellectual activities. Until the third century the Anatolian cities continued to attach supreme importance to the gymnasia. In every city care was taken to keep the buildings in good repair and there was often eagerness to build a new one whenever necessary. The institution continued to be alive throughout that period, but the attitude of the Romans to this attachment is worth noting. It is most cogently expressed in a letter the emperor Trajan wrote to Pliny the Younger, who had been sent as legate to Bithynia with the task of controlling the economy and putting the administration in order: 'These petty Greeks (*Graeculi*, Trajan calls them), I know, have a foible for gymnasia; hence, perhaps, the citizens of Nicaea have been somewhat too ambitious in planning one; but they must be contented with such a one as will be sufficient to their circumstances.'[17]

The taste for *thermae* began to spread in Anatolia, and great bath-houses were constructed all over Asia Minor. Trajan uses the verb *indulgere* to express the passion Greeks and hellenized Anatolians had for the gymnasium, but the Roman passion for indulging in water of different temperatures was no less keen and evidently contagious.

Ephebic training, the backbone of citizenship in the Greek pagan world, is last heard of in the first part of the fourth century AD. The gymnasium became extinct because of Christianity and its influence. The buildings which had risen to provide for that institution and had come to adorn so many cities were deserted and the magnificent baths of the Graeco-Roman age were turned into Byzantine basilicas by the addition of an apse. Bathing was first frowned upon and then given up altogether. The Church disapproved of nudity, the cult of athletics, and of a system of education based on pagan principles, ideals and culture generally. The public educational system changed radically in character and so that spirit died out which had for so many centuries informed city life.

Pagan sacrifices were prohibited and the temples were either destroyed by mobs inflamed with intolerance or allowed to decay and gradually pulled to pieces for building material. In a few cases they were turned into churches. On the other hand orphanages and hospitals were established by the Church, but they failed to form part of that integral city life of which the citizen of the past had been an organic member, nor were they built in a manner that formed part of an architectural whole and solid enough to withstand the inclemencies of time. Ashlar masonry consisting of finely cut rectangular blocks of stone fitted together without mortar, a most distinctive feature of Greek architecture in Anatolia which endured throughout the Roman principate, gave way to building with much smaller stones of any shape stuck together with mortar which tended to crumble away in the course of centuries. The very fine church of the Alahan monastery in the Tauros mountains retains strong pagan architectural features including ashlar masonry because it was built in the fifth century AD. Thereafter this form of masonry disappears. In the Byzantine age architecture was no longer meant for external display in which the eye delighted. The beauty of Byzantine churches is inside the building. Man turned inward. Monasticism, imported from Egypt by Saint Basil in the fourth century, swept through Anatolia, bleeding the city of its population by drawing away men and women to a life of contemplation and prayer.

Not only did the Church disapprove of the educational system which the gymnasium embodied and discountenance the temples even when paganism was virtually extinct, but it also opposed theatrical performances because they were closely connected with the pagan world of the past and its moral indulgence. So the theatre, that very characteristic feature of the *polis* where all sorts of cultural activities took place, was banned or fell into disuse.

The pagan world passed into the Christian world, a totally different world socially and culturally, let alone religiously. Though the change came gradually the break in the end was profound and radical. The splendours of the Byzantine world were indeed of a very different nature.

A mere look at the ruins of these Greek cities in Anatolia, such as they are to be seen today, is enough to make one realize how their adherence to a uniform pattern closely reflected a specific way of life. There came a time when that life disintegrated and so the buildings lost their *raison d'être*. They could only survive as ghosts of the past, at the mercy of the disruptive forces of time. But this remarkable past, surviving in us in some way, is of importance. The amazing process of transformation whereby the indigenous Anatolian people became hellenized and greatly contributed to the cultural heritage of the Hellenistic and Graeco-Roman world is worth following by taking stock of the sites of their cities and architectural remains and by delving into their history as far as the surviving records enable us to do.

We shall begin in those regions in the south-west of Asia Minor bordering on the Aegean sea, Caria and Lycia, where before anywhere else in Anatolia Greek civilization percolated inland. We shall then proceed eastward and northward in the footsteps of that thrust to which Alexander the Great gave momentum – in Pamphylia, Pisidia, Isauria, Cilicia and Lykaonia. Finally we shall return to the west through Phrygia and Lydia, ending our survey in the northern regions bordering the Euxine Sea.

By successive encounters with the surviving architecture of the Greek cities, most of them of barbarian origin, that arose and flourished in the lesser as well as in the better known regions, we may look into this mirror of the past, whether on the shores of a blue lake or in a sequestered valley, among thistles and mountain herbs on precipitous heights or in a wild forest glade, in thickets of jungly vegetation or on the cliffs of an awesome gorge, where a most civilized way of life can be conjured up.

HELLENISTIC & GRAECO-ROMAN ARCHITECTURE

BEFORE APPROACHING WHAT SURVIVES OF THE HELLENISTIC AND Graeco-Roman buildings of Anatolia, and delving into their historical background site by site, let us first consider their architectural nature on a comprehensive basis. The remains surveyed in this volume, which are those that survive more conspicuously in the landscape, extend historically over a period of about six hundred years, from the end of the fourth century BC to the beginning of the third century AD. This architecture is therefore Hellenistic and Graeco-Roman, terms which are used throughout the text. But strictly speaking it is impossible to draw a chronological line between the end of the Hellenistic architecture and the beginning of the Graeco-Roman style, since most of the essential elements of Greek architecture endured until late in the Roman age; the whole period could quite appropriately be termed Hellenistic. The architects were Greek or hellenized non-Greeks and continued to be so. When Pliny the Younger, Trajan's legate in Bithynia, applied to the emperor for a suitable architect to be sent out to him from Rome for the reconstruction of some buildings in Nicaea, the emperor wrote back that there were plenty of architects in Anatolia who could do the job and that in any case Greece was far nearer to him; architects went from Greece to Rome, not in the opposite direction.[1]

Of course certain characteristic Roman elements such as the arch, the vault, the unfluted column, begin to appear in the first century AD and there are a few sites, like those of Side and Aspendos for example, where the ruins are predominantly Roman in character as well as in origin chronologically. But by and large throughout the whole period covered by this survey, the typical Hellenic elements of architecture predominate on all the sites of ancient cities, whatever the century their remains belong to, elements that are basic: the Ionic and Corinthian orders, the architrave, entablature and pediment, Doric triglyphs and dentils, the shape of the theatre always carved into the hillside which has to exceed the semi-circle, polygonal and ashlar masonry and other elements. Many of these were adopted by the Romans, though not all.

The *polis*, or city state, was the social, administrative and political organization which in the form of self-contained nuclei of habitation extended all over the Greek world, each of them more or less independent according to circumstances and periods of history. The principal buildings appertaining to this way of life, which the *polis* needed in order to function and which characterized it architecturally, were: the temple for divine worship, the gymnasium and palaestra for physical training and education, the theatre for theatrical performances, the stadium for running competitions and games, the council chamber, or bouleuterion, in which meetings would be held for political and administrative deliberations, the odeion for musical performances, the stoa for shops, to which can be added the nymphaion, or fountain house, baths, and the aqueduct for water supply characteristic of the Graeco-Roman age. The agora, or market place, essential to the life of the *polis*, was not a building but an open space round which stoas were erected and from which sometimes flights of steps rose to a higher level in order to accommodate the citizens for deliberations. The *ekklesia*, or assembly of the citizens, would usually meet in the agora, which as a pivotal centre of activity would give rise to the layout and general features of the city. Important buildings would often stand in its vicinity such as the bouleuterion. Conspicuous remains of these buildings can be seen not only on the sites of the well-known Ionian cities of the Anatolian coast, such as Ephesus, Priene and Miletus, and at Pergamon, the capital of the Attalid kingdom, but also on the sites of the hellenized cities of the interior.

In the western Greek world there are temples still standing more or less complete which were built as early as the sixth century BC; in Anatolia not one survives, even partially, from that period or even considerably later. Of the archaic Artemision at Ephesus, which burned down towards the end of the fourth century BC, and of its rebuilt successor little more than foundations remain *in situ*. Some columns of the beautiful temple of Athena at Priene, re-erected in recent years, belong to the middle of the fourth century BC. At Didyma there are only three columns still standing of the great temple, which belong to the second century BC. But apart from the scanty remains of these magnificent edifices all the temples of the coastal cities have fallen into pitiful ruin, most of them practically obliterated like the huge temple of Hadrian at Cyzicus which was even larger than the Artemision of Ephesus.

The earliest temple in Asia Minor of which enough is still standing to convey a visual idea of what it was like when it was erected, as well as an impression of its pristine beauty, is the temple of Zeus at Olba in Cilicia Tracheia. It is also the earliest Corinthian temple we know of, having been built at the very beginning of the third century BC.

Three other temples in Anatolia, all built considerably later, have survived more or less to the same extent: the Ionic temple of Aphrodite at Aphrodisias (Pl. 9) built in the first century BC, the Ionic temple of Zeus at Aizanoi (Pl. 44) built in the days of Hadrian and the Corinthian temple of Zeus at Euromos (Pl. 2) which also dates from the second century AD. The beautiful temple of Artemis at Sardeis (Pl. 45) is still very impressive, though only two columns are standing to their full height while others only rise to about half or a third of their original stature. However the impression is of a structure of great magnificence, and full of fascinating details, delightfully set in a beautiful landscape. But the impression remains somewhat confused, partly because it was built in stages and not completed until centuries after its original planning. These four temples were built in hellenized cities whose inhabitants were originally indigenous, in other words barbarians.

In the Hellenisitic age the Doric order for temples fell gradually into disuse. In fact there came a time when it was regarded as no longer suitable for temples, a view held by Hermogenes the great Hellenistic architect and innovator of the second century BC, who was held in high esteem. Vitruvius apparently thought that he was a native of the hellenized city of Alabanda,[2] whereas he was born at Priene. Moreover, according to Vitruvius he invented the pseudo-dipteral temple, which is not quite true since there were a couple built before his day. However, this type of temple was widely adopted in Anatolia under the influence of Hermogenes after he had built the famous temple of Artemis Leukophryene at Magnesia on the Maeander, which was immensely admired; only some stones survive lying in a jumble on the ground. Unfortunately the writings of Hermogenes are lost and we know of them only through Vitruvius. The architectural innovations of Hermogenes brought about a new style which characterized Hellenistic temple architecture and deeply influenced Roman and Renaissance architecture through Vitruvius, who devoted much attention to him. The temples of Aphrodite at Aphrodisias and of Artemis at Sardeis were also pseudo-dipteral, as was the temple of Zeus at Aizanoi in Phrygia. So, too, was the temple of Augustus and Roma at Ankara, built towards the end of the first century BC, of which only the cella is still standing. There are remains of pseudo-dipteral temples on other sites, but in poor condition.

A peripteral temple is a building with a single colonnade, or peristasis, surrounding the cella. The temple of Athena at Priene built by Pytheos, the architect of the Mausoleum of Halikarnassos, is peripteral, as are the Corinthian temples of Zeus at Olba and at Euromos.

A dipteral temple is a building with a double peristasis, like the temple of Artemis at Ephesus and the Didyma temple.

The pseudo-dipteral temple is an edifice which could be regarded as a dipteros but without the inner peristasis, or pteron as it was also called, so that a much wider space is left between the single peristasis and the cella than in the peripteros or than the equivalent spaces in the dipteral temple. Moreover a wider intercolumnar space between the two central columns of the front row and of the back row of columns was sometimes a feature, as in the temple at Magnesia on the Maeander, and also other intercolumnar innovations. But the greater space surrounding the cella was the main innovation. As well as being regarded as pleasing visually it provided much greater room to walk about in, an amenity much appreciated by the citizens and worshippers. Hermogenes' idea, which gained ground in Hellenistic architecture, was to achieve greater lightness in the character of the structure as compared with the massiveness of earlier temples.[3]

The prostyle temple, a more modest type of building consisting of a cella, or naos, with a columnar porch in front, is often found on the sites of hellenized cities in Anatolia. Even more frequently seen is the distyle-in-antis temple, consisting merely of two columns in the porch between the antae, i.e. projections of the side walls of the naos. This was a much less expensive kind of building than the peripteral or pseudo-dipteral temple and therefore more within the reach of the economy of small cities. Excellent specimens of the prostyle temple can be seen still standing at Adada in Pisidia whose ashlar masonry is particularly fine. They date from the second century AD.

As time went on a more secular way of life seems to have developed. Although the cult of the deified Roman emperor gained a central place in the institutionalized affairs of the city state in the Graeco-Roman age, this was a rather formal aspect of its life due to political circumstances. The many rich patrons of that era seem to have preferred to lavish their generous donations on the construction or repair of big theatres and other sumptuous edifices or on festivals, in order to enhance the amenities of life, rather than on large and expensive temples. This impression is confirmed by the sites of many Anatolian cities.

Columns are vulnerable and easily collapse in the course of centuries; walls are more enduring, but in Anatolia the theatre has proved to be the structure that has withstood weather conditions and the violence of earthquakes, as well as human interference, far better than any other building essential to the life of the *polis*.

Nearly all the two to three hundred Greek and hellenized cities which came to life across Anatolia could boast of having a theatre. Of these at least sixty survive in a good or fair state of preservation. No one travelling in Asia Minor can avoid being struck by the impressive presence of the theatre not only on the sites of the famous ancient Greek cities of the coast but also on those of the very many hellenized inland cities. Except for a few that are typically Roman in structure, these theatres are all basically Hellenistic, including those that were built in the Graeco-Roman age, for they follow the characteristic Anatolian Greek model of construction and plan. Many, of course, have been modified or remodelled in the Roman age to suit the stage requirements and tastes of those times.

Vitruvius has given us a detailed description of the rules that govern the plan of the Greek theatre and those that determine the nature of the Roman theatre, showing the difference between the two very clearly. The Hellenistic theatres in Anatolia by no means always comply with these norms. However they are basically Greek in planning and their features differ from the Roman type of theatre in several respects.

The *cavea*, or auditorium, is always built into the hillside which holds its bulk except for the two projecting ends on either side. These are supported by walls, the *analemmata*. In the Roman theatre on the other hand the *cavea* is usually, though not always, held up by walls all round.

In shape the Greek *cavea* always exceeds the semi-circle to a greater or lesser extent, whereas the Roman *cavea* is always semi-circular.

The stage building, consisting of *skene* and *proskenion*, always stands detached from the *cavea* leaving a passage at both ends, the *parodoi*, for the public to enter. In the Roman theatre the stage building stands right up against the *cavea* and an arched entrance to the auditorium is provided at each end.

In the Hellenistic theatre the *proskenion* was supported by pillars which rested on the same level as that of the orchestra and rose to a height which varied between eight and twelve feet (2.4–3.6 metres). It was used mainly as a background for the actors who played their parts in the orchestra. At a later stage in the Hellenistic era the platform on top of the *proskenion* became a proper stage to which the actors had access by an inner ladder or steps and on which they would perform parts of the play's action. The *skene* rose as a wall behind the *proskenion*, at first with one door or opening in the centre and later with three in many cases, through which the actors would come and go.

In the Roman theatre the stage building was raised to a height equal to that of the *cavea*; the stage itself, or *pulpitum*, stretched from one end to the other at a low level a few feet above the orchestra, the *skene* rising behind elaborately adorned with architectural features. The actors would play their parts on the stage only, the orchestra being used as part of the auditorium with rows of wooden seats for the spectators, which could be easily removed leaving the pit free for shows of wild beasts and gladiatorial contests.

When many Hellenistic theatres were to a greater or lesser extent Romanized in the Graeco-Roman age, the stage building was reshaped or rebuilt and in some cases brought close up to the *cavea*, cutting across the *analemmata* as we can see in the theatre of Alinda. Excellent examples of un-Romanized Hellenistic theatres are at Pinara, Antiphellos and Arycanda, still in a remarkably good state of preservation. There are others that have been only slightly modified in later times. Some, though built in the Graeco-Roman period, retained certain Hellenistic characteristics nevertheless, for instance the theatre of Patara.

What was represented, we may well ask, in all these theatres? Of course classical dramatic works continued to be performed, but with the advent of the New Comedy it was especially this type of play that became extremely popular. Comedies were being constantly written, competitions organized at festivals and prizes for them awarded. Unfortunately the texts of most of these plays have failed to come down to us. When mimes became increasingly popular they tended to oust the play proper, finally supplanting it towards the end of the Graeco-Roman era.

Most Anatolian theatres, with their stage-building detached from the *cavea*, were structurally unsuited to the Roman type of spectacle, gladiatorial contests and wild-beast shows, so we can assume that they were never used for this purpose. But of course several were modified to serve exactly that end, like for instance the theatre of Aphrodisias, or were actually built for it primarily, as the Xanthos theatre probably was. Although the pleasure derived from the sight of gladiatorial contests and of wild beasts fighting with one another was something alien to the psychology of Greeks and hellenized Anatolians, and therefore the need to provide buildings for such performances was never felt throughout the Hellenistic age and early Graeco-Roman period, none the less there came a time when the influence of Rome in this particular field started to spread. By the middle of the second century AD these performances had become fashionable even in Anatolia.

It is worth noting, however, that the amphitheatre, that typically Roman circular building for spectacular shows of a ruthless nature, is absent in Asia Minor except for one, at Pergamon. Strabo refers to an amphitheatre at Nysa, but the archaeological remains show that he must have meant the stadium, which was modified or rebuilt in Roman times. It was made to curve round and close the end of the course which would otherwise always be left open. Of this Romanized type of stadium the one at Aphrodisias is in a much better state of preservation.

Being usually built into a hillside or within natural slopes, the stadium, like the theatre, has escaped the disruptive forces of nature to a greater extent than most other structures. Many can therefore still be seen in Anatolia. These stadia, or running-tracks, played a very important part in the life of the *polis* and most cities could boast one. Every citizen had been brought up in the gymnasium, where he had been trained to run and compete with his fellow youths in the palaestra. The stadium was used for the great running competitions, an important feature of the festivals which were held at regular and frequent intervals.

The structure consisted of a levelled-out space 600–700 feet in length, or about 200 metres, surrounded by rising steps in stone except at one end. On the sites of hellenized cities we sometimes see stadia shorter than the standard

Olympic length owing to the nature of the terrain, as for instance at Arykanda. Aphrodisias, on the other hand, has a magnificent specimen of a very large stadium (Pl. 10).

Of the other buildings belonging to the *polis* the bouleuterion and the odeion have survived relatively well, though not nearly so well as the theatre.

The bouleuterion, where the councillors met, could be a rectangular building in which rows of steps for the councillors to sit on were placed at right angles to one another – there is a classical example of this type at Priene; or a rectangular building with semi-circular, theatre-like accommodation inside, of which the Miletus council chamber was an outstanding specimen. But the bouleuterion could also be a semi-circular structure built into elevated ground, of which there is a splendid example at Nysa, the *gerontikon*, designed for the elders of the city to meet in. It is still in an excellent state of preservation (Pl. 8).

The odeion, in which musical performances and competitions were held, was usually semi-circular inside, with a timber roof in most cases, like the beautiful structure at Aphrodisias which of course has lost its perishable roof (Pl. 9). There is another well-preserved odeion of this kind at Kibyra. At Termessos a very fine Hellenistic odeion is still standing to a height of over 30 feet (10 metres), which might as well have been a bouleuterion since it is situated fairly close to the agora. It is a rectangular building with curved rows of seats inside, unfortunately still covered with rubble.

The gymnasia in the hellenized cities of Anatolia have not fared very well as far as structural survival is concerned, somewhat surprisingly so, one might think, given the importance of the institution which every *polis* had to have. Remains of many are to be found, but except for a few they are now in a poor condition scarcely able to catch the eye in the landscape. This may be due to their large and relatively sprawling structure compared with the compact theatre or odeion. The few better-preserved gymnasia are of the Graeco-Roman age, for instance the gymnasium of Termessos dating from the second century AD (Pl. 34). It is a large and architecturally interesting building, waiting to be cleared of the vegetation which at present has completely invaded it. The monumental gymnasium at Sardeis, entirely restored in recent years, is a huge building of the third century AD, architecturally very Roman and somewhat pompous in appearance.

A *heröon* was a small shrine dedicated to a hero, demigod or deified human. The ruins of some can be seen in various parts of western and southern Anatolia, but unfortunately in a poor condition so that reconstruction of them even on paper remains conjectural, however interesting they may be archaeologically.

City gates, towers and considerable sections of city walls dating back to the Hellenistic age have survived on several sites most conspicuously because of the solid nature of their masonry, for instance at Herakleia under Latmos, at Alinda and Isaura (Pls. 4, 38, 39).

A striking feature of many cities was the stoa, a colonnaded structure containing a row of shops which would frequently run along one side of the agora. Some of the larger cities had more than one. In Athens the reconstructed stoa of Attalos gives some idea of the nature of such buildings. There were many in Anatolia, but on the whole they have not fared very well, partly on account of their vulnerable colonnaded structure. Few have survived. The stoa of Alinda, however, is a fine example, its supporting ashlar wall still standing to its full height (Pl. 5).

Nymphaea, large thermae or baths, and aqueducts were Roman innovations, of which many can be seen, imposing structures and sometimes, especially aqueducts, merging into the landsape most pleasingly.

An outstanding and particularly attractive aspect of Hellenistic and Graeco-Roman architecture is its masonry. This is invariably either polygonal or ashlar, usually the latter, of which there are many beautiful examples. Ashlar masonry consists of rectangular blocks of stone so finely cut that when placed upon one another to form a wall, always without mortar, the result is solid enough to withstand centuries of exposure to the inclemencies of weather and other disruptive forces. The surfaces of these blocks are smooth or deliberately rough and embossed, but in either case the nature of ashlar masonry enhances immensely the aesthetic appearance of a building. The Romans introduced mortar, but the cities of Anatolia continued to use ashlar masonry throughout the Graeco-Roman age. It is only with the Byzantines that it disappears and masonry of a slipshod appearance takes over and prevails everywhere – little stones of any shape held together with mortar. This is what makes it easy on many sites to distinguish the ruins of antiquity from those of a later age.

As stone is particularly plentiful in Asia Minor, brick was seldom used until the end of the Graeco-Roman age, although it was often dominant in Roman architecture elsewhere. There is, however, a conspicuous building of brick at Pergamon, the huge temple of Serapis still standing after having been converted into a Byzantine church. The upper parts were once faced with marble.

What about houses? Are there any remains of dwellings to catch the eye in that wonderful landscape of Anatolia? The answer is disappointing. None has survived to anything like the same extent as the ancient civic buildings. Some of the coastal cities have fared better in this respect than the hellenized cities of the interior. In Priene there are ruins of large, luxurious houses which give one some idea of what they were like, often two-storey buildings with an inner court surrounded by fairly spacious rooms on the ground floor. The lower walls consisted of ashlar masonry, but in all likelihood the walls of the upper storey were of dried mud brick. These remains in their present ruined condition constitute the least striking aspect of the site. At Halikarnassos, according to Vitruvius, Mausolos had a magnificent palace built for him, but nothing of it has survived.

Among the remains of the inland cities hardly any traces of dwellings have survived above ground. The houses of the citizens were always unpretentious and probably made of dried mud bricks which adequately suited the purposes of a dwelling as long as the roof was kept in repair, but were doomed to disintegrate in the course of time. They were not made to stand exposure for the duration of centuries as the public buildings were expected to do. Not only the rich citizen of the *polis* but also the man of modest means was prepared to spend money on public buildings, on which his life centred and in which he would take pride, and above all on his tomb which, as his dwelling after death, had to be strong enough to endure for generations when he would no longer be present to make repairs.

In a dry and mild climate like that of Anatolia the inhabitants of cities lived most of the time out of doors. The daily business of citizens and many of their activities were conducted in the open air, in the agora, in the bouleuterion, in the theatre, in the palaestra and in the stadium. Of course for their meals and for the night they would withdraw into their individual houses where the women, and no doubt also the slaves, spent almost all their time. So it is unfortunate that so little has survived of these houses which might have thrown some light on the nature of private lives in those days, of which we have scanty knowledge.

Many of the more conspicuous Anatolian buildings came into being and were kept in repair or rebuilt as the result of the munificence of some of the richer citizens. We may well ask why it was that wealthy men such as Opramoas of Rhodiapolis or Jason of Kyaneai, who lavished funds on several cities for the repair or construction of splendid public buildings, were not tempted to have great mansions built as their homes? There are no traces of any palaces in these cities. Unlike the rich nobles and citizens of the Middle Ages and thereafter throughout western Europe, the Anatolian wealthy citizens went on living in modest houses. 'Man is born for citizenship,' Aristotle asserted,[4] which was what all Greeks felt. So the hellenized Anatolians did not feel the need for magnificent palaces to live in and enjoy their wealth, they displayed it in the public buildings of the city which enhanced their renown and gratified their pride. The essential character of the Greek city *diaita* was non-feudal, which accounts for the absence not only of palaces but also of castles until the Byzantine age.

Did the wealthier citizens of these cities in Asia Minor have villas built for them in the country in order to enjoy their leisure in peace and comfort as many prominent Romans did, such as Cicero and Pliny the Younger? Unlike certain other buildings that reflect Roman habits and tastes, the villa is a particularly attractive feature of Roman culture as well as wealth, remains of which are to be found all over western Europe. But even the second century AD in Anatolia, a period of great prosperity and widespread peace, the age of Opramoas, does not seem to have left any traces of villas, even though certain other aspects of Roman civilization had by then penetrated everyday life, such as a taste for magnificent baths, gladiatorial contests and baiting wild animals, giving rise to the need for new architectural structures or modifications.

Of course there may have been some villas in Anatolia. But as they were situated, by their very nature, outside the city walls, they were in subsequent ages particularly vulnerable and subject to total obliteration. Incursions, raids and destructive wars were to sweep through vast areas of Asia Minor in later centuries.

Philostratos the Elder, who lived at the time of the emperor Septimius Severus (about AD 200), gives us a most vivid description of a picture, somewhat Claude Lorraine-like, in which a magnificent villa on the Asiatic shores of the Hellespont is represented. The description, however, is that of a painting which may or may not have reflected reality.

> The women on the bank are shouting, and they seem to urge the horses not to throw their riders nor yet to spurn the bit, but to catch the game and trample it under foot. And when the youths have finished the hunt and have eaten their meal, a boat carries them across from Europe to Asia, about four stades – for this space intervenes between the countries – and they row themselves across. See, they throw a rope, and a house is receiving them, a charming house showing chambers and halls and indications of windows, and is surrounded by a wall with parapets for defence. The most beautiful feature of it is a semi-circular stoa following the curve of the sea, of yellowish colour by reason of the stone of which it is built. From the stone water pours out; for a warm stream flowing out below the mountains of lower Phrygia and meeting the quarries submerges some of the rocks and makes the outcroppings of the stone full of water so that it assumes various colours . . . In the house a woman lives alone; she has been driven out of the city by the importunity of her suitors. But see how secure the house is; a cliff juts out into the sea; its base bathed by the waves, and, projecting overhead, it bears this house into the sea, a house beneath which the sea seems of a darker blue, and the cliff has all the characteristics of a ship except that it is motionless.[5]

If there were any such villas, whether on the coast of Asia Minor or inland on the shores of a lake, they can only have been very few. Outside city walls only necropoleis and aqueducts have survived. In the Roman age life was still geared to the city.

The layout of the public buildings and houses depended on various factors. Proper city planning did not start until the fifth century BC and in hellenized Anatolia could only apply to those cities which originated in an act of foundation. It would then be based on the so-called Hippodamian system consisting of streets crossing each other at right angles in chessboard fashion. When Miletus was rebuilt after its destruction by the Persians in 494 BC, the city planning was carried out by the architect Hippodamos who was later called to Athens by Pericles for the construction and layout of the Piraeus. His scheme became the classical city plan which in Anatolia, however, could scarcely ever be adopted in its entirety even by the newly founded or rebuilt cities. The terrain seldom permitted its strict application, considerable modifications frequently being necessary as a result of the usually very uneven lie of the ground, which would involve terracing and curved streets for access to the upper levels of the buildings. Hence monotony, which could result from strict application of the Hippodamian scheme, is never encountered.

Most of the cities of hellenized Anatolia originated in barbarian centres of habitation out of which the *polis* came into being, and therefore the planning of the new buildings was to a considerable extent conditioned by the layout of the original houses, even if many or most of them were destroyed to make room for new constructions. Moreover, even the new foundations by the Seleucid and Attalid kings could rarely be laid out in strict accordance with the Hippodamian model, whether the lie of the ground permitted or not, since there was nearly always a nucleus of indigenous dwellings on the sites chosen. These foundations, such as Stratonikeia, Apameia, Nysa, Laudikeia and many others, in fact amounted to re-foundations on the sites of indigenous towns or villages by means of an input of Macedonian and Greek settlers. The main streets were of course wider than the others in the same city and in the Graeco-Roman age were usually paved.

Whenever a new city was founded from scratch on virgin ground, as sometimes occurred, the Hippodamian plan would in all likelihood be adopted if the lie of the land permitted. So for instance on level ground near a Bithynian lake Antigonos founded, at the close of the fourth century BC, the city of Nicaea, or rather Antigonia as he called it before he was defeated and killed by Lysimachos, who changed the name. Strabo described the plan of Nicaea: 'The city is sixteen stadia in circuit and is quadrangular in shape; it is situated in a plain, and has four gates; and its streets are cut at right angles, so that the four gates can be seen from one stone which is set in the middle of the gymnasium.'[6]

Finally the tombs should be mentioned, which sealed the end of individual life with stone. In an effort to prolong existence in some form they frequently assumed the proportions and size of a building which would not only be a home for the deceased nor merely a memorial, but also a kind of continuous, enduring, if not everlasting commemoration in the most visible, tangible and often spectacular fashion. The sepulchre could then become a splendid piece of architecture, of which the classical paradigm was the mausoleum of Halikarnassos, one of the Seven Wonders of the World. Scarcely noticeable in Greece, this striving after, or desire for, self-publicity after death by means of a conspicuous sepulchre was extremely widespread in Anatolia where oriental influences were not lacking.

All over the expanse of Asia Minor tombs of various kinds are present and most visible, not only in the necropoleis of the ancient cities; because of their very nature many have survived remarkably well, as indeed they were intended to do.

Before the advent of Hellenism kings and queens would have great mounds as their sepulchres. There are several Semiramis mounds, believed to have been the burial site of this mythical queen, which are still visible in the landscape. The tumulus type was widespread, often with a vaulted chamber inside. The Lydians had several. The Phrygians went in for rock-cut tombs, some endowed with façades spectacularly designed, the most notable being the tomb of Midas.

With the advent of Hellenism three basic types of tomb can be distinguished. The sarcophagus is very widespread, often extremely simple, but frequently also sculpted and ornate. However this type of tomb can scarcely be regarded as having anything to do with architecture.

The rock-cut tomb was just as popular throughout Anatolia, often amounting to no more than a hole in the precipitous face of a hill or mountain. Entire cliffs are puckered with them. They can hardly be regarded as having anything to do with Hellenism, nor of course with architecture. But when they start putting on a face, or rather having a face cut in the rock for them, and when this face, or façade, consists of columns, pediments and dentils, then Hellenism has left its stamp and we begin to see a definite connection with architecture. Such tombs can play an important part in the very character of the landscape. Most of them are in the south of Anatolia, particularly in Lycia where their forerunners were the typical pre-Hellenic indigenous rock-cut tombs fashioned in the likeness of Lycian timber houses. They were subsequently supplanted by the Greek temple-like tombs hewn into the face of the rock. Their columns, it is to be noted, are always of the Ionic order. A splendid specimen is the tomb of Amyntas at Telmessos (Pl. 17).

The third type is the monumental sepulchre, or mausoleum, which can definitely be regarded as architecture, being built stone upon stone. The classical prototype of this kind, and also the most beautiful to have survived, is the Nereid Monument of Xanthos (Pl. 15), now reassembled in the British Museum, which may have served as a model for the Halikarnassos mausoleum, or at any rate inspired Mausolos in his scheme. Certainly based on the mausoleum of Halikarnassos is the more modest but very fine funeral structure at Mylasa (Pl. 1). Dating from the second century AD, it stands with Corinthian columns and corner pilasters on a high podium and is topped with a pyramid now partly collapsed. There are several examples of the mausoleum type of tomb looking like a small temple in southern Anatolia, built at a time when there were citizens rich enough to afford the construction of such expensive after-death abodes and still in a good or fair state of preservation. Some are gaudy and baroque, others are simple little buildings of perfect ashlar masonry, often exquisitely proportioned and objects of real beauty.

CHAPTER

II

CARIA

THE WESTERN COAST OF ANATOLIA, SPECKLED WITH ISLANDS AT A distance of not many miles, runs from the Hellespont southward with deep gulfs and jutting promontories as though in response to the indented coast of Greece, conversing with it, as it were, across the Aegean Sea. No wonder expansion from the mother country took root here at a very early stage of the history of Greece, with dozens of settlements, the Aeolian, Ionian and Dorian cities of Anatolia, in a geographical configuration of land and sea which provided easy communication and promoted close intercourse. This expansion did not consist of overrunning and occupying foreign territories, like the invasion of Britain by the Angles and Saxons or France by the Franks, but took the form of founding cities, self-contained nuclei of the Greek way of life. Greek civilization expressed itself socially, politically, economically and culturally through the institution of the *polis*, whether democratically governed or under the rule of a tyrant. Any other form of state organization, such as that of the Egyptians or of the Persians, was totally alien to the Greek ethos.

Greek cities flourished on the Anatolian coast, some of them developing into great centres of philosophy, science and literary output as well as of social refinement as early as the seventh century BC. But beyond the range of their lives and the restricted territory under their control outside their city walls lay the vast expanses of Asia Minor and the Asiatic east, scarcely affecting them or affected by them. Other civilizations had flourished there, Hittite, Phrygian and, historically nearer to their growth and development, Lydian. Only with the Lydians some limited contact and cultural exchange were established, not so much as the result of their coming under Lydian subjection for some years, but more especially as the result of Croesus' personal relation to the Hellenic world. By and large, however, the Anatolians of various ethnic origin remained barbarians as far as the Greeks were concerned. This did not simply mean that they spoke other languages than Greek, but more significantly that their way of life, their *diaita*, was radically different. There came a time, however, when a gradual penetration of the continent of both the Greek language and way of life got under way.

If we follow the course of hellenization eastward from the Aegean coast of Anatolia a distinction should first of all be made between the penetration that took place before the advent of Alexander the Great, which was limited to certain areas, and the great thrust that occurred under his successors, the Seleucid and Attalid dynasts, which spread throughout Asia Minor. In the earlier period no new cities were founded inland. Only two Greek cities in western Anatolia were situated out of sight of the sea, both founded by early Aeolian and Ionian settlers, Magnesia on the Maeander and Magnesia ad Sipylum in Lydia. During the Hellenistic age, on the other hand, several cities were founded further and further inland while many old indigenous towns became thoroughly hellenized.

Now let us glance at the map of western Anatolia and take note of its geography in relation to Greece across the sea and to the Greek colonies on the coast. The main regions bordering the Aegean, Mysia, Lydia and Caria, were inhabited by ancient Anatolian people of Indo-European origin mixed with earlier indigenous elements. Of these three regions, followed by Lycia in the south-western corner of Asia Minor which was likewise inhabited by people speaking an Indo-European language, Caria was the first to be penetrated by Hellenic civilization. This had taken place before Alexander's campaigns by a process of osmosis, as it were. There are many sites of ancient cities in Caria, inland at some distance from the sea, which were at first barbarian but became Greek by the middle of the fourth century BC.

The region is articulated by chains of mountains which from altitudes of over 7000 feet (2000 metres) in the western stretches of the Tauros range descend to the Aegean, intersecting each other and forming landscapes of great beauty in a gentle Mediterranean climate. Olive-clad promontories jut out into the sea and deep gulfs open up to the west for contact with Greece and the exchange of sea trade. Here flourished the Dorian city of Halikarnassos, birthplace of Herodotus, which had been colonized by settlers from Troezen and Argos. This city became inhabited also by hellenized Carians with whom the Greeks lived on exceptionally good terms. Vitruvius tells an amusing story about the way in which the indigenous people of Caria came to be civilized by the Greek settlers who had founded Halikarnossos. When the Carians were driven inland by the colonizers they took to the hills, rallied and made raids devastating the land occupied by the Greeks. But one of the newcomers had the brilliant idea of setting up an inn where excellent meals were provided, a restaurant in fact, which was situated close to a spring. The water of this spring was not only crystal clear with a very pleasant flavour, but also had the effect of an aphrodisiac. Drawn by the good food exquisitely cooked and the delicious water of the spring, the barbarians came down from the hills one by one, and mixed with the colonists 'changing of their own accord from their rough and wild habits to Greek customs and affability.' So as the result of this aphrodisiacal water, 'the delights of civilization softened their savage breasts.'[1]

No wonder interbreeding took place, with Greek little by little prevailing over the indigenous language and Greek civilization penetrating inland. This process was aided by a natural affinity between the Greeks and the Carians. The settlers had found in this part of Anatolia an indigenous population whose temperament, ways and customs were not fundamentally different from their own and who therefore proved receptive to a more advanced form of civilization. By the first century BC, Carian was a dead language, but already in the fourth century Greek had been the official language of the cities, most of whose inhabitants were keen to be regarded as Greeks.

At some distance south-east of Halikarnassos, where the fertile valleys of the interior produced corn, olive oil, wine and figs, was situated Mylasa, the old capital of Caria.

Let us see what Herodotus himself has to say about the Carians and their capital, at a time when hellenization of the country was still at an early stage:

The Carians were people who had come to the mainland from the islands; for in old times they were islanders, called Leleges, and under the rule of Minos, not (as far as I can learn by hearsay) paying him tribute, but manning ships for him when he needed them. Seeing that Minos had subdued much territory to himself and was victorious in war, this made the Carians too at that time to be very far the most regarded of all nations. Three things they invented in which they were followed by the Greeks: it was the Carians who first taught the wearing of crests on their helmets and devices on their shields, and who first made for their shields holders, and guided them with leather baldrics which they slung round the neck and over the left shoulder. Then, a long time afterwards, the Carians were driven from the islands by the Dorians and Ionians and so came to the mainland. This is the Cretan story about the Carians; but they themselves do not consent to it but hold that they were aboriginal dwellers on the mainland and ever bore the name which they bear now; and they point to an ancient shrine of Carian Zeus at Mylasa, whereto Lydians and Mysians, as brethren of the Carians (for Lydos and Mysos, they say, were brothers of Kar), are admitted, but none of any other nation though they learnt to speak the same language as the Carians.[2]

Under Persian suzerainty the country was governed by a dynasty of Carian princes who came into prominence with the satrap Hekatomnos in the first quarter of the fourth century. He was a hellenized Carian with whom the process of hellenization gathered momentum. This meant that the cities of Caria adopted the constitution of a Greek *polis* as well as Greek as the official language, and issued coins inscribed in Greek.

Mausolos, Hekatomnos' son and successor who extended his rule as far as the Maeander in the north and over much of Lycia in the south, was an even more eager hellenizer than his father. He transferred the capital of the country from Mylasa to Halikarnassos on the coast and with his wife Artemisia, who was also his sister, became an outstanding patron of the arts attracting to the city some of the most prominent artists of the Greek world. When he died in 353 BC his devoted wife, who succeeded him as a ruler of Caria, took steps to have a tomb for him built on a stupendous scale. The so-called Mausoleum, one of the Seven Wonders of the World, may have been planned by Mausolos himself. The construction of the building, according to Vitruvius, was carried out and completed in 351 by the architect Pytheos, who was also responsible for the beautiful temple of Athena at Priene. But Halikarnassos, as well as the twelve Ionian cities, lies outside the field of our exploration: the expansion of Hellenism into the interior of Anatolia reflected in the architectural remains as we see them in their landscape today.

The old capital of Caria was not neglected by Mausolos in spite of his having taken up residence in Halikarnassos. As Strabo in the first century BC described, it was embellished by Hekatomnos and his successors with Hellenic edifices.

Mylasa is situated in an exceedingly fertile plain; and above the plain, towering into a peak, rises a mountain which was a most excellent quarry of white marble. Now this quarry is of no small advantage since it has stone in abundance and close at hand for building purposes and in particular for the building of temples and other public works. Accordingly this city, as much as any other, is in every way beautifully adorned with porticoes and temples . . . The Mylasians have two temples of Zeus, Zeus Osogo, as he is called, and Zeus Labrandeus. The former is within the city, whereas Labraunda is a village at some distance on the mountains near the pass that leads over from Alabanda to Mylasa.[3]

This Zeus, already mentioned by Herodotus in the fifth century BC, was of course a local Carian deity who by exemplary Greek syncretism became identified with the supreme Olympian godhead.

From being a barbarian village Mylasa blossomed into a typical Greek city. In Strabo's days it produced two notable men 'who were at once orators and leaders of the city, Euthydemos and Hebreas'. There follows in Strabo's account a couple of pages about them and the eminence they achieved in statecraft. But of the splendours of this city's architecture very little survives; gone are the marble temples, porticoes and stoas. The site is now occupied by a thriving small Turkish town, Milas, the ancient name only slightly modified. It possesses some very attractive old houses and a few fine mosques, but of course its character is totally different from the Greek city it once was. As practically nothing remains of the ancient monuments it is impossible to form a clear mental picture of what Mylasa, the capital of Caria, must have looked like in the Hellenistic and Roman age. There is one Corinthian column of a temple still standing, and so is one of the city gates, but the best preserved ancient building is a fine sepulchral structure of the second century AD (Pl. 1). The high base on which its peristasis stands, its encircling fluted Corinthian columns of which the four corner ones are square pillars, and its roof consisting of a stepped pyramid, suggest that it was a small replica of the celebrated mausoleum of Halikarnassos. The prototype may well have been the Nereid monument of Xanthos, reconstructed in the British Museum, which dates back to about 400 BC.

The wish to have a splendid tomb built for an after-life abode, which would stand in the landscape as a monument for everyone to contemplate and admire, was widespread in ancient civilizations and ubiquitously carried out, though not among the Greeks in Greece who were usually content with a comparatively modest stele. The opulent kings and potentates of the east, notably in Egypt, aimed at something more spectacular. Notwithstanding the concurrence of the best Greek architects and sculptors of the period for the construction and adornment of the mausoleum of Halikarnassos, there was something barbarian about this huge structure, at least as far as it is possible to gather from the descriptions, measurements and details left to us by writers such as Pliny and Vitruvius. Nothing like it was ever undertaken in Greece except very late in the Hellenistic age, and it is worth noting that neither Alexander nor his Macedonian successor had mausoleums built for themselves. Though magnificiently rich the recently discovered tomb at Vergina in Macedonia, which is believed to have been that of Philip II, is definitely not a mausoleum.

Mausolos, on the other hand, moustached, long-haired and heavily robed as we see him represented in statuesque form at the British Museum, was profoundly Anatolian in spite of his hellenization and hellenizing activity. The Mylasa tomb, remotely modelled as it may have been after the mammoth-like Halikarnassian monument, is conspicuous but discreet as well as harmoniously proportioned and stands as a characteristic specimen of an Anatolian sepulchre where Hellenic architectural features, as in so many other instances throughout Asia Minor, embellish an oriental idea of entombment. Indeed we find everywhere among the Anatolian people of antiquity this need for self-projection beyond death in architectural form above the surface of the earth.

Mylasa is a typical example of an ancient city that has virtually disappeared from view, partly as the result of decay caused by earthquakes but more radically and significantly on account of a village or small town totally alien in tradition and character having sprung up on the site, whose inhabitants have used the remains of the ancient structures as building material. Being situated on a highway in a fertile plain the site has been exposed to human spoliation. We shall see how those cities fared, with regard to architectural survival, which lay off the beaten track in solitary if not totally uninhabited neighbourhoods, as for instance the sanctuary of Labraunda situated at some distance from Mylasa, or secluded Euromos.

The holy sanctuary of Labraunda is to be found in the mountains at a distance of about ten miles (16 km) from the old capital. The temple of Zeus Stratios stood there, a peripteros of the Ionic order built by Idrieus, Mausolos' brother, about the middle of the fourth century BC. Only its foundations and lower structures remain with some of the column drums. It must have replaced an older temple, for Herodotus mentions it and says it was standing in a grove of plane trees where the Carians took refuge after fighting most valiantly with heavy losses against the invading Persians.[4] The sanctuary was held in great veneration by the Mylasians and Strabo tells us that a paved way led to it from the city. Mausolos devoted much attention to the construction of various buildings on the site and so did his brother and successor Idrieus under whom they were completed. As a result the sanctuary came to consist not only of the original temple of Zeus Stratios but also of several other structures such as stoas, propylaea, spacious terraces and notably buildings of the megaron type called *andron*, a sort of gentlemen's club for religious gatherings. Mausolos had one of these built, but the *andron* that stands in an impressive state of preservation, a most interesting building with windows, was built under instructions from Idrieus (Pl. 3). A very different though no less notable structure is a tomb set into the steep hillside immediately above the terrace where the principal remains are situated. It is large and massive, built of huge blocks of stone superimposed on and inserted into the ground, forming an impressive structure as well as an unusual type of sepulchre. It may have been the tomb of Idrieus himself, but it could hardly be more unlike the mausoleum of his brother Mausolos.

In spite of presenting a certain admixture of the conventional elements of Greek architecture, the remains of Labraunda are of particular interest as tokens of the penetration of Hellenism in the mid-fourth century BC. Nowhere else in Caria away from the sea do we find a manifestation of this development so conspicuously surviving from half a century before the Hellenistic age. The sequestered location has protected the ruins and as the result of recent excavations they have become today even more striking to the eye than they were when first discovered by travellers in the last century. The position of Labraunda, surrounded by pine woods high up in the mountains, is extremely attractive. So far the site is only accessible by a very rough road which protects it from the blight of coach parties. The track winds its way with difficulty into the rugged scenery, arousing wonder at the image of a paved road which led all the way to Mylasa in Strabo's day.[5]

It has been propounded, if not assumed, that paved roads were a Roman innovation, but the existence of this road in the first century BC and referred to by the great geographer surely indicates that it was most likely of Hellenistic construction, particularly because it was not part of a highway of some importance to Roman imperial rule, but was built merely to serve a local religious cult.

In the same region, south-west of Labraunda, is the site of Euromos, which was an ancient Carian city closely connected with Mylasa. In all probability it was hellenized at the same time, but like several other Carian cities it flourished in the Hellenistic and particularly in the Roman age. Although Euromos is more than once mentioned by writers such as Polybius, Livy and Strabo, the references are short and in passing. The information of the surviving inscriptions is also very limited and therefore little is known of its history. First visited by Richard Chandler in 1764, the site has been surveyed by Turkish archaeologists and some useful work has been done where the temple stands, but the old city itself has not yet been excavated, which is perhaps why nothing disturbs the enchantment of the whole place, one of the most picturesque in Anatolia where architecture and nature harmoniously blend. Enshrined in a grove of old olive trees a Corinthian temple suddenly rises before you at the end of a track, sixteen of its fluted columns still elegantly standing, forming a Piranesi-like image seldom encountered in real life nowadays (Pl. 2).

The temple is to Zeus, the same Zeus as at Mylasa or Labraunda, we might surmise, were it not for an inscription recently found which refers to the god as Zeus Lepsynos and would therefore suggest that it was a different local deity. This hexastyle peripteral edifice had eleven columns on its flanks. Some of the columns still standing are unfluted, having remained incomplete after erection. The temple was built in Hadrian's day and therefore owes its beauty to the spell of purism which ruled in the neo-classical age of that emperor and of the Antonines when the style of architecture strove towards elegance and harmony. In Anatolia this was a golden age of architectural achievements as well as general prosperity, to which also the temple of Aizonoi in Phrygia belongs and many other fine buildings.

At Euromos the citizens took great pride in their temple, contributing to its construction and embellishment. This is charmingly told by the inscription on one of the tablets applied to the columns at some height from their base:

Menecrates, son of Menecrates, the chief physician of the city, wearing a wreath, provided this column with its base and capital in memory of his daughter Tryphanete, herself also wearing a wreath, and being a director of the gymnasium.

The other tablets commemorate similar donations or benefactions. Though situated at a distance of only a few hundred yards from the tarmac highway the temple's fair state of preservation is most probably due to its secluded location away from any village or human dwelling in the immediate neighbourhood.

Not far from Labraunda, in the valley of the River Marsyas, a tributary of the Maeander, is the site of an important ancient city of Caria, Alabanda. Early in the fifth century BC the influence of the Greek coastal cities may already have made itself felt on this originally very Carian town, with the adoption of Greek customs and Greek as their language by the more educated citizens. Although the ruins of the public buildings date back to the Hellenistic and Roman age, the process of hellenization, with the establishment of a Greek city constitution, was already well advanced in the fourth century when Alinda, its sister city as one might call it, also flourished in the neighbourhood under the Hekatomnid dynasty. The implanting of Macedonian settlers in the third century, under the Seleucids, was scarcely needed to complete the process.

Strabo appears to be rather shocked by the luxury and seeming debauchery in Alabanda, famous for its lovely girl harp players, which is perhaps why he somewhat spitefully says that the city, as well as the whole district, was infested with scorpions. He quotes Apollonios Malkos, who called the place 'an ass laden with scorpions'.[5] However, he adds that it was the native city of several prominent orators such as Menekles, Hierokles, Apollonios Malkos and Molon. The last-named was Cicero's and Caesar's teacher in rhetoric. According to Vitruvius, the painter Apaturios was a native of Alabanda, too. He was active at Tralles where he was held in high esteem and renowned for his skill in acheiving *trompe l'oeil* effects. Also according to Vitruvius, Alabanda was the home town of Hermogenes, a fact which is nowadays disputed. It would have been an even greater honour for Alabanda if credence could be given to Vitruvius, since Hermogenes was one of the major architects of antiquity.

Alabanda is frequently mentioned by Polybius and Livy as a city actively involved in various military conflicts in the second century BC. Its citizens do not seem to have been debilitated by their alleged luxury and debauchery. We find them courting, with some degree of success, the support of the Romans who in the first quarter of that century were already beginning to play a significant part in the affairs of Asia Minor.[7] During the Roman empire Alabanda continued to prosper.

The site of the city spreading out into the plain from the lower slopes of a gentle hill can hardly impress the visitor today. Unlike the sites of certain other cities in Anatolia it is far from spectacular, though it does not lack a certain charm, and the ruins, as we see them today, are not at all striking. They have suffered not only from earthquakes but also from erosion caused by a parasitic village eating into them. But they are not uninteresting. The walls of the city were built in fine ashlar masonry in the Hellenistic period. The remarkable bouleuterion, the agora, the pseudo-dipteral temple of Apollo mentioned by Vitruvius and the theatre, all of the Hellenistic era with subsequent modifications, evince the typical characteristics of the Greek *polis*. But unfortunately, apart from the council chamber, these buildings are all severely damaged and do not emerge from the ground sufficiently to strike the eye as a coherent whole. After more thorough excavation they may perhaps stand forth more conspicuously in the landscape, as they no doubt did in the past.[8]

To the west of Alabanda, over a ridge of hills and on the other side of a fertile valley, are the splendid remains of beautiful Alinda. Situated on the steep slope of a lofty olive-clad hill, among gnarled trees and prominent granite outcrops, the major part of its ruins are placed far enough above the village, which now spreads at the foot of the hill, to escape the ravages that result from human proximity. Approaching the site from across the valley, the visitor's eye is struck by the sight of a great wall of perfect ashlar masonry which rises from a slope above the village to a height of over 50 feet (15 metres) like a magnificent Renaissance palace, stretching out to a length of 320 feet (100 metres) along the whole extent of a platform (Pl. 5). This is the wall of the agora and stoa dating back to the Hellenistic age, with square pilasters all along the inside rebuilt in the Graeco-Roman period, which have Doric half-columns on each side and which are still standing above a row of square rooms, no doubt the shops of the stoa. Ruins of a number of other buildings are to be seen lying on the ground nearby, but the way up to the theatre and acropolis is impressive, strewn with potsherds among granite outcrops and knotted tree trunks. Commanding a view of the valley and the mountains beyond, the theatre, which survives in a fair state of preservation, nestles into the steep hillside. Beautiful olive trees grow around it, between the seats and in the orchestra without detracting from its architectural features. This Hellenistic theatre with a single *diazoma* exceeds the semi-circle very slightly on account of considerable modifications carried out in the Graeco-Roman age. The *skene* is now up against the *cavea* united to the *analemmata* on either side, having been brought forward in conformity with the style of stage buildings in later times; in Hellenistic days it stood detached, leaving passage free through the *parodoi*. The fine city walls and towers which dominate further up the hill are also Hellenistic: some may even date back to the days of Queen Ada in the fourth century BC. At the top of the olive-clad hill was the acropolis, enjoying a magnificent position over the valley. On the edge of the site one of the towers stands in a remarkable state of preservation (Pl. 4). Others can be seen emerging from the walls some distance away.

On the same level as the acropolis but a little beyond, the necropolis begins among fantastically shaped boulders of dark granite and pieces of dazzling white marble lying on the ground here and there as if disgorged by these black monsters of rock. The tombs, no doubt those of the more prominent and prosperous citizens, are particularly interesting because of their unusual shape. They rise conspicuously in this setting, cubes tapering in reverse from a somewhat wider top to a slightly narrower bottom.

Alinda is one of the most attractive sites in Anatolia, not only because of its fine and relatively well-preserved ruins but also because of the beauty of its natural setting. Perhaps much of its exceptional charm is due to its secluded, untouched, unspoilt character, its ruins harmoniously merging into the vegetation and rock, for the site has not yet been excavated, nor has it been disturbed by the inhabitants of the village, at any rate in its upper part. But though situated off the beaten track it has already begun to be featured on package tours. Luckily the rough climb to the site of the acropolis affords some discouragement.

Alinda experienced its heyday in the fourth century BC when much attention and care were lavished upon it by the Hekatomnid dynasts, in particular by Queen Ada, the younger sister of Mausolos. She was her brother Idrieus' wife, marriage between brothers and sisters being a Carian custom. When Idrieus, dynast of Caria after Artemisia, died in 343, Ada became the ruler, 'government by women having been a familiar thing in Asia from the days of Semiramis onward', asserts Arrian. But her younger brother Pixodaras ousted her and made himself satrap of Caria with the approval and support of the king of the Persians. Ada withdrew to Alinda which, being a well-fortified stronghold, she was able to retain. Both Strabo and Arrian tell us that when Alexander came to capture Halikarnassos, Ada received him with open arms at Alinda where she entertained him and got on so well with him that she offered to adopt him as her son. He did not refuse the offer and assigned to her the siege of the acropolis of Halikarnassos after the rest of the city had been taken. Under her command the acropolis fell. Alexander then made her queen of the whole of Caria. But she did not forget Alinda which she kept as her capital and embellished with many new buildings. As we can see from the ruins of various edifices, the city continued to flourish right until the Roman age when it began to decline, being eclipsed by Alabanda, for after Ada's death this city of luxury and debauchery, of scorpions and beautiful harpists, was able to oust Alinda and become the most important city of the region.

About 15 miles (24 km) west of Alinda as the crow flies over the hills is the site of Herakleia under Latmos on the shores of Lake Bafa. Until the River Maeander silted up its access from the sea, late in the Roman age, the city was an Aegean port inhabited from its earliest days by Carians who, according to Strabo, called it Latmos after the name of the mountain that towers above it. Being at that time open to the sea and situated not far from Miletus, it received a small influx of Ionian and Aeolian settlers early in the history of Greek colonial expansion, who changed its name from Latmos to Herakleia. But it remained basically Carian until the fifth century BC; then the penetration of Hellenism was stepped up, becoming predominant in the days of the Hekatomnid dynasty, Mausolos having expanded his dominion as far north as the Maeander. Herakleia under Latmos can therefore be regarded as coming within the field of our survey. The present-day ruins date back to the beginning of the third century BC, when

Lysimachos, one of Alexander's most powerful successors, built or completed the present walls of the city. Their splended ashlar masonry can be seen in the considerable surviving sections as well as in the towers still standing in a fair state of preservation. These walls have aroused much interest[9] because of the remarkable degree of military defence they provide compared with fourth-century and Hellenistic walls elsewhere. They could be patrolled unobserved and the battlements are built in such a way as to furnish protection against missiles.

Some of the city buildings were added or modified in the Roman age and much was also built in the Byzantine period, when the site became a centre of monastic activity.

The charm of Herakleia, which cannot fail to enthrall the visitor even from a distance, whether approaching by boat or along the inland dirt road, derives first of all from the romantic situation of the site on the edge of a lake. Huge granite and conglomerate outcrops, with their weird dark shapes like pachyderm humps of prehistoric mammals, have come to crowd the rim of the valley embedded in olive trees at the foot of Mount Latmos which, jaggedly crested, beetles over the site of the city encircled by its walls. On a promontory jutting southward into the lake the picturesque ruins of a Byzantine castle stand among olive trees below which, on the edge of the lake, lies the necropolis whose tombs are cut in the white rock of the hillside. To the west, on a small island a hundred yards from the shore, the walls and arches of a Byzantine monastery rise framed by the blue waters and encircling mountains (Pl. 6). The island used to be the far end of a promontory which was cut off from the mainland by the rising waters of the lake in the course of centuries.

Most unfortunatcly, a village has sprung up among the ruins of the ancient city which have suffered from more recent building activities. The new houses stand among, or right on top of, what remains of the ancient buildings. However, the temple of Athena rises prominently on the brow of the upper edge of the site overlooking the lake, a Hellenistic prostyle edifice. It has lost the columns and pediment of its porch but otherwise stands almost intact. Near the temple the remains of a Hellenistic agora can be seen, bordered by a fine wall which supports it on its south side. Further up the hill among olive trees is the theatre built in the Hellenistic age, much of it awaiting proper excavation. Remains of a bouleuterion and of a nymphaion are also to be found. Lower down the hillside is situated the sanctuary or tomb of Endymion of which much remains standing. It is a prostyle temple consisting of a pronaos and an apsidal cella. But perhaps the most impressive feature of Herakleia is the stretch of city walls with their towers on the east side of the site. They rise, some to their full height of 30–40 feet (10–12 metres), well away from the houses of the village in a setting of olive trees and huge boulders, dark brown and full of fragments of white marble. These extraordinarily shaped boulders look as if they were hurled by giants down the mountainside, tumbling into fantastic positions over which the towers dominate as they look out to the west over the lake and to the east, up Mount Latmos, to its jagged peaks.

The magic of Herakleia is enhanced by the myth of Endymion which still clings to the place and the whole surroundings. He was a Carian shepherd and because of his surpassing beauty Selene, the moon, fell in love with him while he was lying asleep in a cave on Mount Latmos. According to one legend Selene bore him fifty daughters. Thereafter as she was kissing him one day he fell into a deep sleep from which he never awoke, and in his sleep preserved the bloom of his youth for ever. Various stories were told about the cause of his sleep. Some said it was brought on at his own request because he feared old age, others that it came about because Selene preferred kissing him asleep to being made love to the whole time and so becoming a mother too often. In the days of Apollodorus and Pausanias travellers were shown the tomb of Endymion by the inhabitants of Herakleia, and they still are by the present-day villagers.

At the end of the pagan era, when Herakleia had ceased to be a Greek *polis* in the proper constitutional sense of the term, an influx of monks and hermits was drawn by the secluded nature of the site, which by then no longer provided an anchorage and was virtually cut off from the outside world. The bay had been turned into a lake by the silt of the river Maeander. Its waters ceased to be salt as a result of an inflow of freshwater springs. Many monasteries were built, some on islets in the lake, and the remains of several are still standing picturesquely in the landscape. In some of the nearby caves there are interesting Byzantine frescoes which were painted by the monks. For several hundred years the monks were left more or less undisturbed, but when in the eleventh century the Seljuk onslaught wrecked their peace, Abbot Christodoulos departed with most of them and founded the celebrated monastery of Saint John on the island of Patmos.

The outlines of Herakleia's city walls and towers, the city gate arch, the temple of Athena and Endymion's sanctuary, the dilapidated Byzantine monasteries enshrined in olive boughs, Mount Latmos surging aloft with its crest of granite and its caves where the moon kept kissing Endymion and where the hermits prayed to hold Satan's temptations at bay, the rough paths of stone spangled with thistles, the smell of oregano and thyme, and the blue sheet of the lake stretching away sprinkled with islets on which cormorants flock and chatter – all these elements join together, strains of shape, colour, light and shadow, to leave an unforgettable impression of nature and architecture, myth and history, blending and harmonizing.

In the fertile valley of the Maeander, on the border between Caria and Lydia, lay Tralles, originally a barbarian town like all the inland centres of habitation in Caria. Little by little it became an important Greek city and flourished as such. The penetration of Hellenism started in the fifth century BC

△　**1**　The Mylasa tomb

△ **3** The *andron* at Labraynda

◁ **2** The Temple of Zeus at Euromos

◁ **4** A tower of the walls at Alinda

▽ **5** The stoa wall of the Agora at Alinda

△   **6** The Byzantine monastery of Herakleia

△ **8** The council chamber of the Elders at Nysa

◁ **7** The theatre at Nysa

◁ **9** The odeion at
Aphrodisias

▽ **10** The stadium at
Aphrodisias

△ **11** The Temple of Aphrodite at Aphrodisias

△ **13** Rock-cut tombs at
Kaunos

◁ **12** The propylon at
Aphrodisias

▷ **14** The Corinthian temple
at Patara

◁ **15** The Nereid monument from Xanthos, now in the British Museum

▽ **16** The Harpy tomb at Xanthos

△ **17** The tomb of Amyntas at Telmessos

◁ **18** The theatre at Pinara, with the Massikytos range in the background

▽ **19** The theatre at Antiphellos

◁ **20** A tomb at Myra

▷ **22** (*overleaf*) The Lycian
  tomb at Limyra

▽ **21** Tombs at Limyra

by a mere process of symbiosis, the Greek settlements of the coast being not far off. In the next century, when Mausolos extended his dominion as far as the border with Lydia, Tralles became totally hellenized. It continued to prosper throughout the Hellenistic and Roman ages, right into the Byzantine era, and was the native town of a number of distinguished personages in the world of art and culture generally, among others Artemidoros the sculptor, who lived in the first century BC, and Anthemios in the sixth century AD, the mathematician and architect of Saint Sophia in Constantinople.

Of its many edifices unfortunately almost nothing has remained visible, although much was still standing in the last century. The flourishing Turkish town of Aydin has obliterated its vestiges but for a gymnasium dating back to the third century AD, of which a few ruins can still be seen.

Nysa, by contrast, situated a few miles further east in the same Maeander valley, lies at some distance from the nearest village, Sultanhissar. Its buildings have therefore only suffered from natural decay brought about by weathering and earthquakes and from the effects of farming which, however, have perhaps added to the charm of the situation. We can there still enjoy the sight of three major structures, a theatre, a council chamber and a library.

The very fine theatre (Pl. 7), to which Strabo refers, is in a good state of preservation and has recently been cleared, although a few old olive trees have been allowed to stay where they grew between the rows of seats, casting their dappled shade on the brilliantly white limestone of the masonry. We can assume that the theatre was built in the Hellenistic era not only because Strabo mentions it a time when the Roman age had only just started, but also because it slightly exceeds the semi-circle, as in the case of all Greek theatres in Anatolia, though no doubt it was reconditioned in Roman times when the stage building was built and the *diazoma* most probably provided.

The conspicuous remains of the library stand in a rural setting of olive trees, west of the theatre. It is a rather interesting structure, originally a two-storey building with rows of arched niches in which the manuscripts were kept. Strabo does not mention it in his description of Nysa, evidently because it was built in later times. In fact the masonry, which is rather coarse, suggests that it dates from an age subsequent to the Antonines, probably to the third century AD. Most elegantly built, on the other hand, is the marble council chamber of the elders, the *gerontikon* (Pl. 8), to which Strabo makes reference. So very likely it was built in Hellenistic days, though the structure we see is a renovation of the second century AD, the golden age of so much good architecture in Anatolia when the Hellenistic spirit of proportion and measure came to life again and endured until the end of that century. The *gerontikon* has survived in an almost perfect state and is enchantingly situated in an olive grove east of the theatre and the gorge that divided the ancient city into two. Several bulls' heads are carved in the marble, a decoration which may have had something to do the Pluto and Persephone cult in a cave not far from Nysa. Strabo tells us in this connection that at Acharacha, a village which belonged to the Nysaeans, a festival was held every year where naked and anointed young men of the gymnasium would grasp a bull, carry it up into the cave and let it loose. It would then run forward a short distance and fall dead.

As a young man Strabo studied at Nysa where he was a pupil of the grammarian and rhetorician Aristodemos. So the description he gives us is graphic and probably quite accurate – the city divided in two by a gorge, the bridge joining the two halves, a tunnel or underground passage for the torrential waters, an amphitheatre, a theatre, a gymnasium for youths, the agora and the *gerontikon*. By 'amphitheatre' Strabo must have meant a stadium with both ends rounded and closed, since in the first century BC no Roman type of amphitheatre was built in Anatolia, where displays of gladiators and wild beasts took place only late in the Roman age. Of all these structures of Nysa only the council chamber, the theatre and the library can be seen today with their architectural features still clearly recognizable and therefore able to carry us back to the days of Nysa's prosperity. Of the other structures, including the stadium, only traces remain.

As early as the second century BC, Nysa produced a distinguished philosopher, the Stoic Apollonius, and it rapidly developed into a centre of studies. Strabo gives us a list of philosophers, grammarians and rhetoricians who were natives of that city and active in his days. Nysa however, it should be noted, not only flourished as a centre of studies but also prospered as a result of its geographical position in the neighbourhood of the sanctuary of Pluto, and so received from everywhere numerous visitors who came to participate in the rituals, as well as people in need of cures.

The citizens of Nysa, like those of most Anatolian cities, claimed ancient Greek ancestry for the origin of their city. They said, as Strabo tells us, that it was founded in ancient times by three brothers from Sparta. This account was of course more mythical than historical. In fact Nysa was founded by Antiochos I Soter, son of Seleukos, at the beginning of the third century BC. But whatever the number of Greeks and Macedonians who at that time came and settled, there must have been a considerable indigenous substratum of the population which was then hellenized and absorbed.

Perhaps the most spectacular site in Caria today, where the architectural remains are such as to strike the eye of the visitor with a vision of past splendour even more vivid than other ancient sites are able to conjure up, is Aphrodisias, again in the remote past a barbarian centre of habitation which grew into a magnificent city.

Thanks to the thorough and painstaking excavations carried out by Professor Kenan Erim in the course of more than twenty years, many of the buildings damaged by earthquakes and vandalism, and covered up by the rubble and earth of centuries of decay, have now come to light. They dazzle us with their beauty and elegance as we see them today, but travellers in the eighteenth and nineteenth centuries were impressed by the ruins even as they then were, particularly by the pseudo-dipteral temple of Aphrodite of which fourteen columns are still standing.

Aphrodisias came into the picture of history relatively late, remaining obscure during the greater part of the Hellenistic age while Mylasa, Alabanda, Nysa and other cities of Caria were intellectually and artistically active. Practically all the remains of its buildings date back to the Roman era, a few to the very late Hellenistic age, though the site was the centre of a very ancient Anatolian cult, the worship of the goddess Nino or Nina, one of the names of Babylonian Astarte. She was a fertility goddess similar to Cybele and basically the same. In fact according to Stephanos of Byzantium, a sixth-century writer, the city was known as Ninoe before it became hellenized. When this occurred in the late fourth century BC and subsequently under the impact of Alexander and his successors, Nina became Aphrodite, goddess of love and fertility, not unlike Artemis of Ephesus, and the old sanctuary became a Greek temple. What we see today was built in the first century BC. Unfortunately the information concerning this cult that can be gleaned from ancient writers is very meagre, but there can be no doubt that the city greatly benefited by it, and much of its wealth derived from its observance, until late in the Roman age when Christianity put an end to it.

By the third century BC, Aphrodisias was a Greek-speaking city with a Greek city constitution, but its period of real prosperity, reflected in its architecture and sculpture, started in the first century BC under the patronage of Augustus. It was declared a free city, or in other words was granted autonomy as far as local administration was concerned and exempted from taxation. Several cities in Caria, having developed and cultivated friendly relations with Rome, obtained this privilege, cities such as Mylasa and Alabanda, but Aphrodisias succeeded in ingratiating itself to an exceptional extent. It had received a golden crown and a double-axe for its sanctuary from Sulla, and subsequently it was favoured by Mark Antony, Caesar, Augustus and later emperors. What gave rise, we may well ask, to this special link between Aphrodisias and Rome?

The answer may be marble. Aphrodisias was a city of marble buildings on account of a quarry in the foothills of Mount Salbakos, now Baba Dag. Its architects were experts in marble building and Rome, until the first century BC, was a city of brick. The introduction of marble which then started, and under the emperors reached its full magnificence with new buildings and the embellishment of old ones, may have been in part due to the architects of Aphrodisias. And it was at Aphrodisias that a school of sculpture developed and achieved surprising excellence in the first century BC and the following ones. The work of these sculptors took shape in the classical tradition of ancient Greece, but not in the least, as one might expect, like the rather cold and dull copies of the Greek statuary of that period that are generally seen. The sculptors of Aphrodisias were genuinely gifted artists and the work which came from their hands and which we can see in the well arranged museum on the edge of the site, discloses exceptional vitality as well as beauty. We know that a few of these sculptors had the name of Zeno, but whether they were of the same family is not clear.

Aphrodisias was not only a city of sculptors. In the days of Nero and the Flavians it was the native city of a distinguished medical writer, Xenocrates, and a century later of Chariton, one of the early and most gifted Greek novelists, author of 'Chaerea and Kallirhoe'. In the third century AD the Peripatetic philosopher Alexander, who taught at Athens, came from Aphrodisias. He was regarded as the ablest commentator on Aristotle and one of his extant works, *On Fate*, is the most comprehensive ancient treatise on free will.

The city began to decline at the end of the fourth century for economic reasons and on account of earthquakes and Christianity. When it became a bishopric the new religion began to dominate, the pagans were persecuted, vandalism set in, many statues had their heads knocked off and theatrical performances were brought to an end. The cult of Aphrodite, which had been for centuries a centre of pilgrimage and a source of wealth, was abolished. The temple was turned into a church and the Byzantine city was renamed Stravropolis, the City of the Cross. Its decline ended in obliteration when the Seljuks came.

The ruins are situated on a plateau at about 2000 feet (600 metres) above sea level under Mount Salbakos. The scenery is not spectacular but alluring none the less, delicately rimmed with hills on the horizon and bathed in a translucent light which seems to penetrate the ruins, enhancing their architectural features.

On approaching, the visitor is greeted at a distance by the fourteen Ionic columns of the pseudo-dipteral temple of Aphrodite (Pl. 11) built in the first century BC, which still stand, the most striking feature of the whole site. Scarcely less pleasing to the eye and evocative of the splendid past are the huge stadium (Pl. 10), the odeion (Pl. 9) and the recently excavated theatre in an almost perfect state of preservation. When Richard Pococke saw it on his visit to Aphrodisias nearly 250 years ago it was virtually buried in the hill in which it had been set and almost entirely 'ruined'. It was built in the Hellenistic age but greatly modified in Roman times when the *skene* was widened and made to cut across the orchestra, the stage building becoming one unit with the *cavea*, and the orchestra deepened by the sacrifice of a few rows of seats in order to provide for wild beasts and gladiatorial shows.

The other edifices of which some remarkable vestiges still stand are the propylon gateway, recently restored and extremely picturesque (Pl. 12), Hadrian's baths and the agora surrounded by porticoes with columns of the Ionic order.

Away to the south-west, on the other side of Caria, are three sites not to be overlooked in this survey: Kedreai, picturesquely situated on an island in the Ceramic gulf; Stratonikeia about 30 miles (50 km) inland north of the gulf, which was a Seleucid foundation and therefore part of the hellenizing drive that followed Alexander; and far south on the coast Kaunos, a Carian town close to the Lycian border, which became a Greek city through contact with the Greek coastal colonies, particularly the island of Rhodes which lay facing it not far off.

The ruins of Kedreai lie enshrined in an olive grove a few hundred yards off the rocky southern shore of the Ceramic gulf. Since these remains are on an island we might assume that they are those of a city built by Greek settlers. In fact the inhabitants of Kedreai were indigenous Carians who in the days of Xenophon were still 'half barbarians'.[10] But when the city became a deme of Rhodes, being situated in that coastal area which came under Rhodian rule and was known as Rhodian Peraia, the inhabitants and their way of life were thoroughly hellenized, as the ruins attest. The site is enchanting, though nothing conspicuous remains standing except a few towers, an impressive city gate and sections of ashlar walls. Most of these belong to the fortifications, but some are supporting the agora. The un-Romanized theatre is in a good state of preservation and particularly attractive, nestling among olive trees, its fine *analemmata* converging at an angle in the traditional Greek style. The *skene*, however, as well as the orchestra and the lower part of the *cavea*, lies embedded in the ground.

Kedreai never issued coins of its own as far as we know, even though it was already partly hellenized before it came under Rhodian rule, for in the fifth century BC, when it was an independent city, it paid a small tribute to the Delian league. The principal gods worshipped were Pythios and Kedrieos Apollo.

Of far greater importance than Kedreai was Stratonikeia. The little that is known of it cannot fail to stimulate a wish for more information, but the surviving records are very limited. Apart from Strabo's account it is only from short references to the city by a few other authors that we can extract any additional information.[11]

Stratonikeia was founded with Macedonian settlers at the beginning of the third century BC by Antiochus I, who named the city after his wife Stratonike. She had been his stepmother, the wife of his father Seleucus, a woman of great beauty with whom he had fallen desperately in love. When he became seriously ill as a result, his father generously ceded her to him.

Strabo devotes a whole paragraph to Stratonikeia and tells us that the city was in the course of time greatly embellished with costly improvements by the Seleucid kings. He says that there were two temples within the city's territory. The more famous one, dedicated to the cult of Hekate, was situated at Lagina in the neighbourhood. The other one was close to the city, the temple of Zeus Chrysaoreos or the golden sword, which belonged to all the Carians in common who gathered there to offer sacrifice and deliberate on their common interests. Apparently they formed a league called 'Chrysaorium' which consisted of the various Carian villages, each with one or more votes according to its size. The Stratonikeians were also represented in the league, so Strabo states, although they were not of Carian stock, because they possessed villages that were members of it. As time went on the people of these villages were hellenized under the dynamic influence of Stratonikeia.

In spite of Rhodian interference, when for a while the city came to be included in that stretch of Carian coast under Rhodian rule, a control which was rescinded by the Romans in AD 167, Stratonikeia flourished throughout the Hellenistic age as well as in the subsequent Roman period as a centre of various activities. It was the native town of a number of prominent men in the intellectual world, among others Metrodoroa, a noteworthy philosopher of the second century BC and follower of Epicurus and Carneades, and Menippos, a distinguished orator much praised by Cicero.

The site of Stratonikeia is at Eskihissar near Yagatan, a village now virtually deserted on account of mineral mining activities which are also seriously threatening the ruins of the ancient city. A team of archaeologists from Ankara has been working on the sites and has uncovered remarkable remains of a gymnasium and much of the agora. Most conspicuous are the walls of a large temple dating back to the second century AD, which still stand to a considerable height, 10–13 feet (3–4 metres). The ashlar masonry consists of unusually wide blocks of stone. Within these walls recent excavations have disclosed a semi-circular structure with tiers for seating like a bouleuterion. The whole building is supposed to have been a temple of Serapis because one of the many inscriptions on its north wall is an *ex voto* to Helios Zeus Serapis, but it is not certain whether Serapis was indeed the deity to whom this unusual edifice was dedicated.

On the slope of the acropolis hill to the south of these remains is a fairly large theatre in a fair state of preservation, but invaded by shrubs and badly in need of clearing. Beyond the theatre are the ruins of a marble temple which has not yet been identified, but may well have been the temple of Zeus Chrysoareos mentioned by Strabo.

Unlike the rather disappointing picture Stratonikeia presents today, considering the importance of the city in ancient times, partly on account of the disfiguring mining operations which are about to eat into the site, Kaunos, some forty miles to the south, stands out as one of the most enchanting and evocative ancient sites of Caria. The ruins are situated close to the sea on the edge of an outlet from a lake, right away from human habitation. Lake Koycegiz, as it is called today, used to be a bay of the sea which became dammed up in very ancient times with the silt brought down by the rivers that flow into it. A natural canal several miles long has formed itself as the outlet, and on the promontory that edges along it rose the city of Kaunos.

What you encounter at the end of the road is a green strip of lagoon-like water two or three hundred yards wide, the canal, which winds its way along to the sea framed in by feathery bulrushes. Cliffs rise on the other side with pedimental tombs carved into them (Pl. 13). Olive trees, oaks and thistles cover the promontory; walls and towers emerge, and down by the water a crowded procession of reeds breathes in the wind, rimmed by the bold line of a high range of mountains way to the south. The site is accessible only by boat.

Who were the ancient inhabitants of this wonderful site, the Kaunians? Herodotus[12] says that to his mind the Kaunians were 'autochonous', aborigines of the soil, and that they spoke the same language as the Carians, though they themselves believed that they had originally come from Crete. They seemed to have been cheerful people who enjoyed the good things of life. Their chief pleasure, so Herodotus tells us, was to gather together for drinking bouts, men, women and children.

In many respects their customs were similar to those of their neighbours, the Lycians, who likewise believed they came from Crete. But whereas the Kaunians believed that they had come from Crete, the Carians, as Herodotus tells us, held that they were aboriginal dwellers of the mainland from the start. The two beliefs were not as inconsistent as they seem, for although the view of ancient writers differed on the matter, migrations from the Anatolian mainland to the Aegean island and back to the mainland did in all likelihood occur. So far, however, no relevant information has emerged from archaeological excavations.

Kaunos was sacked and burnt by the Persians, but rose again and flourished. Its inhabitants, like those of the other Carian cities, were hellenized in the days of the Hekatomnid dynasty under whose dominion they came for a time. Subsequently they came under the sway of the Rhodians from whom they revolted, but to whom they were restored by the Romans. Finally they were declared a free city under the Roman principate. The inscriptions as well as the surviving architecture show that they were entirely hellenized by the time Strabo wrote.

What Strabo says about the climate of Kaunos in those days may be worth noting. He tells us that it was regarded as extremely unhealthy, especially in the summer and the autumn on account of the heat and the abundance of fruits. The inhabitants had consequently a pale-green complexion. From this we may deduce that they suffered from malaria, though the nature and cause of the disease were of course unknown at that time.[13]

On the summit of a hill an acropolis, protected by walls restored in the Middle Ages, overlooks the site. On the opposite side, with the site of the city lying in between, a row of fine Hellenistic walls emerges from the hills, ashlar and polygonal.

In recent years excavations have disclosed the existence of four temples and brought into conspicuous view a nymphaion, a stoa, a tholos, a basilica which was originally a palaestra, baths and a theatre. Practically all these buildings belong to the Roman age when the free city was able to prosper in peace. Those that delight the eye in their natural setting overlooking the little sandy cove which used to be the harbour, because much of their structure survives, are the theatre, the nymphaion, which is beautifully built, the basilica, the baths and a columned building which at first sight might seem to have been a tholos since its shape is concentric, but apparently the exact nature of the structure is not yet clear. Particularly attractive is the theatre, which is in a fairly good state of preservation though much of its stage building has gone. The nature of the whole structure is Greek since the *cavea* exceeds the semi-circle, with lateral *parodoi* one of which, however, seems to have been deliberately obstructed. There are two fine back entrances which are arched and which therefore may have been added or completed in Roman times.

Away to the north-east is the necropolis with its imposing rock-hewn tombs in the sheer mountainside clearly visible from afar. Over the marshy expanses to the south-west the snow-capped heights of Lycia rise into the sky where another world opens out.

CHAPTER

III

LYCIA

No territory of Anatolia, no autochthonous region of Asia Minor apart from the Troad, was so closely connected with Greece in mythology as Lycia. Its magnificent scenery, with mountains rising to heights of over 10,000 feet (3000 metres), with its lakes, woods and forests, its rocky coast indented with creeks and sprinkled with islands, its superb ruins of two dozen cities, could hardly reflect more splendidly, even today, the ancient link that held them together.

Just think of Bellerophon and the Chimaera, or of Sarpedon and Glaucus, heroes of the *Iliad*, and Lycia is brought to mind. Bellerophon became king of Lycia after having slain the fire-spitting Chimaera. His grandson Glaucus and his companion Sarpedon, princes of Lycia, led the Lycian troops most valiantly in support of the Trojans in their struggle with the Greeks. 'Sarpedon and peerless Glaucus were captains of the Lycians from far off Lycia.' Sarpedon was slain by Patroclus and Glaucus by Ajax. And Pandarus, who had received his wonderful bow as a gift from Apollo, was also a Lycian. Throughout the *Iliad* the Lycians are constantly mentioned as foremost among the allies of the Trojans. What better credentials could a non-Greek nation boast for holding an eminent place in the Homeric saga and the ancient Greek world?

Xanthos the city and Xanthos the river, where only a few centuries later some of the most beautiful pieces of Greek sculpture took shape, were already then part of the landscape of ancient Greece. Homer does not mention Xanthos the city but lets Sarpedon exclaim, when he spurs on Glaucus in the battle fray of Troy: 'We possess great estates by the banks of the Xanthos, a fair tract of orchard and wheat-bearing ploughland.' For at Xanthos, Glaucus' grandfather Bellerophon had established a lasting foothold.

Homer gives us a whole picture of Lycia in those days when myth and history were merging into one. Up in the Solymi mountains overlooking the sea the Chimaera was indeed spitting fire and still does so today. Her fame reached out to Etruria, taking form in a wonderful piece of bronze sculpture. Moreover, Lycia also deserves our interest as the native country of a famous Christian saint almost as mythical as Sarpedon or Glaucus – Saint Nicholas, bishop of Myra. He was born at Patara not far from Xanthos and has survived among us as Father Christmas.

When myth started to give way to the more solid ground of history the transition is reflected in the information with which Herodotus provides us. Myth is not rejected as out of keeping with his factual account of a remarkable custom the Lycians seemed to have had in his own days, which should be of special interest to the feminists of our times:

The Lycians came originally from Crete, which in ancient times was occupied entirely by non-Greek peoples. The two sons of Europa, Sarpedon and Minos, fought for the throne, and victorious Minos expelled Sarpedon and his party. The exiles sailed for Asia and landed on Milyan territory, Milyas being the ancient name of the country where the Lycians live today, though it was occupied then by the Solymi. During the rule of Sarpedon, the Lycians were known as Termilae, the name they had brought with them from Crete – and which is still in use among their neighbours; but after Lycus, son of Pandion, had been driven from Athens, as Sarpedon was from Crete by his brother Aegeus, and had taken refuge among the Termilae, in the course of time they adopted his name and came to be called Lycians. In their manners they resemble in some ways the Cretans, in others the Carians, but in their customs, that of taking their mother's name instead of their father's, they are unique. Ask a Lycian who he is, and he will tell you his own name and his mother's, and his grandmother's and so on. And if a free woman has a child by a slave, the child is considered legitimate whereas the children of a free man, however distinguished he may be, and of a foreign wife or mistress have no citizen's rights at all. (I.173)

Before Herodotus' day Lycia as a nation consisted of an indeterminate number of townships. The largest and most important was Xanthos, whose original Lycian name was Arna, but several other centres of habitation had grown into towns of some size, each with its organization governed by a local prince. But all of them, though often at war with one another, were already conscious of a certain communal inter-relationship, in other words of belonging to one nation. They succeeded in remaining free from outside intervention until the middle of the sixth century BC. They had their own language, basically Indo-European, which we find inscribed on their more ancient tombs and sepulchral reliefs – where they always referred to themselves as Termilai – a language they tenaciously clung to for a long time, even when the influence of Hellenism had penetrated deep. It has not been entirely deciphered and is not yet fully understood, though the script is related to the Greek script.

When the Persians came in 545 BC the citizens of Xanthos put up a desperate resistance. Herodotus relates how when Harpogos, King Cyrus' general, led his army into the plain of Xanthos, the inhabitants came out to meet him:

> They did valorous deeds in battle against odds. At length, however, they were defeated and forced to retire within their walls, whereupon they collected their women, children and slaves and other property and shut them up in the acropolis of the city, set fire to the place and burnt it to ground. Then having sworn to die, they marched out to meet the enemy and were killed to a man. (I.76)

Little by little, however, Xanthos recovered. Initially the Persian satraps may have been domineering if not arrogant, but soon the Lycians were able to re-establish a considerable degree of local autonomy under their own dynasts whom we find ruling the main cities of the country throughout the fifth and fourth centuries, such as Perikles of Limyra, Kherei and Arttumpura of Xanthos. The doors were being progressively opened to the influence of the Greek world and in the sculpture of the fifth century we see a most interesting confluence of Lycian, Persian and Greek streams of culture, with the Greek manner rapidly increasing. By 400 BC it had become predominant; though the national language still persisted, inscriptions, which had hitherto been exclusively in Lycian, now begin to appear in Greek and in these the Lycians refer to themselves as Lycians, no longer as Termilai. In the fourth century the people were not only bilingual, but many also appear to have become entirely hellenized. The Greek historian Menekrates, who lived in that century, was a native of Xanthos and wrote a history of Lycia, *Lykiaka*, which regrettably is lost.

In the relief sculptures of tombs and throughout Lycia, Greek mythology is now the dominant theme and whatever the indigenous deities may have been they emerge as gods and goddesses of the Olympian pantheon. Indeed, the Lycians proved particularly receptive to Greek art and culture generally, and remarkably creative in the field of sculpture which manifested itself in hellenized form. Some of their best pieces of sculpture were probably made by artists from the mainland of Greece or the islands, like for instance the three female figures and the reliefs of the Nereid Monument now in the British Museum, which dates back to the very beginning of the fourth century BC. But even in the early fifth century the reliefs of the so-called Harpy Tomb (Pl.16), also now in the British Museum, were executed either by Greek sculptors or by Lycians who had received training from the Greeks. There can be no doubt that there were by then many gifted Greek-speaking Lycians who worked with Greek artists and learned from them. Very likely most of the relief sculptures we see on the tombs, which vary greatly in quality, were executed by hellenized Lycians.

As regards architecture the remarkable Lycian tombs, many of them rock-hewn or standing aloft in pillar form, show the distinctive mullioned features of the original timber dwellings that at first prevailed in the country, but often combined with the characteristic components of Greek temple architecture. Not infrequently what looks like a small Greek temple is in fact a tomb. As their actual buildings were of timber they could not of course last very long. Evidently the Lycians were more concerned about the durability of their abodes in the after-life than of those needed in this life, which accounts for the appearance of architecture in the proper sense of the term only when they became hellenized. Then theatres were built, agoras, stoas, council chambers and so on, constructed in fine ashlar masonry. These public buildings were the expression as well as the physical embodiment of the *polis* way of life which they had achieved. Even so, these solid stone buildings were vulnerable; the majority have been destroyed by earthquakes, which are frequent in Anatolia, and human spoliation. Because of their construction, the rock tombs and the theatres are the best preserved; they survive most conspicuously among the Lycian remains.

In the fifth century the Lycians were freed from the Persians by the Athenians who under the command of Kimon won, in about 468 BC, the famous battle of the Eurymedon in Pamphylia against the Persian fleet. This was one of the greatest victories of Athens which virtually liberated the entire Aegean and the coasts of Caria and Lycia from Persian rule. In that century Lycia was already regarded as part of the Hellenic world, for as from 446 BC its cities became, or were induced to become, members of the confederacy of Delos, jointly paying a contribution to Athens for their defence. Eventually, however, this payment was felt to be an unacceptable burden. The Lycians were then governed by their own princes who resented being subjected to this obligation. So when Melisandros was sent by the Athenians in the year 430 with a number of ships to extract the overdue tribute, he met with disaster. Thucydides tells us that when he landed he was defeated and killed in battle, with the loss of many of his troops. This may well be the event we find recorded in the Lycian inscription of the Kherei tomb which is situated on the north side of the Xanthos agora. The sculptures, which were found by a team of French archaeologists and which are now in the Istanbul museum, as well as the inscription itself containing a Greek epigram, recall the dynast's triumph over his Greek opponents.

Later the satraps of Lydia under Artexerxes II succeeded in regaining control of Lycia, but the local dynasts continued to retain much of their power, though frequently in conflict with one another. From about 360 BC, Mausolos and his successors extended their dominion over western Lycia under purely nominal Persian suzerainty, but were opposed by Perikles, dynast of Limyra. A few years before Mausolos started to push further south-east into the country

Perikles, who was an enterprising prince, succeeded in seizing Telmessos on the border with Caria and in extending his rule for a while over much of Lycia. Although eventually he had to yield most of the territory he had occupied to the Hekatomnid dynasts, Carian hegemony did not last long. Xanthos and the other Lycian towns were beginning to shake themselves free from their petty princes. When a few year later Alexander came, they submitted to him voluntarily and so were able to retain a considerable degree of freedom. Under his inducement or encouragement they developed into proper cities with a democratic constitution. Not long after Alexander's death they came under the dominion of the Ptolemies of Egypt for the best part of a century.

The process of hellenization in Lycia had already started in the 5th century BC. It gained momentum in the subsequent century when closer political contact took place between Greeks and Lycians following the defeat of the Persians. Greek inscriptions start appearing and gradually oust those in Lycian language and script. The architecture and sculpture of the tombs becomes distinctly Hellenic, at any rate in form. Greek mythology is adopted and eloquently expressed in the reliefs, as for instance in reliefs of the Trysa heröon. But much of the iconography is still native, or more exactly Lycian with oriental elements – Assyrian and Persian.

With the advent of Alexander the Great and his successors hellenization received an overriding impulse. Greek became the language of the country. It was indeed in the third century BC that the Lycians voluntarily gave up their native language and script for Greek. Hellenization was soon complete. But it is interesting to note that it was also in the third century that their solidarity as a nation greatly developed by their organizing themselves into a confederacy. There is no historical evidence of its having existed in the preceding century when the country was still under the rule of various princelings, though to some extent a cohesive element was already then present in the ancient Amphictyony of Apollo with its sanctuary at Patara. There are indications of this council in coins dating from before the formation of the confederacy. When the extremely characteristic institution of the Lycian confederacy came into being it consisted of twenty-three cities joined together in a league with proportional representation. It issued coins in silver with the head of Apollo on one side and his lyre on the other. The lettering varied according to the individual city in which the coin was struck. The League also issued copper coins with the heads of Artemis and Apollo. Strabo's description of the organization is, I think, worth quoting in full:

There are twenty-three cities that share in the vote. They come together from each city to a general congress, after choosing whatever city they approve of. The largest of the cities control three votes each, the medium-sized two votes each, and the rest one. In the same proportion also, they make contributions and discharge other public services. Artemidorus[1] says that the largest were

Xanthus, Patara, Olympus, Myra, Pinara and Tlos, the last-named being situated near the pass that leads over to Kibyra. At the congress they first choose a *Lyciarch*, and then other officials of the League; and general courts of justice are designated. In earlier times they would deliberate about war and peace and alliances, but now they naturally do not do so, since these matters necessarily lie in the power of the Romans, except, perhaps when the Romans should give them permission or it should be for their benefit. Likewise judges and magistrates are elected from the several cities in the same proportion. And since they lived under such a good government, they remained ever free under the Romans.[2]

Unfortunately the considerable degree of freedom they enjoyed did not survive long after Strabo's days. In AD 43 the emperor Claudius declared Lycia a Roman province. But though its powers were reduced the league was not disbanded and much of the country's administration remained in its hands. With an age of great prosperity setting in, the number of city members increased to over thirty. The League had then an assembly and a council, and in addition to the Lyciarch, the highest official, it had a chief priest elected annually who, apart from his religious tasks, held the office of Secretary of the Federation.

It is worth noting that throughout his account of the Lycians and their league Strabo makes no mention of the matriarchal customs described by Herodotus. We can assume that by the first century BC they had died out, the priority of fatherhood having prevailed as the result of hellenization.

Strabo gives us a picture of the happy state of affairs in Lycia under the Romans, but not until the Pax Romana was firmly established under Augustus and his successors did the member cities of the League always escape unpleasant experiences caused by Roman interference or highhandedness. Not long before Strabo was writing, prosperous and peaceful Xanthos suffered another catastrophe similar to her destruction by the Persians five centuries before. Plutarch gives us a graphic account of what befell the city in 42 BC when Brutus demanded money and men from the citizens, and being rebuffed attacked them. Pursuing those who had confronted him and who had taken refuge within the walls, he besieged the city. Plutarch relates that fire broke out and that the solders of Brutus tried to assist the inhabitants in putting out the fire but were prevented.

The Lycians were of a sudden possessed with a strange and incredible desperation; such a frenzy as cannot be better expressed than by calling it a violent appetite to die, for both women and children, the bondmen and the free, those of all ages and all conditions strove to force away the soldiers that came to their assistance from the walls; and themselves gathering together reeds and wood, and whatever combustible matter they could find, they spread the fire over the whole city, feeding it with whatever fuel they could, and by all possible means exciting its fury, so that the flame having dispersed itself and encircled the whole city, blazed out in so terrible a manner that Brutus, extremely afflicted by their calamity, got on horseback and rode round the walls, earnestly desirous to preserve the city, and stretching forth his hands to the Xanthians, begged of them that they would spare themselves and save the town. Yet none regarded his entreaties, but, by all manner of ways, strove to destroy themselves. Not only men and women, but even boys and little children, with a hideous outcry, leaped into the fire, others from the walls, others fell upon their parents' swords, baring their throats and desiring to be struck. After the destruction of the city there was a woman found who had hanged herself with her young child hanging from her neck, and the torch in her hand with which she had set fire to her own house.

It was so tragic a sight that Brutus could not endure to see it, but wept at the very relation of it and proclaimed a reward to any soldier that could save a Xanthian. And it is said that only a hundred and fifty were found to have their lives saved against their wills. Thus the Xanthians after a long space of years, the fated period of their destruction having run its course, repeated by their desperate deed the former calamity of their forefathers who after the very same manner in the Persian war had set fire to their city and destroyed themselves.[3]

One cannot but suspect that Plutarch's account does not quite tally with what actually happened. Plutarch seems to have committed himself to depict a portrait of Brutus as a man extremely just, honest and humane, and so he makes him weep over what happened, But if Brutus did weep, his tears, I guess, were crocodile tears. He may have tried to put out the conflagration, but was it not in his own interest to do so since he wanted money and men from the city? Besides, it is unlikely that the Xanthians should have gone to such lengths as wilfully to destroy themselves without cause, in other words unless they had reason to fear that they would be losing their freedom. They had always been brave and freedom-loving people. In any case, whatever happened could have hardly been so disastrous as to leave only 150 inhabitants alive, since Strabo, writing a mere generation or two after the event, states that Xanthos was the largest city of Lycia. It prospered throughout the Roman age and in the fifth century AD it could still boast of a neo-Platonist school. Proklos, the most prominent of the later neo-Platonist philosophers was from Xanthos, in fact he was born there according to Marinos, his successor at the Academy in Athens who wrote his biography. Certainly his parents were Xanthians. In the Byzantine age the city was the seat of a bishop under the metropolitan of Myra, but its fortunes then declined for it became exposed to the raids of pirates and Saracens. It was therefore deserted and fell into ruin.

When Sir Charles Fellows visited Xanthos in the years 1838–42 the ruins of the city lay untouched in their beautiful and at that time scarcely inhabited valley under the splendid ridges of Mount Makissytos. The river, deep yellow-green, wound its way gracefully at the foot of the acropolis. As early as the seventh century BC the lyric poet Alkman compared the beautiful hair of a maiden of Sparta with the yellow streams of the Xanthos and her song with the song of a swan of that river. In those days the whole neighbourhood was more wooded and picturesque than it is today. Intensive farming, asphalt roads, tractors, archeological activities and tourism have greatly altered the atmosphere, but the site still retains some of its dignity and evocative beauty. From the top of the rocky hill, where the Roman acropolis was situated, the view is truly magnificent.

Fellows was able to remove most of the surviving pieces of sculpture he found on the site and with the help of the Royal Navy had them transported to London where they are to be seen in the British Museum, well conserved against the rigours of weather and the ravages of time. It is these remains, particularly the Nereid Monument which he found collapsed on the ground, and the tomb of the Harpies (Pl. 16) (in fact of the Sirens as it should be called), that reflect the penetration of Hellenism in the fifth and fourth centuries, rather than anything we can see *in situ* such as the striking and typically Lycian rock-cut, gabled or pillar tombs.

The monolithic pillar of the so-called Harpy Tomb still stands to the height of about 28 feet (8.5 metres), together with the sepulchral chest that crowns it, but the reliefs which encompass the funerary chamber are plaster casts of the originals. These rank among the finest pieces of Greek scultpure of the early fifth century BC, most probably executed by Greek sculptors imported by the ruling Lycian dynasty at a time when Greek culture was beginning to penetrate the country. The Harpy Tomb as a structure is still typically Lycian, but the reliefs are manifestly Hellenic.

The hellenization of Lycia compared with Caria presents a particularly interesting and unusual aspect. In Caria the native culture, whatever it was, had not greatly evolved and had little to show, so the penetration of Hellenism into the country and the wholesale adoption of the Greek way of life were a natural development of a people temperamentally akin to the Greeks. But in Lycia, as we see from the tombs and inscriptions all over the country, a high degree of indigenous evolution had been achieved, so much so that the native language was clung to with greater tenacity than in Caria even when Hellenism had infiltrated deeply. If we look at the picture of the situation presented by the sepulchres, we see first the typical rock-hewn tombs which mirror the structure of the timber houses, then the rock tombs with temple-like façades, the first to reflect the adoption of Greek architecture, and thirdly tombs not cut in the rock but free-standing in the form of a Greek temple, often but not always on a high podium. The pillar tombs, prominent only in the dynastic age, remained

characteristically and exclusively Lycian in character even when furnished with
hellenized or hellenizing reliefs as the Harpy Tomb was.

The most significant surviving structure of Xanthos to embody a process
of hellenization already advanced at the outset of the fourth century BC is the
Nereid Monument (Pl. 15) which now stands in full view in the British Museum,
most of its parts having been successfully put together. The monument is
remarkable not only because the structure is attractive as architecture and
displays some of the finest pieces of ancient Greek sculpture, particularly the
three Nereids, but also because it is the first model of a typical Anatolian
sepulchral building in which Hellenic architectural features are applied and
adapted to a Lycian conception of entombment. The high podium on which the
deceased was placed and the size of the whole structure, a glorified after-death
abode well above and insulated from the unstable ground, are in accordance with
an oriental ideal. But the temple-like structure resting on the podium and
consisting of six Ionic columns on the flanks and four on the front and back
holding an entablature is typically Hellenic. Most probably the main architect
and the main sculptor or sculptors were Greek, though they may well have had
Lycian assistants trained by them, which would account for the difference in
quality we see in the reliefs of the friezes and bands that encircle the podium.
These consist mainly of battle scenes. The artists seem to have been inspired by
the the Erechtheion and by the friezes of the Parthenon with which they were
certainly acquainted, but we find a curious coming together of Hellenic and
oriental elements in the reliefs as well as in some of the architectural parts.

It has been suggested that Arttumpara, who was beaten by Perikles of
Limyra at Telmessos in the seventies or sixties of the fourth century, might have
been the dynast who had the monument built as his sepulchre. But in my opinion
the style as well as the entire character of the building points to a somewhat
earlier date, closer to the turn of the century. More likely it was Arttumpara's
predecessor, whose name remains unrecorded, a dynast unbeaten in battle and
proud of his warlike spirit reflected in the lower frieze of the podium.

Almost certainly Mausolos saw this monument as he advanced into Lycia
to seize control many years after its erection, for there can hardly be any doubt
that it inspired the planning and design of his own monumental sepulchre at
Halikarnassos.

The well-preserved theatre dates from the Roman period and indeed its
architectural features are extremely Roman. The orchestra lies well below the
level of the first row of seats to protect the public from the wild beasts and
desperate gladiators contesting with one another. But the arch of the emperor
Vespasian, the first structure to be seen on the way up to the city, is handsome.
The city gate near by, of which little remains, was built in the Hellenistic style
and is interesting not only because it is one of the very few structures still visible
at Xanthos from a time when the city was experiencing a spell of prosperity, but

also because it bears an inscription honouring Antiochus III. It may therefore date from 197 BC, when he sailed along the coast to receive the surrender of the Lycian cities which had been under Ptolemaic control for over a century.

With a good guidebook in hand the visitor today can find the way through these ruins up the rough hillside to the necropolis where the famous Payava tomb stood before it was taken away to the British Museum. This tomb of the fourth century BC is noteworthy on account of its reliefs which show the coming together of two cultures – the relatively static Persian world and the dynamism of Greece. The seated notable, probably Autophradates satrap of Lydia, who to some extent gained control of Lycia between 390 and 350 BC, is typically robed in Persian fashion and so are his retainers. By contrast the Lycians are represented naked as Greek athletes or partially clad as Greek warriors. Some of them, however, are bearded and unlike the Greeks of that period wear their hair down to their shoulders. Despite the penetration of Hellenism they kept this characteristically eastern trait, as Mausolos himself still did.

In the neighbourhood of this site, a little below the top of the hill where the remains of the so-called Roman acropolis are to be seen, a splendid fourth-century pillar tomb nearly 23 feet (7 metres) in height shows no apparent trace of the current of culture at that time coming from the Aegean. By contrast particularly interesting for our pursuit is, I think, a less spectacular tomb also of the fourth century, which once stood outside the walls on the eastern side of the hill but which, overthrown by an earthquake, lay broken on the ground when Fellows came there. He removed its parts and, with the other finds on the site of the city, had them transported to the British Museum where we see them today reassembled. It is known as the Merehi sarcophagus, from the name of the entombed Lycian warrior inscribed upon it. On the gabled top of the tomb we see represented in Hellenic style a chariot drawn by four prancing horses and driven by two warriors, both beardless and dressed like Greeks; one is bare-headed, his haircut Greek, the other is wearing a crested helmet. Our special attention, however, should focus on the bottom righthand corner of the whole representation where, crouching beneath the feet of the two foremost horses, the monster Chimaera is to be seen. There is no Bellerophon, however, and no Pegasus. We can only assume that one of the warriors was Merehi himself who probably wished to indicate his descent from Bellerophon. The Chimaera opens up a vast Graeco-Lycian landscape going back to the days of Homer. The myth was evidently deeply rooted in Lycian iconography by the fourth century BC. Bellerophon and Pegasus appear on a tomb relief at Tlos 18 miles (30 km) north of Xanthos as the crow flies, although not the Chimaera. But all three are represented in a relief of the Trysa heroon, again of the fourth century, now in the Kunsthistorisches Museum in Vienna. The site of Trysa where it was found is about 45 miles (70 km) east of Xanthos.

To what extent was the myth, or part of it, indigenous? Where did it arise, in Greece or in Lycia? A definite answer to the question has not yet been found, first of all because there are no Lycian relief sculptures totally uninfluenced by Hellenism and secondly because the Lycian language is not yet fully understood. We simply do not know what Lycian mythology might have been before the penetration or influence of Hellenism, although we know the names of some of their deities.[4] The rather inorganic structure of the Chimaera, with the head of a lion, the upper part of a goat and a snake as its tail, could suggest an oriental origin, perhaps Hittite.[5] On its way from the east this fire-breathing monster may have found the burning gas jet in the foothills of Lycian Mount Olympus a congenial locality for its den and developed into a nation-wide myth. Strabo, however, localizes it not in eastern Lycia as Pliny and others do, but in a ravine of Mount Kragos not far from Xanthos. Whatever the exact nature of its origin, the myth of the Chimaera had already spread from Lycia across the Aegean to Greece in pre-Homeric days. Homer, who is the first to describe her, states that she was of divine stock, while Hesiod is more specific in his account of her awesome pedigree as well as of her body structure and fierce nature.[6] He tells us that Keto gave birth to the 'fierce goddess' Echidne who was 'half nymph with glancing eyes and fair cheeks, and half again a huge snake, great and awful, with speckled skin, eating raw flesh beneath the secret parts of the earth.' The monster Typhaon, 'outrageous and terrible, was joined in love to the maid with glancing eyes. So she conceived and brought forth fierce offspring,' among others Cerberus the hound of Hades, the Hydra of Lerna and the Chimaera.

Typhaon was born in the Corycian Cave of Cilicia, so it is not surprising that his daughter Chimaera should also be an Anatolian monster. But the whole story of Bellerophon and Pegasus is typically Greek, namely of the winged horse that sprang from the head of Medusa severed by Perseus and of the Corinthian hero Bellerophon who riding it flew over Lycia to fight the Chimaera at the behest of Iobates king of Lycia, who was intent on having him killed because of the grudge his daughter Anteia, queen of Tiryns, bore him for having rejected her advances. The myth existed in Greece before there was any real penetration of Hellenism into Lycia, and also before there was any likelihood of there taking shape in Anatolia a mythical story of the kind with its hero a Corinthian. On the other hand the rumour of a monster spitting fire was most likely carried from Lycia into the Homeric world through the Greek settlements on the coast of Asia Minor and the Aegean islands from where it spread and became an integral part of a Greek myth. When the process of Hellenic penetration of Lycia started in the fifth century BC much of Greek mythology, including the deities of the Olympian pantheon, was soon adopted and superimposed upon whatever native mythological background there may have been. So from the fourth century onwards we find represented in the reliefs of Lycia the traditional feats such as battles with the Amazons, Lapiths fighting centaurs and of course Bellerophon mounted on Pegasus slaying the Chimaera, this last being probably regarded by the dynasts and the people as a national myth. And so the Chimaera represented alone could become a national emblem.

As far as architecture is concerned little has survived *in situ* at Xanthos which is conspicuous in appearance and which at the same time reflects the great wave of Hellenism that swept through Anatolia, compared with the remains at certain other sites in Lycia, such as those of the Letöon and Patara in the neighbourhood of Xanthos itself.

Near the outlet of the river, in what has been marshy land for a very long time, there arose a confederate sanctuary of Lycia known as the Letöon, dedicated to the cult of Leto who gave birth to Apollo and Artemis. She was of Anatolian origin[7] and Ovid in his *Metamorphoses* relates how she was loved by Zeus and consequently aroused the vindictive jealously of Hera who, having discovered that she was pregnant, proceeded to pursue her unremittingly from place to place. Even after having given birth to Apollo and Artemis in the island of Delos, Leto was driven away by pitiless Hera carrying her two infant children.

And now, having reached the borders of Lycia, home of the Chimaera, when the hot sun beats fiercely upon the fields, the goddess weary of her long struggle, was faint by reason of the sun's heat and parched with thirst, and the hungry children had drained her breasts dry of milk. She chanced to see a small lake far down in the valley; some peasants were there gathering bushy osiers. Leto came to the water's edge and kneeled to the ground to drink the cool water and quench her thirst. But the rustic rabble would not let her drink. Most pitifully she beseeched them: 'Even as I speak, my mouth is dry of moisture, my throat is parched and my voice can scarce find utterance . . . Life you will give me if you let me drink.' But despite all her entreaties they kept denying her request with threats if she did not go away, soiling the water with their feet in the pool and stirring up the mud. Then, in anger the goddess lifted her hands up to heaven and cried: 'Let them live for ever in the pool.' Whereupon they were turned into frogs.

Ovid (*Metamorphoses*, VI, 339ff.) goes on to describe most vividly how the frogs behaved in the muddy pool ever afterwards, leaping and croaking. And indeed even today the frogs at Letöon are still noisily croaking.

The story Ovid relates was based on an old legend which mythographers before him had recorded and which reflects the close connection of Leto with Anatolia, particularly Lycia where the cult of the goddess, a fertility deity, went back to prehistory. The unfriendly behaviour of the peasants may suggest that, coming as a foreign goddess, she met with local opposition before her cult was established. On the other hand it is known that Leto was the Greek name for a Lycian divinity who in Greek mythology was hellenized, and inasmuch as the

Letöon, the sanctuary, was hellenized at an early date, the goddess was worshipped there in her Greek form.

Thanks to French archaeologists, who have been conducting excavations on the site with remarkable success in spite of the swampy ground, the ruins at the Letöon are both interesting and striking, though practically nothing of the buildings is still standing today. But the bases of three temples of the fourth and third centuries BC, a large nymphaion dating back to the age of Hadrian, magnficent porticoes of the Hellenistic and Graeco-Roman period, a fairly large theatre of those days in a good state of preservation and a smaller theatre of the Hellenistic era which awaits excavation, all betoken the vitality of the Letöon cult which lasted nearly a millenium and evidently embodied several different activities. Of special historical interest is an inscription, found near one of the temples and now in the local museum, which is in Greek, Lycian and Aramaic, dating from about 358 BC. The text is of a decree which established at the Letöon a new cult of a Carian and a Lycian god, Basileios Kaunios and Arkesimas. The decree was issued by the satrap Orna, apparently the oriental name of Pixodaros. It would appear, therefore, that Pixodaros for a short while succeeded in deposing his brother Mausolos as satrap of Caria with the support and approval of Artaxerxes III. No wonder then that he ousted his sister after his brother's death. However, it is most unlikely that Mausolos ever lost control of government throughout his rule; there is no other evidence that this occurred. So a very plausible theory has been put forward that the dating of the inscription, which appears in the Aramaic version, has been incorrcctedly interpreted as 358 and should be understood as 337 when Pixodaros was indeed satrap.[8]

The fact that the inscription is in these three languages is of particular interest inasmuch as it would seem to indicate that at that time decrees would still be issued in the offical court language of the Persians, Aramaic. Greek would be used for the information of the cultivated upper classes of Lycia, while Lycian would also have to be used since it was still the language of the people or a proportion of them.

The site of Patara lies embedded in sand a few miles south of the Letöon. Although invaded by dunes the visible remains of its buildings are enough to give an idea of the importance of the city as the principal port of Lycia on which much of the country's economy depended. Although remarkable Lycian tombs are to be seen among its ruins, the signs of hellenization and of Graeco-Roman prosperity are more conspicuous at Patara than at Xanthos, not least because the visitor is at once confronted, on approaching the site, with a stupendous city gate in the form of a triple arch containing consoles to support busts, which was built about AD 100.

Patara had a distinguished mythological past. The city was said to have been founded by Pataros, a son of Apollo by Lycia, daughter of the river god Xanthos. It became famous for its sanctuary of Apollo and his prophetess. The oracle functioned, however, only in the winter when the prophetess was shut up in the god's temple during the night because he would then want to rest and find her in the sanctuary.

A surviving token of the importance of Patara as a port for the Romans, whose fleet bearing grain to Rome could anchor there in safety, can be found in the remains of a large granary built at the time of Hadrian, much of it still standing though embedded in vegetation. Near by is a pseudo-peripteral structure which might have been a monumental tomb. On the opposite, south-eastern side of the harbour, a fine little Corinthian temple (Pl. 14) is worth noting, a prostyle edifice without a row of surrounding columns, which is still standing in a fairly good condition. Its perfect ashlar masonry and fine marble door are striking. The building dates back to the days of Hadrian or the Antonines when purism and good taste prevailed. But perhaps the most impressive ruin at Patara is the theatre, partly because of its situation carved into the hillside and overlooking the whole site. Although an entire section of it is now buried in sand, its characteristic features still emerge quite clearly. An inscription tells us that the *skene* was built in the days of Vespasian, but the *cavea* most probably predates it.

Before the Romans, Patara came under the rule of the Ptolemies of Egypt for a while. Ptolemy II Philadelphos changed its name to Arsinoe in honour of his beloved wife. When the Seleucids came, however, the name of the city reverted to its original form.

Patara, it should be recalled, was not only the birthplace of Saint Nicholas, bishop of Myra, but also an important halting place for Saint Paul who embarked there on his way to Rome. The large harbour from which he sailed is now a reedy swamp, for it gradually silted up towards the end of the Roman age. So having become useless as a port Patara declined and was abandoned, leaving a world of space, solitude and grandeur to take over which breathes through the ruins, trees and shrubs like the wind that silently blows over the dunes from the white-crested waves, bearing sand and more sand.

North of Xanthos, the hub of ancient Lycia, are situated the sites of six important cities, members of the confederacy: Sidyma, Pinara, Tlos, Telmessos, Kadyanda and Kibyra.

Nearest to Xanthos and nestling in a hollow of the Kragos range are the ruins of Sidyma. But little has survived of this city. When Fellows visited the site in 1840 the remains were still considerable and he came across only 'three or four inhabited huts amidst the ruins'. At the close of the last century temples, the agora, the theatre and very many large tombs were conspicuous remains. But now a village has sprung up on the site which has eaten into the remains leaving only a few walls, a few stones of a temple dedicated to Artemis, a heröon and some tombs dating back to the Roman age, when the city was extremely prosperous. At that time Sidyma had a *gerousia*, a society of elders headed by the gymnasiarch and consisting of 51 councillors and 50 commoners.

If we are to believe the information Fellows obtained when he visited the site, lions, leopards and bears were not lacking in the surrounding neighbourhood. Today you hear only of wolves. No doubt in ancient times the lion was fairly common in Anatolia, which would account for the frequent appearance of lions' heads sculpted on monuments and tombs throughout the country.

About another ten miles (16 km) further north, up against the spurs of Antikragos, the remains of ancient Pinara are to be found most dramatically situated. Pinara was a major Lycian city with the right to three votes in the League, one of the six cities with this privilege mentioned by Strabo.

On a shelf of the rugged mountainside, about a thousand feet above the fertile valley of Minara, whose lush vegetation and natural beauty Fellows most graphically describes, lay the lower part of the city. Then above a steep escarpment, a terrace extends on which the upper section of the city was placed. Towering above, on the summit of a huge truncated cone, stood the acropolis. 'Pinara' meant 'round' in ancient Lycian, according to Staphanus Byzantius, and the name may have derived from the shape of the great cliff which, however, gives the impression of being more square than round. Its precipitous limestone face, honeycombed with hundreds if not thousands of hollowed-out tombs, presents a spectacular sight. Of the acropolis buildings practically nothing remains – the result of earthquakes. On the other hand the ruins of the city on the upper terrace are considerable and include the remains of an odeion, a temple, a mausoleum, the agora and many tombs, but all difficult to identify on account of the indifferent state of preservation and the thick overgrowth of vegetation which covers the entire site. However here the stately pines rise, striking features of the setting, and looking down to the theatre, which nestles in the hillside on the eastern edge of the lower terrace, the view across the valley of the Xanthos to the snow-capped range of Massikytos is truly magnificent (Pl. 18).

Unfortunately the lower part of the city, where many more ruins were visible in the days of Fellows and of Spratt and Forbes who visited the site a year later, has greatly suffered from the farming activities of the villagers of Minara, while the upper part of the city has been much reduced as the result of stones being removed for building. The only structure which still survives as a real architectural feature in the landscape is the theatre, beautifully situated and, having been cut in the rock of the hillside, in an excellent state of preservation. It is of the Greek type, its *analemmata* converging to the centre of the orchestra, and was built not later than the second century BC,[9] showing how the Hellenic way of life had by then taken hold of the city. Of notable interest are also the tombs carved in the rock of the escarpment, particularly one in which the outlines of a Lycian city are represented, more clearly visible, however, in the days of Fellows. These tombs are Lycian in character and were probably made early in the fourth century BC, but some are surmounted with pediments which indicates that the influence of Hellenism was already felt before the theatre was built. They are approached through a delightful grove of plane trees where a brook of clear water purls down from a nearby spring.

Many of the inscriptions found on the site are in Lycian, but some also in Greek. In Strabo's days the link with Homer was strongly felt for he tells us that Pandaros, the Trojan ally of Lycian extraction, was held in great honour by the inhabitants of Pinara.[10]

The city surrendered to Alexander the Great on his march through Lycia. After his death it was annexed to the Attalid kingdom, while retaining its municipal autonomy, and subsequently enjoyed considerable prosperity under the Roman principate. It suffered greatly, however, from two earthquakes, in AD 141 and 240, after which the city declined although it remained inhabited for several centuries.

Away to the north-east, majestically situated across the valley of the river Xanthos, is the site of Tlos, another important city of the Lycian League with the right to three votes. Its position, perched on a steep rocky hump under the lofty ridges of the Massikytos range, cannot fail to strike the visitor with wonder. The acropolis occupied the summit now crowned by the walls of an Ottoman fortress, which of course rests on very ancient foundations. Cut in the north-eastern side of the limestone cliff, which here falls sheer clothed in plane, walnut and kermes oak trees, various tombs show up conspicuously as the visitor approaches the site, some entirely Lycian in character, others with composite elements, others still with Greek temple-like façades. The most interesting one is in the form of an Ionic temple which impressed Fellows and several travellers after him because it contains a relief showing Bellerophon mounted on Pegasus. There is no Chimaera, as far as it is possible to see, but Bellerophon was a hero dear to the Lycians and his feats were not limited to the slaying of the fire-spitting monster. He and Pegasus were often represented on Lycian coins. Unfortunately the relief sculptures, which Fellows was able to see clearly, have since then greatly deteriorated.

The actual buildings of the hellenized Lycian city lie in a saddle between the acropolis and the main declivities of the Massikytos range. They mostly date back to the Roman age and now consist of remains of a gymnasium, a palaestra, traces of an agora and a stadium as well as a temple. But they are too ruined and smothered in vegetation to emerge clearly as enjoyable architectural elements of the scenery. Though encumbered with shrubs the theatre, which Opramoas the rich patron of Rhodiapolis built or reconstructed, is sufficiently well preserved to form a most satisfying feature in the landscape with the acropolis rising in the background behind the remains of the *skene*.

At about 30 miles (48 km) west of Tlos the ancient city of Telmessos was situated beside the sea in a beautiful bay not far from the border with Caria.

Having greatly suffered from earthquakes, nothing has survived of its buildings which are now covered by the modern town of Fethiye, rebuilt in 1957 after having been razed to the ground by a cataclysmic earthquake. But in the 1830s, when Charles Texier visited the site, a temple of Apollo was still standing and the theatre was practically intact. Of this theatre, built in the Graeco-Roman age and situated close to the sea, virtually lapped by the waves, Texier says: '*On n'a pas en Europe un seul monument de ce genre aussi bien conservé et d'aussi bon style.*'[11] Both temple and theatre have now vanished.

The only conspicuous remains of Telmessos are its famous rock tombs. The magnificent fourth-century BC tomb of Amyntas (Pl. 17), a wealthy citizen, is indeed a striking feature in the landscape. Looking like the façade of a temple in antis of the Ionic order, it is excavated in the face of a great cliff which dominates the town. The tomb can be approached only at a steep gradient from below.

Although very little of Telmessos has survived the city had an interesting history which should not be overlooked. In the first half of the fourth century it was occupied and held for a while by Perikles, prince of Limyra, in his contest with Mausolos. Thereafter Alexander was able to seize the city peacefully with the help and intercession of Aristander, a sage and seer native of Telmessos who had for many years been close to Philip king of Macedon and then accompanied Alexander on his eastbound campaign. After Alexander's death Telmessos came for some time under the suzerainty of the Ptolemies, but in 189 BC was handed over by the Romans to Eumenes king of Pergamon. Later, like the other cities of Lycia, it was given by the Romans to the Rhodians and so came to form part of what was known as the Peraia, meaning 'the country on the opposite side' of Rhodes. The Rhodians were far from popular, however, so much relief was felt when the city was finally embodied in the Roman province of Lycia and Pamphylia. Throughout these vicissitudes Telmessos succeeded in retaining a considerable degree of autonomy, subject to tribute or taxes having to be paid to the sovereign power. In 168 BC it joined the Lycian League: coins were issued to commemorate the event.

North-west of Telmessos at a distance of about 20 miles (30 km) the remains of Kadyanda are situated. The site occupies the top of a mountain at an altitude of 10,000 feet (3000 metres) and is embedded in a pine forest surrounded by scenery of striking grandeur. Fellows, who was alive to the wonders of nature and landscape, described the view on reaching the site after a steep climb:

The view was overwhelmingly beautiful. To the south-west lay the Bay of Macry, with its islands and the coast of the south of Caria, while beyond lay the long and mountainous island of Rhodes. Cragus, with its snowy tops, broke the view towards the south, and the coast and sea off Patara measured its elevation by carrying the eye down to the valley of the Xanthos, whose glittering waters were visible for probably seventy miles, until lost in the range of high mountains on a part of which we were standing; in this chain it has its rise in the north. The crags of limestone around us were almost concealed by a forest of fir-trees and green underwood. Before us was the city, surrounded by beautiful Cyclopian walls.[12]

From what he goes on to say it is evident that the ruins were more prominent than they appear today. Barely emerging above an accumulation of dead branches and pine needles they consist of an agora, a stadium, a gymnasium, a temple, a Hellenistic theatre, baths, some tombs and some fine inscriptions in Greek. Except for the theatre, carved in the mountainside, which is in a fair state of preservation, these ruins are in poor condition. No doubt much more than is at present visible lies buried in the ground, though the buildings have suffered not only from earthquakes but also from human spoliation. Tombs have been rifled and many pits have been dug by treasure hunters. As yet only a survey of the site is being carried out by a team of French archaeologists. The settlement may date back to the fifth century BC. In the fourth century, jointly with Pinara and Tlos, Kadyanda honoured Pixodaros, dynast of Caria, with gifts. The baths, the walls of which survive in part, were a donation of the emperor Vespasian, which shows that the city was on good terms with the Romans. But this is about all we know of Kadyanda's history so far.

Kibyra, with its remarkable ruins and interesting history, should not be over-looked in this survey of the main cities of northern Lycia, even though it hardly belonged to Lycia proper and its citizens never spoke Lycian. Away to the north, at a good distance from Tlos and overlooking lake Gölhissar, which lies in a plain a few miles east of the site, the region in which it is situated could just as well be regarded as part of southern Phrygia, or Pisidia, or Lydia, or even Caria to which the city was for a while attached by the emperor Diocletian, since all these regions here converge. However its history was in due course more closely connected with Lycia whose confederacy it joined in 84 BC after having to submit to Licinius Murena, who put an end to its political independence though not to its autonomy. Before then it had formed a league of its own consisting of three lesser cities in the neighbourhood in addition to itself. It is worth quoting what Strabo says of this city in a very explicit paragraph of his 'Geography'.

It is said that the Kibyratae are descendants of the Lydians who took possession of Kabalis and later of the neighbouring Pisidians, who settled there, and transferred the city to another site, a site very strongly fortified and about one hundred stadia in circuit. It grew strong through its good laws; and its villages extended alongside it from Pisidia and the neighbouring Milyas as far as Lycia and the Peraea of the Rhodians. Three bordering cities were added to it, Bubon, Balbura and Oenoanda, and the union was called Tetrapolis, each of

the three having one vote, but Kibyra two; for Kibyra could send forth thirty
thousand foot-soldiers and two thousand horse. It was always ruled by tyrants;
but still they ruled it with moderation. However, the tyranny ended in the time
of Moagetes, when Murena overthrew it and included Balbura and Bubon
within the territory of the Lycians. But none the less the jurisdiction of Kibyra
is rated among the greatest in Asia. The Kibyratae used four languages, the
Pisidian, that of the Solymi, Greek and that of the Lydians; but there is not
even a trace of the language of the Lydians in Lydia. The skilful embossing of
iron is a peculiar thing of Kibyra.[13]

The Moagetes whom Strabo mentions is obviously not the same tyrant as
the one Livy refers to by the same name in his account of the campaign in
Anatolia which the Roman consul Cnaeus Manlius carried on against the
Galatians a hundred years earlier, shortly after the defeat of Antiochos III at
the battle of Magnesia. Though threatened by the Roman army this Moagetes,
ruler of Kibyra, succeeded in retaining the independence of his city by
clever negotiations, agreeing to pay the Roman army one hundred talents and
to supply a certain amount of corn. Livy gives us a picture of a cunning,
cringing, despicable tyrant, but it must be borne in mind that he was writing
as a Roman and so from the enemy's point of view. Polybius, writing earlier
but in the same spirit, tells the story in very similar terms. By contrast
Strabo's picture of what the government of Kibyra was like is impartial and well-
balanced.

Loss of political independence did not mean impoverishment or stagna-
tion. Kibyra's autonomy was sufficient to provide incentive of various kinds. As
Strabo tells us its wrought iron craftsmen were well known for their skill and
output. It played its part in the Lycian confederacy when it jointed the League
and like the other cities of Lycia and Caria Kibyra benefited from the Pax
Romana and prospered.

Strabo uses the past tense in referring to the polyglot nature of the
Kibyrites, so it is not clear whether by then Greek had already ousted the other
languages to the same extent to which Greek had wiped out the Lydian language
in Lydia. No doubt it was the official language, the city having become totally
hellenized as the coins, the incriptions and the remains of the buildings attest,
notably the stadium carved in the hillside and overlooking the lake in the distance
and the splendid theatre (which could do with some clearing) beautifully situated
on the uppermost slope of the site. The stage building is in ruins, but a fine door
is still standing. Close by is a large odeion in a fair condition dating from the
Roman age. It stood to its full height until not long ago, but at present its entire
lower part is covered with earth, possibly as the result of a landslide. Scattered
around over a large area lie the ruins of many other buildings including a
temple of the Roman age. There are also fine ashlar city walls of an earlier

period. So hellenized had the Kibyrites become that they claimed to be of Spartan descent.

Of the other three cities which with Kibyra formed the tetrapolis mentioned by Strabo the remains of Oinoanda are the most striking. The mass of ruins which spill over the mountain crest overlooking the Turkish village of İncevelier some 30 miles (50 km) south of Kibyra are remarkable and show that Oinoanda, which began to flourish in the second century BC, was a city of importance scarcely overshadowed by Kibyra.

The theatre is not as large as the one at Kibyra and its stage building is in no better condition, but its *cavea* is in a fairly good state of preservation. The fine stone pavement of a spacious agora still survives, backed by a solid ashlar wall and some arches of an unidentified building of the Roman age surge majestically over a mass of confused ruins. Many walls still rise to a height of ten feet (3 metres) or more over a considerable area.

Oinoanda was first described by Spratt and Forbes, who visited the site in 1842, subsequently by E. Petersen who surveyed the site epigraphically in 1882.[14] He argued that Oinoanda in its Hellenistic days must have come under the rule of Pergamon, namely when Eumenes II was king (197–159), since several of the architectural features of the walls have a marked Pergamenian character. This period must have preceded the city's membership of the Kibyritian tetrapolis which was dissolved by Murena in 84 BC. Oinoanda became then a member of the Lycian confederacy under Roman supremacy.

The Council and the People head the decisions taken by the city which are recorded in several of the inscriptions and which reflect the democratic and Hellenic character of the constitution. Some of the magistrates are mentioned, e.g. the gymnasiarch, the city clerk and the controller of victuals, literally the 'measurer of corn'.

Petersen points out how the nomenclature as shown by the inscriptions changes chronologically. First Lycian or Pisidian names appear, then Greek, followed by Roman names, such as Licinius, the name of a notable patron and benefactor in the second century AD. In the Roman age citizens were inclined to adopt Latin names, while the city life and language continued to be Greek as in all the hellenized cities of Asia Minor.

From the many inscriptions that have survived we can see that Oinoanda did not lag behind in the intellectual life of the second-century Graeco-Roman world. Particularly interesting is a long inscription recording the Epicurean philosophy of a certain Diogenes who was a citizen of Oinoanda. It deals with the formation of the world and affirms Epicurean tenets such as: 'The key to happiness is our physical condition, a thing in our control.'

We now turn south again and proceed eastward from Xanthos, which was the main city of Lycia and which with the Letöon and Patara may be regarded historically as the heart of the country. But was it really? Two major cities lay away to the east, whose voices in the confederacy were equal to that of Xanthos.

First we come to a central group of cities which occupy an area in the southernmost region of Lycia bordering on the sea, some right on the coast, others close inland. Of this group Myra was the most important for it was one of the six members of the League that had the right to three votes. But all are remarkable for being characteristically Lycian, in other words indigenous, with at the same time outstanding evidence of the penetration of Hellenism, of which the most significant indication was the theatre. Wherever a theatre is to be found the Greek *diaita* had set its foot, without necessarily extinguishing certain characteristic features of native culture. For instance at Antiphellos, the western-most of this group, we see one of the most perfect truly Hellenic theatres in Lycia and then, only a few hundred yards away, standing in the present village of Kaş which occupies the ancient site, a magnificent, typically Lycian gabled tomb, which may not have preceded the construction of the theatre by many years.

Habesos was the original Lycian name of the city, as Pliny tells us, but when it became hellenized in the fourth century the inhabitants changed its name to Antiphellos, which is a Greek word literally meaning 'before the cork tree'. This name arose from its being the harbour of Phellos, a larger and originally more important city at some distance in the mountains of the hinterland. So out of a small centre of habitation Antiphellos grew and flourished, its prosperity deriving from the export of timber and the sponge trade. It became a member of the Lycian League and evidently never felt the need for extensive fortifications, since there are only a few defensive walls to be seen.

The Hellenistic theatre (Pl. 19) overlooks the sea with a magnificent prospect of the whole bay of Kaş. It is relatively small, without a *diazoma*, exquisitely proportioned and, although the *skene* is missing, in a very good state of preservation, without having undergone later modifications such as Romani-zation. Carved in the hillside the projecting ends of the *cavea* are held up by beautiful ashlar masonry.

The very scanty remains of a temple can be seen on the left side of the road leading to the theatre from the village. In a much better state of preservation because cut out of the rock is a tomb of the Hellenic temple type further up the hillside, with a fine door between two pillars in relief.

Apart from a few other tombs nothing else at Antiphellos has survived from ancient times, partly on account of the growth of Kaş. From a group of three houses in Fellows' day, called by the Turks Andiffelo, it has become a prosperous village and tourist resort invaded by thousands of holidaymakers and hundreds of yachts in the summer months. Its position by the sea is indeed stupendous, in a bay embraced by articulated stretches of land with the beautifully shaped island of Kastelorizo facing the harbour and completing a picture of form, colour and light.

Some 15 miles (24 km) due east of Antiphellos is another wonderful bay, the ancient Asthene known today as Kekova, virtually encircled by hilly tongues of land and islets. Like the bay of Kaş it is much visited in the summer months by yachts because of the shelter it affords and by holiday makers because of its natural beauty. On the shores of this bay and a few miles inland the sites of a number of Lycian cities follow one another closely – Aperlai, Apollonia, Theimiussa, Simena, Istlada and Isinda. Their remains are not striking, but they are interesting and attractive thanks to their setting in a remarkable landscape.

None of these settlements was big, in fact most of them were very modest towns and therefore several could not afford a theatre, which is found only in the more sizeable cities. In order to have adequate say in the confederacy a smaller city would be represented by a larger one, as in the case of Simena which was represented by Aperlai. Some of these cities, moreover, joined together to form what was known as a sympolity in order to create a weightier political and economic entity, namely Aperlai, Apollonia, Simena and Isinda.

Nearest to Antiphellos and situated close to the sea is the site of Aperlai, some of whose remains date back to the fourth or fifth century BC. The ruins consist mainly of polygonal walls and towers from various periods.

The remains of Apollonia lie at some distance inland on top of a rugged hill. This city was of some importance as well as size for it had a theatre which has survived (not, however, in a good state), and a remarkable heroon. There are also traces of baths and other structures including cisterns and tombs, some of these being upright stelai. As far as we know the settlement was called Apollonia from the start, which would seem to indicate that it was established in circumstances already permeated with Hellenism.

Istlada is another site situated a little inland and, overlooking it at no great distance, is the site of an unidentified Lycian centre of habitation near the present village of Kapakli, formerly Hoyran, with an acropolis high up on a rocky hill as well as interesting tombs. Some of these are typically Lycian, but others bear reliefs which show the influence of Hellenism. Both sites, like the ruins of Isinda situated inland further west, are probably of fortified fiefdoms rather than real cities.

Charmingly located down by the sea are the ruins of Theimiussa, a small city of which little has survived apart from tombs. One of these bears the figure of a youth in relief.

Simena, also beautifully situated by the sea in the bay of Kekova, is dominated by a medieval castle on a hill, within whose walls a delightful small theatre nestles, carved into the rock.

The remains of these cities in the whole Kekova region are not in any way outstanding from a visual and architectural point of view, but they are attractive because of their picturesque tumbledown walls and numerous tombs set in a scenery of great beauty. The buildings have suffered too much from the inclemencies of nature and time to form features in the landscape that can conjure up an image of their past city life. Only the tombs, because of their structural nature, have survived in a fairly good state. The inscriptions that have been found on them are in Lycian and in Greek; these, with some reliefs and coins, constitute the only records which can provide some indication of their past history, but give us very little information.

Further inland, however, and right away from the sea, are two sites of particular interest with regard to the history of Lycia and the penetration of Hellenism – Kyaneai and Trysa.

Perched on top of a high cliff is the site of Kyaneai. The name is Greek; the actual word means dark blue, perhaps in this case the name of a nymph. Did the city have a Lycian name in pre-Hellenic times? Or did its foundation take place only after the third century BC when Greek had become the language of the country? This question remains unanswered since neither the inscription nor any of the ancient writers provide a clue. The city was of some size and wealth as its remains show, particularly the fine theatre with framed seats along the lower *diazoma*, which commands a magnificent view over the surrounding rugged countryside and the indented coast of Kekova. It was built in the Hellenistic age and restored, after an earthquake in the second century AD, with funds donated by the Lyciarch Jason, a rich citizen of Kyaneai and a generous patron who, like Opramoas of Rhodiapolis, contributed a great deal to the erection and repair of many buildings in southern Lycia. When Lieutenant Spratt and his friends visited the site in 1842 the two sustaining walls of the *cavea*, the *analemmata*, 'of solid masonry' as he describes them, were intact. Unfortunately they are now in ruins, but the rest of the *cavea* is in a good state of preservation and still very impressive.

Besides the theatre at Kyaneai and the much older ruins of a heröon near the western gate, very little of the public buildings survives. The tombs are many and as usual conspicuous, some carved into the face of the cliff with Ionic temple-like façades, thus showing marked Hellenic influence, others typically Lycian in character clustering together in the necropolis, some richly decorated with elaborate lids covering the sarcophagi, others decorated with reliefs.

But perhaps the most significant hellenized Lycian remains of the region are those of Trysa, situated near the edge of a plateau overlooking the Demre gorge to the east. Nothing much remains there to be seen today, the most important and interesting survival having been removed. The ruins still *in situ* amount merely to traces of the acropolis walls in addition to a few tombs and some walls of the famous fourth century BC heröon which contained a tomb – famous on account of its fine friezes. They were taken away by a team of Austrian archaeologists in the 1880s and are now to be seen in Vienna's Kunsthistorisches Museum. Among various mythological scenes Bellerophon is here represented riding Pegasus in his contest with the Chimaera, which shows how widespread and deeply rooted this myth already was in Lycia in the fourth century BC. The other mythological scenes are the usual traditional ones, namely the battle with the Amazons, the war of the Seven against Thebes and the Lapiths fighting the Centaurs. Greek mythology was by then the dominant mythology of Lycia.

At the foot of this plateau under the rock face of a great cliff where the Demre river, the ancient Myros, flows to the sea through an intensely cultivated strip of plain, lay the city of Myra, one of the six cities of the Lycian League with the right to three votes. The site is now occupied by the village of Demre. Apart from numerous tombs, a few walls of the acropolis on the cliff overhanging the site and the well-preserved theatre, practically nothing remains to be seen today of the ancient city in spite of its original size and importance. After the catastrophic earthquake of AD 141, which brought about destruction throughout Lycia, the theatre was rebuilt by Licinius of Oinoanda, and its scale reflects the large size of the city population at that time. For its construction and the erection of many other public buildings, now effaced or hidden beneath the houses of the present-day village, funds were lavishly donated by Opramoas and Jason.

The site of Myra, however, remains extremely striking on account of the spectacular tombs which tier above tier are carved into the rock of the overhanging cliff. With their mullioned window-like fronts and curious pediments over rows of small round dentils, which may indicate the use of reeds for the roofs of the timber houses, they are typically Lycian in character. But the reliefs which some of them bear are entirely Greek, showing again the extent to which Lycian sculptors of the fourth century BC had been influenced by Hellenism. Though impressive in their setting, the workmanship of these sculptures is somewhat coarse. They were painted, but the colouring which Fellows noticed with interest has now faded away almost entirely.

A particularly fine rock tomb of a later date is carved into the flank of the great cliff further east, overlooking the Myros river, where the view is more striking than the prospect from the theatre and its neighbouring tombs. This tomb is temple-like in shape, with pediment and dentils, and is flanked by two Ionic columns. Within the pediment a lion is represented grasping a bull by the neck. Unfortunately the condition of the whole tomb has deteriorated pitifully within the last hundred years.

Another very fine tomb of an entirely hellenized style (Pl. 20) can be seen in the neighbourhood of Myra, a couple of miles west of the site. This is a mausoleum and stands alone in the landscape like a temple. Its beautiful ashlar masonry, pilasters with Corinthian capitals at the four corners and monumental door, the whole resting on a three-stepped podium, create a picture of dignified simplicity and harmony characteristic of the purism of the early Roman age in Anatolia.

Like the other cities of Lycia, Myra enjoyed peace and prosperity throughout the Roman period. It was visited by Saint Paul on his way to Rome in AD 60 and in the fourth century Saint Nicholas of Patara became bishop of Myra, the metropolitan diocese of Lycia. Subsequently a monastery arose where he was buried and a church was built in the eleventh century which still stands, though greatly restored. The city was occupied by the troops of the Caliph Harun-al-Rashid in 808, then taken back by the Byzantines, though only for a while.

Andiriake near the sea, a few miles away from Demre, was the port of Myra; its ruins consist mainly of walls of the Roman age and later, now partly standing in a wooded, marshy setting of idyllic charm.

About 20 miles (30 km) north-east of Myra, where the Arykandos valley opens out into a plain bordering the sea, flourished the city of Limyra. Though it did not have the right to three votes on the League and therefore was not of the six major cities of the confederacy enumerated by Strabo, nevertheless Limyra was a city of eminence. It was the home and capital of Perikles, the fourth-century dynast who, under the influence of Hellenism then already prevailing, took his name from the celebrated Athenian statesman and gained control over most of Lycia. Of course in his days the confederacy had not yet taken shape and so there was no question of one or more votes.

At a time in the history of Lycia when there are few names even of outstanding individuals about whom any information has reached us, Perikles, prince of Limyra, emerges as a strong personality, hellenized, ambitious and enterprising. Not only did he repel the Carians for a while, who under the Hekatomnid dynasts were penetrating deep into Lycia, but he extended his rule as far as Telmessos. We can only regret that so little information has survived regarding this intrepid dynast.

Unfortunately, on reaching the site it is difficult if not impossible to discern what the city was or might have been like. As in the case of so many other sites there are only a couple of fine structures or walls remaining, and as they now appear in the landscape above the ground they are unable to provide, even with much imagination on our part, an image of what the original organic ensemble, the *polis*, could have been. There is a large, well-preserved theatre carved into the hillside and pleasing to the eye, which was built or reconstructed in the second century AD with the help of Opramoas who generously donated the necessary funds. Below the theatre and beyond a little stream where the ground is level, are some not very interesting ruins of the Roman age – a temple, the tomb of Gaius Caesar who was the adopted son of Augustus and died at Limyra in AD 4, the remains of a basilica and of a bishop's palace as well as some other Byzantine ruins in a setting the plan of which remains at present incoherent to the eye.

On the hillside not far above the theatre, where the necropolis extends eastward and westward, stands a very striking Lycian tomb (Pl. 22) of the gabled sarcophagus type, mounted on a podium which bears fine reliefs. This is the tomb of Katabura, probably a brother or other relative of Perikles, and the scenes sculpted upon it represent funeral ceremonies and the judgement of the dead. On one side Katabura himself is shown in the nude and *en face*, his features most expressive and forthright. The tomb is typically Lycian, but the reliefs show the marked influence of Hellenism. In the western part of the necropolis there are some interesting tombs which show a curious combination of Lycian and Hellenic structural elements.

Several other fourth-century BC tombs are decorated with reliefs showing various scenes of life and parting with life that bear the mark of Hellenism which patently inspired the remarkable sculptural production of Limyra at that time. In this respect the most interesting tomb, or rather mausoleum, consists of a structure known as the heröon and placed high up on the rugged hillside at an altitude of 654 feet (218 metres) overlooking the plain and the lower part of the city. Unfortunately little now stands above the ground. The architecture of this mausoleum in the form of a temple with friezes, which rested on a platform measuring 57 by 52.5 feet (19x17.5 metres), had much in common with that of the Nereid Monument of Xanthos. Its superstructure, however, was born not on columns but by caryatids. Some of these have been found and placed in a shed on the site, where they now stand behind wire netting presumably to ensure their safety. The friezes represented a military procession with chariot and warriors. Statues probably stood between the columns as in the Nereid Monument. There can be little doubt that Perikles himself, inspired by classical Athenian architecture, had the monument erected which may have subsequently served as his tomb.

During the centuries that followed Perikles' death, when Lycia came under the control of so many different powers, Limyra lost its eminence as a capital, but like several other cities of Lycia retained its autonomy, joined the League, went on striking its coins and prospered, especially in the Roman age. It suffered greatly from the earthquake of AD 141, but was rebuilt. By then it had ceased to function as a port, access from the sea having become silted up; it was able, however, to use the harbour of Andiriake for its active trade.

Archaeologically and historically the importance of Perikles' city cannot be overstressed. But from the point of view of scenic beauty, natural position, city plan and surviving buildings that embodied the Hellenic way of life and provide a picture we can visually grasp, nothing in the whole area, in the whole of Lycia for that matter, surpasses Arykanda some 20 miles (30 km) north of Limyra.

The approach up the Arykandos river, the Baçkoz Su of today, and its lofty position deeply impressed Fellows a century and a half ago. He expressed himself in a manner characteristic of those days when there was perhaps more responsiveness to, or awareness of, the beauty and magnificence natural scenery can display and less reticence in giving full expression to emotions resulting from what was termed 'the sublime'.

My tent is pitched about twenty miles up the valley of the ancient Arycandus, to the north of Limyra. A journal, after all, is only a register of the state of mind as impressed by the objects of the day; I shall therefore not hesitate to describe my own feelings, and confess that I never felt less inclined or less able to put to paper any remarks than the impressions produced by my ride during the last five hours. I have heard others speak of a melancholy being caused by the overwhelming effect of the sublime; but it is not melancholy when better analysed; it is a thoughtfulness and feeling of gratified pleasure which affect me, and I long to express what is perhaps better indicated by the prostration of the Oriental worshipper than by any verbal description; I feel as if I had come into the world and seen the perfection of its loveliness, and was satisfied. I know no scenery equal in sublimity and beauty to this part of Lycia.

The mere mention of mountain scenery cannot give any idea of the mountains here, which are broken into sections forming cliffs, whose upheaved strata stand erect in peaks many thousand feet high, uniting to form a wild chaos, but each part harmonized by the other; for all is grand, yet lovely. Deep in the ravines dash torrents of the purest water, and over these grow the most luxuriant trees; above are the graver forests of pines upon the grey cliffs, and higher than these are ranges of mountains capped with snow, contrasting with the deep blue of the cloudless sky.[15]

Although the track up the river on which Fellows rode is now an asphalt road busy with lorries connecting the coast with Elmali, the chief centre of inland Lycia, little has so far changed to disturb the eye. The plane trees still shadow the course of the river, their branches stretching over the rushing stream. The limestone crags puckered with rock-cut tombs or anchorite caves still beetle overhead while beyond, gleaming yellow or pink in the sunshine, the silken surfaces of bare ridges and peaks ten thousand feet high rise above the pine forests.

At the hamlet of Arif, where the main source of the river comes pouring out of the cliff in a waterfall, there is a great wall of russet rock which surges Delphi-like many hundreds of feet above the road. Here, until a few years ago, a coffee-house stood on planks overhanging the stream where the traveller could rest with refreshing drinks of icy cold water abundantly available. It has recently been washed away in a storm by a landslide. A narrow track leads steeply up to terraces above, where the remains of Arykanda stretch over a sizeable area higher and higher until they virtually cling under the pine trees to the limestone cliff which springs mightily aloft. A magnificent view opens out at your feet as you look down the valley where the pines and then the plane trees steeply descend and cluster along the rushing river.

Arykanda was one of the cities of the Lycian League and as such no doubt played its part in the life of the nation, but we do not know whether it had more than one vote in the administration. They were pleasure-loving citizens in the habit of living lavishly beyond their means. Thoroughly hellenized as they became, they certainly showed no stint in providing the city with all the necessary buildings for a civilized life, a city not large but well proportioned. Thanks to Athenaios and his garrulous gourmets we have a pertinent quotation from the fifth book of a 'History of Europe' by the historian Agatharchides, a work which but for a few fragments[16] has been lost. The historian tells us here that the Arykandians 'became involved in debt through their prodigality and extravagance of living, and being unable to pay their debts because they were lazy and pleasure-loving, they lent themselves to the ambitious projects of Mithradates, thinking they would have as reward the abolition of their debts.'[17]

This Mithradates may have been Mithradates III king of Pontos who gave one of his daughters in marriage to Antiochos III and may have helped the Seleucid king in his campaign to seize Lycia from the Ptolemies at the beginning of the second century BC. But more likely Agatharchides is referring to a son of Antiochos III by the name of Mithradates who assisted his father in that campaign. Unfortunately we do not know whether the Arykandians succeeded in having their debts remitted. At any rate they survived that crisis quite happily and even during the unpopular period of Rhodian dominion the city went on minting its own coins as a member of the confederacy. During the first two centuries of the Roman principate it enjoyed great prosperity, like most other cities of Lycia, fully attested by the remains of its buildings many of which date back to that period.

In the Byzantine age Arykanda became a bishop's seat, Christianity having prevailed after a bitter struggle with the pagans of the city. Persecution of the Christians was inevitable when the spreading new faith was felt as a threat by the pagans who in their turn were persecuted when Christianity triumphed. Marking its conquest Fellows found a cross cut in the wall of a building with the word NHKA.

Arykanda then declined and in the ninth century, after a life of well over a millennium, the site was abandoned by the dwindling inhabitants at a time when the whole of Lycia had become insecure as the result of Arab incursions.

On discovering the site and indentifying it with Arykanda from the name of the city he found inscribed, Fellows was thrilled. 'There is a great excitement and pleasure,' he says, 'in discovering these cities, once so splendid, and whose sites have been for twenty centuries unknown.' But the remains he was able to see in his days were not nearly so conspicuous as they are now, after the excavations carried out by Turkish archaeologists in 1978.

An exceptional group of buildings, fairly well preserved and characteristic of the *polis* way of life, are harmoniously set in a wonderful natural position. The essential edifices are all there on display, for on the successive terraces that descend from the base of the sheer cliffs you have a stadium, a theatre, an odeion, a stoa, an agora, a council chamber, a gymnasium and baths. The town planning is determined by the descending terraces at an incline similar to that at Delphi.

Delightfully shaded by overhanging trees the stadium (Pl. 25) is situated on the topmost terrace, as at Delphi, among pines right under the great wall of rock. It is probably Hellenistic, restored in the Graeco-Roman age and only about 260 feet (83 metres) long, but it may have been shortened by a landslide. On the terrace immediately below is situated the theatre (Pl. 24), an enchanting structure in a perfect state of preservation, well proportioned with most of its *skene* still standing and entirely Greek in character. There is no sign of Romanization. That it is a Hellenistic and not a second-century AD building, as was thought, has been confirmed by a recently found triglyph-metope decoration. On approximately the same level as the theatre a few hundred yards further west is the bouleuterion or council chamber which, though partly carved out of the rock, has survived in a poor condition.

Particularly interesting on the terrace below the theatre is the odeion (Pl. 23) with its three portals and its portico, which was decorated with mosaics. It opens out on a spacious agora overlooking the remains of a temple, which was later turned into a church, and a nymphaion. Conspicuously standing to their full height on the lowest terrace are the gymnasium and the Roman baths.

To the east of the city, on a terrace of its own, the necropolis stretches out into a row of splendid tombs, several of which are well preserved. Not one of them is typically Lycian like the tombs at Limyra, Myra and elsewhere, namely rock-hewn, pillar-shaped or gabled, for they stand as real buildings resembling small Greek temples distyle-in-antis. The largest one in fact, with a Corinthian façade, was for some time believed to be a temple. These sepulchures, or mausolea as we might call them, with doors beautifully decorated date from the Graeco-Roman age. The inscriptions are of course all in Greek. But characteristically Anatolian are the size of these structures, their prominent display and the fact that they constituted an integral part of the city. A few typically Lycian rock-cut tombs of a much earlier date are also to be found at Arykanda, but at some distance and not within view from the site of the city itself which must have been hellenized at an early stage of its history.

East of Arykanda and Limyra stretches a whole region as far as the Pamphylian gulf which may be regarded as Eastern Lycia. Here the sites of the ancient cities are set in a landscape where mountain shapes and vegetation vie with each other in creating an unparalleled pattern of sublime beauty. This is not merely brought about by the mountains rising to altitudes of nearly eight thousand feet close to the sea, nor merely by the magnificent pine forests that clothe the declivities, nor just by the wine-blueness of the Mediterranean which hugs the promontories, creeks and beaches, but above all by the unique configuration. The articulated shapes of the ground, of earth and rock, modulate into climaxes of grandeur from a seductive intimacy which the immediate surroundings most generously offer.

The main cities of the region, members of the League, were Korydalla, Rhodiapolis, Gagai, Olympos and Phaselis. The ruins of Korydalla have been virtually obliterated by intensive cultivation and at Gagai by the sea little has survived; but Rhodiapolis, the easternmost city of the group, has still much to show that is of interest.

We have already come across several fine theatres the construction or reconstruction of which was made possible by the generosity of a wealthy patron, Opramoas of Rhodiapolis. So where was his own city situated? Remotely tucked away and embedded in a forest of pines, the site is to be found on top of a hill at some distance north of the large village of Kumluka. It can only be reached on foot after a long climb, which accounts for the wild, undisturbed nature of the ruins. Under overhanging branches and among fallen leaves the remains of the buildings emerge. The masonry of the taller ones now standing is in most cases Byzantine, but resting on the fine ashlar masonry of older buildings belonging to Opramoas' days. At present the most striking structure dating back to that period or earlier is the theatre buried in woodland.

In front of the theatre are some remains of a monument which bore, according to travellers of the last century, 64 inscriptions honouring the patronage Opramoas bestowed upon the cities of the League. These Greek inscriptions consisted of 12 letters from the emperor, 19 letters from procurators and records of 33 meetings of the League. Unfortunately the inscriptions have now totally disappeared. Lieutenant Spratt and his companions were able to make a copy of the inscriptions when they visited the site in 1842 and the ruins were in a far better state.[18] There are still, however, some fine tomb inscriptions in Greek lying on the ground.

The name of Rhodiapolis might suggest that the city was founded in the days of the Rhodian dominance in Lycia, but there are some Lycian rock tombs on the way up to the site with inscriptions in Lycian. So the settlement must have dated back to a much earlier age than the Rhodian and been later renamed. Or perhaps Rhodiapolis derived its name from *rhódeos*, and so may have meant 'city of the roses', a simpler explanation, or alternatively from Rhode, daughter of the soothsayer Mopsos.

At present the ruins lie in a confused medley, most of the older ones buried under an accumulation of pine needles and dead branches, so it is difficult to make out the plan of the city. Excavation would no doubt reveal a great deal, but at the same time would destroy the magic of this secluded, rarely visited site.

On the eastern coast of Lycia, about 20 miles (30 km) north-east of

Rhodiapolis, was situated another notable city, member of the confederacy. At the foot of cliffs by the sea and on the banks of a stream, the ruins of Olympos nestle among plane trees, pines, overhanging creepers and entwining shrubs. A couple of clear springs come welling up from the ground as you approach on stepping-stones through the shallow water.

Olympos came relatively late into the history of Lycia. Nothing is known of it before it started to strike coins in the second century BC as a member of the League. But the polygonal masonry of the remains of a quay wall date back to a period which could hardly have been much later than 300 BC. By the second century it was not only a large and thriving city, as well as totally hellenized, but also one of the most important members of the League with the right to three votes. Strabo, who as well as Olympos briefly mentions the other five large cities with the same right, bases his account on the geographer Artemidoros who lived a couple of generations earlier. Unfortunately nothing has come down to us of this writer's work, so the historical data for this period are meagre. We happen to know more of the vicissitudes Olympos experienced in the next century, when it was seized by an enterprising pirate, Zeniketes, who made it his stronghold. Zeniketes may have been a Cilician pirate who captured both Olympos and its neighbouring city Phaselis further up the coast to the north by making his attack from the sea. More probably, however, he was a local chieftain of the Solimoi people who lived in the high mountains of eastern Lycia. He evidently succeeded in forming a kingdom of his own in the unsettled days that followed Mithradates' invasion of southern Anatolia.

From the heights and fastnesses of Mount Olympos, which towers not far from the city, Zeniketes overlooked the whole coast of the gulf and so could control the approaches to the flourishing cities of Pamphylia. In connivance with the pirates of Cilicia across the gulf he carried on his buccaneering depredations with impunity for some years. Hellenized though he was, as were all Lycians by then – Zeniketes is a Greek name – he may well have had Zoroastrian leanings, a Persian legacy perhaps in common with the Cilician pirates, for it was at Mount Olympos that according to Plutarch[19] they made strange sacrifices and performed the rites of Mithras. Zeniketes' days of luck were numbered, however, for the Roman senate decided to put an end to his lawlessness. Publius Servilius Isauricus, proconsul of Lycia, defeated the pirates at sea in a naval battle and vigorously attacked the strongholds of Zeniketes, who, realizing the hopelessness of any resistance and brandishing a burning torch, set fire to his house at Olympos and burned himself to death.[20] From far out at sea the flames could be seen that night, while higher up the hillside the Chimaera burned her own perennial flame.

The whole region was then annexed to the province of Cilicia and Olympos, once a rich city according to Cicero, declined into virtual insignificance. But it revived little by little under the first Roman emperors and in the second century AD flourished once more. Thanks to that generous donor Opramoas many fine buildings were constructed, but unfortunately they suffered greatly, first from the incursions of the Arabs and then from spoliation by the Genoese and Venetians who built a new stronghold on the hill overlooking the ancient site. These medieval walls are still standing and are plainly visible from the beach. Scanty remains of a theatre can still be seen on the southern side of the stream and a dilapidated building which may have been a gymnasium. The only structure that strikes the eye is the magnificent door of a temple nearly 15 feet (5 metres) high set in a wall of fine ashlar masonry, its jambs characteristically a little inclined toward the lintel (Pl. 27). The inscription of a statue which was found lying at the base tells us that it was dedicated to Marcus Aurelius, but the temple itself may have been of an earlier date. Lying near by are fragments of columns which confirm that the building was a temple. George Bean was mystified by the apparent lack of room for a temple of any size between these remains and the edge of the lake a few yards beyond,[21] but there is no reason why the lake should not have expanded in the course of centuries.

On reaching Olympos, Fellows was disappointed and totally uninterested in what he came across, which is perhaps not surprising in view of the poor state of preservation of the remains, most of which were and are still covered with vegetation. Their quality as well as their condition scarcely warrants excavations nor any action to clear the site which would only destroy its main asset, the natural beauty and poetry of the place.

On a hillside not far above Olympos are some vents of burning gas; the larger one produces a flame from a hole in the ground sufficiently bright to be seen at night far out at sea. This gave rise to the belief that the fire-spitting Chimaera had her den here. In the daytime the site of this natural phenomenon is more curious than impressive or attractive. Near by are the ruins of a little temple, most aptly dedicated to Hephaestus.

Almost 25 miles (40 km) north of Olympos lie the remains of Phaselis in one of the most beautiful natural situations of the Lycian eastern coast under the towering cone of Mount Olympos, the Tahtali Dag of today, and not far from the spectacular peaks of Mount Climax. Although close to the Pamphylian border and in many respects belonging to the world of the Pamphylian cities, Phaselis was nevertheless regarded as a Lycian city and for a considerable period of its long history was a member of the Lycian League. Strictly speaking, however, it does not come within our field since it was never hellenized, nor did its foundation occur as the result of Alexander's thrust and the policy of his successors. Phaselis was Greek from the start, an ancient Greek settlement like most of the Pamphylian cities. But as a member of the Lycian confederacy Phaselis was part of the hellenized world of Lycia and so should perhaps receive some attention in our pursuit.

The city was founded by colonists from Lindos in Rhodes at the very beginning of the seventh century BC and flourished as a port, the Phaselians being industrious traders. Herodotus mentions it as one of the Dorian cities which early in the sixth century took part in founding the sanctuary of Hellenion at Naukratis in Egypt. When later in that century the Persians overran the whole of Asia Minor, Phaselis had to submit to their rule like the other cities of Anatolia, but was able to retain some degree of autonomy. It evidently continued to prosper contentedly, for its citizens let themselves be 'liberated' most reluctantly, as Plutarch tells us, by Kimon who in 469 BC, at the head of the Athenian fleet, defeated the Persians in the famous battle of the Eurymedon in Pamphylia. So Phaselis had to become a member of the Delian League established by Athens for the defence of the liberated cities and had consequently to pay a financial contribution for this doubtful privilege. It is worth noting that after the collapse of the Delian League and the restoration of Persian rule, Phaselis behaved in a manner scarcely in keeping with the interests of the Lycian cities and their spirit of independence, for it contracted an alliance with Mausolos and aided him in his conflict with Perikles of Limyra.

In the fourth century Phaselis produced a distinguished rhetor, philosopher and playwright, Theodoktes. He removed himself, however, to Athens, intellectually a more stimulating city, where he came to know Plato, Isokrates and Aristotle. Of the many tragedies he wrote only a few fragments have reached us. It is to be particuarly regretted that the work entitled 'Mausolos' should have failed to survive, for no doubt it would have been of great historical interest in view of the close understanding there had been between his native city and the Carian dynast. It was unusual for a dramatist to choose a contemporary personality as the subject of his tragedy: his other plays dealt with the conventional heroes and heroines of Greece. After Theodoktes' death the Phaselians honoured him with a statue which, as Plutarch tells us, drew the attention of Alexander the Great:

> At Phaselis Alexander stayed for some time, and finding the statue of Theodoktes, who was a native of this city and was now dead, erected in the market-place, and after he had supped, having drunk plentifully, he went and danced about it, and crowned it with garlands, honouring not ungracefully, in his sport, the memory of a philosopher whose conversation he had formerly enjoyed when he was Aristotle's pupil.[22]

In the centuries that followed Phaselis experienced more or less the same vicissitudes as the other cities of Lycia and in the second century BC we find it a member of the Lycian League. This is a rather interesting development since there are no characteristic Lycian tombs to be found on the site and no inscriptions in the Lycian language. Thoroughly Greek from the time of its foundation, Phaselis had always kept aloof and followed an independent line of policy. Of course it should be borne in mind that by the second century the whole of indigenous Lycia had been hellenized. The new participation did not, however, last long: only a little more than half a century later the city found it expedient to break away. Then, like Olympos, it fell into the hands of the pirates and evidently submitted to the domination of Zeneketes. Perhaps the citizens did not do too badly in the lawless trade that ensued. After the defeat of the pirates by Servilius Isauricus we find Phaselis once again a member of the League. It continued to be a fully fledged member during the Roman empire without interruptions, enjoying with the other cities of Lycia the prosperity that resulted from the Pax Romana at the inevitable cost, however, of its history becoming uneventful and slowly sinking into oblivion.

Although visited and described, or mentioned, by many travellers since the days when Captain Beaufort landed there in 1811, the best account of the history of Phaselis and the best description of its ruins have been left to us by George Bean. His guidebook is indispensable to the traveller wishing to become thoroughly acquainted with the sites of southern Anatolia. But Bean visited and surveyed Phaselis in the early 1960s, when the site was still entirely deserted and accessible only by jeep or by boat, and so retained its wild natural beauty. Now, however, a tarmac road leads up to it for the benefit of coach tours, a large, newly-built museum stands conspicuously white in the pine wood close to its access, general tidying-up has taken place including archaeological excavation, and the sight of cars parked in the close vicinity of the ruins cannot be avoided. Much of the enchantment has therefore been eroded. Nevertheless, Phaselis remains one of the most attractive ancient sites of Lycia. Though not spectacular the ruins, which consist chiefly of a paved street flanked with shops, an agora, a gate of Hadrian and a theatre carved into the hillside, gracefully span the two ancient harbours among stately pine trees. Close by, on the edge of a swamp, the arch of a splendid Roman aqueduct frames a view which opens out to the hinterland where Mount Olympos surges majestically (Pl. 26).

Lycia turns into Pamphylia in the western corner of a wide gulf by a succession of limestone peaks and indented ridges which descend steeply to the sea through pine forests and exotic vegetation. Sublime is perhaps not quite the right adjective, for there is a dramatic element in the picture which is breathtaking and arouses excitement as well as wonder.

CHAPTER

PAMPHYLIA & PISIDIA

F ROM THE APEX OF M OUNT C LIMAX AND THE S OLYMOI RANGE, WHERE there once dwelt the warlike people whom King Iobates dreaded and Bellerophon fought, the view reaches far out to the east over the plain of Pamphylia. For fifty miles the plain stretches along the coast of a wide gulf as far as the foothills of the Cilician Tauros where the pirates flourished. From the sea it extends northward for about ten miles to where the Pisidian Tauros begins to rise in waves of increasingly bold ridges. Irrigated by three large rivers, the Kestros, the Eurymedon and the Melas, the plain is fertile and green. We are unable to peer through the mist of time which hangs over it, back into the remote Hittite past, but by the end of the second millennium BC settlements of invaders have begun to emerge, Greek settlements, dimly visible in the haze of a world still mythical. The names of two heroes stand out, Mopsos and Amphilochos, who, according to an ancient tradition which cannot be regarded as entirely legendary, led a migration through Anatolia after the fall of Troy. Mopsos was a diviner, a son of Apollo and Manto, and a grandson of the famous soothsayer Teiresias. After founding the city of Mallos in Cilicia with Amphilochos son of Amphiaraus, another seer, Mopsos fell out with him. The quarrel led to a duel in which both were killed. But before they arrived in Cilicia, Mopsos and Amphilochos had settled in Pamphylia many of the multitude of migrants from whom, according to Herodotus, the Pamphylians were descended.[1]

There is no reason to reject the tradition that a migration and settlement of pre-Dorian Greek-speaking people took place, since the Pamphylians, before the *koine* Greek speech became universal, spoke a sort of pre-Dorian dialect of which an inscription at Sillyon, bearing the name of Mopsos, is the best surviving specimen. There is no trace of the early indigenous people; whoever they may have been, they were absorbed by the Greek immigrants at the end of the first millenniun BC. So Pamphylia was never hellenized in the same way as Lycia or Caria were. Perge, Sillyon and Aspendos were Greek from the start and so do not lie in the field of our survey, but the case of Side, situated by the sea in the far eastern corner of Pamphylia, is different, in spite of its claim to have been founded by Greek settlers. This city calls for our attention.

The general history of Pamphylia does not differ in many respects from that of Lycia where, however, there rose in course of time more than thirty cities compared with merely half a dozen in the neighbouring region to the east. But most of these, in size and population, were much larger cities as their extensive remains attest. They never joined together in a confederacy, as the Lycian cities did. However, as far as the outside world was concerned, the general situation was by and large the same, except that the Rhodians never came into the picture.

In the sixth century BC, Pamphylia, like Lycia, fell under the sway of the Lydians and soon after under that of the Persians who overran the whole of Anatolia. The famous naval battle of the Eurymedon won by the Athenians in 465; they freed the whole coastal region of Anatolia from Persian domination until the end of the Peloponnesian war. The cities of Pamphylia were enrolled in the Delian League, which was formed allegedly for their protection, but whether they were happy to join seems doubtful. With the collapse of the Athenian hegemony Pamphylia reverted to Persian rule under the governorship of a satrap. The cities, however, were able to retain a considerable degree of local autonomy and issue their own coins. When Alexander came he was well received by Perge, but Aspendos submitted to him reluctantly and Sillyon opposed him defiantly. Having secured, however, the submission of the other three cities he desisted from laying siege to Sillyon, which enjoyed a superbly strong position, because he felt that the time needed for a successful siege would only delay him in his eastward march of conquest.

In the Hellenistic age Pamphylia was contested by the Seleucids and the Ptolemies of Egypt, and then by the Attalids of Pergamon. Towards the middle of the second century BC, Attalos II was able to secure control of most of Pamphylia, except the main cities and their harbours. He refrained for fear of displeasing the Romans whose ally Pergamon had always been and whose power in Asia Minor had been steadily growing since the battle of Magnesia in 190 BC at which the powerful Seleucid King, Antiochos III, was defeated. So Attalos II, not having the use of a port, founded Attaleia, the present-day Antalya, well situated by the sea. Attalos III bequeathed his kingdom and territories to the Romans, but the republic of Rome was not at that time over-anxious to take possession of territories in Anatolia beyond the limits of the Province of Asia which consisted of Mysia, Lydia and Phrygia. So Pamphylia was for a couple of generations left alone by foreign powers, which enabled the Cilician pirates to penetrate the region.

Side was affected by this penetration more than any other Pamphylian city, but even Attaleia allowed them a foothold thereby making it easy for Zeniketes to establish himself as the ruler of the Solymoi region of Lycia and carry on his lawless but lucrative trade with the backing of the Cilician pirates. This situation lasted until Servilius subdued the pirates in eastern Lycia and western Pamphylia, which were turned into a Roman province. But Side remained independent and flourished as a slave market as the result of the pirates of Cilicia being able to carry on selling their captives there unimpeded, until they were finally crushed by Pompey. Thereafter the Pamphylian cities enjoyed for some centuries the prosperity resulting from the Pax Romana. This is reflected in their splendid buildings of which impressive remains are still standing.

Pamphylia is a Greek word meaning 'the land of many tribes', which may refer only to the multitude of immigrant settlers. To what extent the people who lived in the country outside the cities differed from the citizens ethnically as well as linguistically is impossible to tell. The inscriptions found are in Greek and have all come from the cities; no other records exist that could give us some relevant information. In any case the indigenous elements which must have prevailed at an early period were soon absorbed by the overwhelming Hellenic stream. In neighbouring Pisidia the situation was different.

Of the five major cities of Pamphylia, namely Perge, Sillyon, Aspendos, Side and Attaleia, the last-mentioned, beautifully situated by the sea on travertine rocks, was a comparatively late foundation which occurred as the result of the expansionist pursuits of Alexander's successors. As a port it flourished especially during the Roman empire and, being the only proper harbour of Pamphylia with easy access from inland as well as from the sea, it retained a certain importance through the ages up to our times. Unlike the other cities of Pamphylia it was never deserted and modern Antalya is nowadays a large town, but virtually nothing of ancient Attaleia has survived. Apart from a somewhat squat tower, at present used as a clock tower, which was originally a mausoleum, only Hadrian's gate, a splendid piece of architecture, is still standing.

From our point of view Side is of particular interest, for although its citizens claimed to be the descendants of a Greek colony they were in fact hellenized. Before the advent of Alexander they spoke an indigenous language of their own in spite of a colony from Kyme, an Aeolian city near Smyrna, having settled at Side, as Strabo tells us. This occurred in the second half of the seventh century BC and has been confirmed by Greek pottery of the period found on the site. Instead of hellenizing, the immigrants were apparently absorbed by the indigenous inhabitants, who must have outnumbered them, and so came to speak the local language, records of which have been found on inscriptions and coins. Arrian relates, however, that:

There is a tradition among them that when the first settlers from Kyme sailed thither and landed from their ship to found a new home, they promptly forgot their native Greek and began to talk in a foreign tongue – not the language spoken, but an entirely new dialect of their own; and from then on the men of Side had remained foreigners, distinct in speech, as in everything else, from their neighbours.[2]

So unlike the main cities of Pamphylia where a Greek dialect was spoken, until the Hellenistic age the inhabitants of Side spoke a native tongue, undoubtedly one of the original Anatolian languages whatever the tradition reported by Arrian may have meant. Then, in the wake of Alexander's immense prestige and under the overriding influence of Greek culture, they became entirely hellenized. The language in use for inscriptions and coins in the third century BC was Greek.

In the second century Side prospered as the main port of the slave market where, as Strabo informs us, 'the dockyards stood open to the Cilicians who would sell their captives at auction there.'[3] But in spite of this prosperity practically nothing, apart from a section of the city walls, has survived from this period, the interesting age of hellenization. The edifices of the period were evidently obliterated by the building activities that went on during the years of great affluence which the city enjoyed throughout the first two centuries of our era. In the third century Side began to decline on account of the unsettled fortunes of the Roman empire, but it could still afford such a sumptuous building as the so-called State Agora, whose exact nature or use is still not clear. In the fourth century the impoverished city shrank in size, but in the early Byzantine age, unlike most of the other cities in Anatolia, it experienced a revival as the ruins of that period show. The city expanded once more and became an important metropolitan diocese under the patriarch of Constantinople. Tribonianus, a close councillor of the emperor Justinian and the principal collaborator in the compilation of the famous Codex Justinianus, was a native of Side. Then in the seventh century the Arab incursions proved disastrous for the city. It finally fell to the Arabs and though it was recaptured and held for a while by the Byzantines it rapidly decayed. By the tenth century it was in ruins.

The first description we have of the site of Side after a millennium of obliteration comes from Captain Francis Beaufort who in 1811 was cruising in His Majesty's ship *Frideriksteen*, under his command, along the southern coast of Anatolia surveying the ancient sites of which he wrote and published a graphic account entitled *Karamania*. His response to what Side looked like in those days, its ruins overgrown with vegetation and yet conspicuously grand, was full of appreciation. Fellows' reaction, on the other hand, was not without reservations. When he visited Side some 27 years after Beaufort there was still not a single house or hut on the site; only a few tents of the roaming nomads were to be seen. Now there is a thriving parasitic village full of hotels, motels and pensions occupied in the summer by crowds of Turkish holidaymakers and foreign tourists, with advertising placards, restaurants, gift shops and postcards galore covering up what used to be a magnificent colonnaded street. These recent and less recent structures, several of which may date back to when a group of Muslim refugees from Crete were settled there at the end of the last century, now sprawl over much of the ground in which many ruins lie buried. However, considerable archaeological work has been undertaken and a large number of important remains have been cleared which strike the eye on approaching the site. The imposing Roman theatre, now emptied of the accumulation nature and time collected, was full of trees in Fellows' day and the whole promontory offered a picturesque sight of ruins entwined in wild vegetation. But Fellows was disappointed by the remains he saw and complained that 'the Greek style is scarcely to be traced in any of the ruins, but the Roman is visible in every part.' He was right. Indeed they are splendid, these remains of the main edifices – the theatre, the agora, the state agora, the baths, the nymphaion or city fountain. But the general picture we now get is one of Roman ostentation, in which the presence of the emperor is everywhere felt, rather than an image of Greek tradition, discretion and refinement such as we find at sites like Nysa, Alinda, Euromos, Arykanda, Termessos and others, where though many of the remains date from the Roman age they are informed with a spirit which is essentially Greek. Perhaps there was at Side too much wealth, too much money, as undoubtedly there also was at Hierapolis in Phrygia. The ruins that most vividly evoke the Hellenic heritage rather than the Roman world, even in their present dilapidated condition, are perhaps the two peripteral temples of Apollo (Pl. 28) and Athena, both of the Corinthian order, which stood side by side close to the sea. Though built in the second century AD they replaced two older temples on the same site, something of which they seem still to reflect. Strado mentions the temple of Athena, but surely next to it in his days stood also the predecessor of the temple of Apollo.

Of special interest and fascination from our point of view is the site of Seleukeia in Pamphylia. It was one of the two Hellenistic foundations of the region, the other being Attaleia, and the earlier by more than a century since it was founded by Seleukos Nikator or by one of his immediate successors, as were several other cities of that name scattered over Anatolia and Syria.

Very little is known of this Seleukeia, the surviving records amounting to virtually nothing. It is mentioned neither by Polybius, nor by Diodorus Siculus, nor by Pliny, nor by Strabo who refers to several other cities of the region most of which have left scarcely any traces. Seleukeia, on the other hand, has some splendid remains still standing. The geographer Artemidoros may have said something about this city, but we cannot tell since almost his entire work is lost. By Stephanus of Byzantium it is only very briefly mentioned under the name of Sardessos.

So the history of Pamphylian Seleukeia remains shrouded in mystery. Not only ignored, as far as we know, by historians and ancient geographers, Seleukeia was scarcely visited by the travellers of the last century who were zestfully locating and discovering ancient sites in Anatolia.[4] George Bean went there in the 1960s and has left us a description of the ruins at that time and a useful plan of the core of the city.[5] In 1974 a team of Turkish archaeologists from the university of Istanbul, under Professor I. Inan, carried out some excavations and the much needed clearing of the site, though luckily it still retains its natural beauty and poetry.

Situated inland at a distance of about 12 miles (18 km) from Side and hidden in a forest of pine trees on the brow of a prominent hill, the site of Seleukeia was, until recently, accessible only on foot by a rough path along which it was easy to lose the way. In many respects the position and character of the site resemble those of Rhodiapolis or Kadyanda, but the ruins are in a far better state of preservation. On account of its secluded situation and the paucity of information about it, Seleukeia has escaped commercialization so far.

After walking on a carpet of russet pine needles in the dappled shade of the trees, the visitor reaches the end of a steep uphill path which has become rough and stony. Suddenly the opening of a glade in the forest reveals the remains of a city. They encircle the agora square (Pl. 30) speckled with golden thistles – columns and arches, the vestiges of stoas, a two-storey building of fine ashlar masonry with framed doors and windows, which contained shops and an odeion or perhaps a council chamber, another edifice standing to a considerable height, its lower wall embossed like the Pitti Palace in Florence (Pl. 31) and other attractive buildings form a harmonious complex. To the west of the agora on a lower level is a long passage with the remains of fluted columns and capitals. Originally it was vaulted, but it still retains attractive architectural features mellowed by lichen and creepers on its walls.

Beyond this core of the city and in the wood that surrounds it stand the remains of a little temple, distyle-in-antis (Pl. 29), still in a fair condition although with a pine tree growing in the middle of its cella. Near by other ruins emerge from the ground, as yet unexcavated. Further to the west, overlooking the valley far below, a large structure stands 30 feet (9 metres) high, most likely baths of the Roman age. Here the site comes abruptly to an end with the cliff overhanging a cave in which there is a spring. This is a numinous spot frequented only by goats and no doubt by Pan in the days of Seleukeia. The visitor will find it with difficulty, so concealed is it under the cliff. Water keeps dripping on a ledge from the overhanging rock and collects in little mossy nooks. Long trails of ivy tendrils hang low from the rock overhead. The sky is concealed by luxuriant vegetation in which towering plane trees emerge from below the edge of the drop.

The buildings of Seleukeia have suffered from earthquakes and weathering in the course of centuries, but have hitherto escaped the plight of being encroached upon by agriculture or of being used as building material for the houses of a village. It is interesting to note that Seleukeia never had a theatre, most unusual for a Greek city. Not so very far away was Etenna which possessed a theatre, though it was barbarian in origin, inhabited by the wild Pisidian tribe of the Etennians who were only little by little hellenized.

Pamphylia is a long narrow strip of lowland bordering the sea. To the north, for its entire length from west to east, at a distance of merely ten to 20 miles from the sea, the foothills of the Tauros range start and here we are in Pisidia. This region extends to the north as far as the lakes Egredir and Beysehir. It is an extremely mountainous territory of great natural beauty, with forests, lakes and bold rocky peaks.

Pisidia was inhabited by hardy tribes with predatory propensities who were regarded by the Greeks as barbarians. They had a language of their own, to which Strabo refers,[6] and they were gradually hellenized, first those occupying the southern part of the region through contact with the civilized Pamphylians, then little by little the others further north as the result of Alexander the Great's campaigns and the expansion of Hellenism. So the lawless tribes came together in centres of habitation. These developed into cities which emulated their southern neighbours, the cities of Pamphylia, erecting buildings appropriate to the *polis* way of life, of which splendid remains can still be seen. They adopted Greek as their official language and issued coins with Greek legends. From the autocratic rule of chieftains they gradually developed more democratic forms of government presided over by councils.

According to Artemidoros, whom Strabo quotes, the cities of Pisidia were Termessos, Selge, Kremna, Petnelissos, Sagalassos, Adada, Tymbriada, Amblada, Anabura, Sinda, Aarassos, Tarbassos and Pityassos.

The sites of these 13 cities have not all been located. We know where Termessos, Selge, Sagalassos, Kremna and Adada are because conspicuous ruins have survived, but the exact location of the others remains hypothetical or uncertain because of the paucity of records and the absence of ruins. Aarassos appears to have been somewhere near Kremna; Amblada north-east of Lake Egredir; Anabura may have been where the village of Enevre now is north of Lake Beysehir, ancient Karalitis; Sinda or Isinda apparently occupied the site of the village of Istanoz in western Pisidia now called Korkuteli; Tymbriada or Tymbrianassos was perhaps near Imrator, a few miles east of Lake Egredir. Where Tarbassos and Pityassos might have been remains unknown. Petnelissos may have been situated, it is believed, at a place south of Kremna and west of Selge near the village of Khozan where there are a few ruins.[7]

It is odd that Artemidoros should have omitted Etenna, which is situated about 10 miles (16 km) north of Seleukeia and where considerable remains are still to be seen. This city was striking coins with Greek legends in the fourth century BC, at least two generations before the foundation of Seleukeia which was regarded as a Pamphylian city, but Etenna was definitely Pisidian according to the little we know of it. Nor does Artemidoros mention Pisidian Antioch, remotely situated in the north of the region, a city interesting on account of its history and ruins, an omission perhaps due to the fact that it was never inhabited by Pisidians. Strabo refers to 'Antioch near Pisidia', not 'in Pisidia'. There were other lesser cities in Pisidia which Artemidoros does not include in his list.

Of chief interest to us, of course, are those sites where the ruins enable us to picture the city's past existence. In southern Pisidia there are two such sites, that of Termessos and that of Selge, the former more outstanding than the latter. The site of Etenna might be added, even though we know so little of its history.

One of the most fascinating sites in Anatolia is without any doubt Termessos, high up in the Solymoi mountains on the border with Lycia at an altitude of over 3000 feet (900 metres), its remarkable remains rising from rocky outcrops and enveloped in a most varied vegetation under the towering limestone hump of Mount Solymos itself. It is still a world of its own, untouched and full of grandeur, miles away from human habitation, but nowadays easy to reach by road and consquently much visited by tourists owing to the relative closeness of Antalya and the publicity the site is receiving. However the road ends well below the site and a quarter of an hour on foot along an uphill path is needed to reach the main ruins, so the core of the ancient city is protected from buses parking close by; the sequestered character of this extraordinary site remains unaffected.

Unlike most other ancient sites in Pisidia, Termessos has retained a few strands of its history in the records of ancient historians, which throw some light on its noteworthy past. We do not know when the city was founded and before the advent of Alexander the Great relevant information is extremely meagre. All we really know is that its inhabitants were Pisidians speaking a Pisidian dialect of which unfortunately no records have survived, all their inscriptions being in Greek. They were hard, proud and warlike people addicted to plundering, but in the fourth century BC they already struck coins with Greek legends, which shows that the world of nearby Hellenic Pamphylia was beginning to influence their lives. So 'when Alexander civilized Asia and Homer became common reading'[8] the Termessians claimed to be the descendants of the Solymoi people, which Strabo regards as correct, while believing somewhat inconsistently that Bellerophon had founded their city.

Three events in the history of the Termessians, well recorded by ancient historians, highlight their courage, belligerent nature and spirit of independence. The first of these occurred in 334 BC as reported by Arrian. He relates how Alexander clashed unsuccessfully with the Termessians on his march through southern Anatolia and describes the site of the city as well as the reaction of the inhabitants to Alexander's impending attack.

The people of Termessos are an Asiatic race of Pisidian blood; the town stands on a lofty and precipitous height, and the road which leads past it is an inconvenient one, because the ridge runs right down to it from the town, breaking off short with the road at the bottom, while opposite it, on the other side, the ground rises again in an equally steep ascent. The two cliffs make a sort of natural gateway on the road, so that quite a small force can, by holding the high ground, prevent an enemy from getting through. And this is precisely what the Termessians did . . . Alexander accordingly gave the order to halt at once, convinced that when the enemy saw his men taking up a position for the night they would no longer hold the road in force but withdraw the majority of their troops into the town near by, leaving only a small part to keep watch. His guess proved right, the main body retired and only the outposts remained. So Alexander was able to overcome them, pass through the narrow passage and take up position close to the town.[9]

Something strange then happened. Representatives from Selge, a rival city and old enemy of Termessos, came to offer Alexander the support of their citizens. Alexander accepted the offer at first, but changed his mind. He evidently came to the conclusion that Termessos could not be reduced without a long siege, so he turned away and proceeded to Sagalassos. Now, was this the result of the advice given to him by the representatives of the Selgians, enemies of the Termessians, contrary to what one would have expected? Arrian does not tell us, but very likely they knew that it would have been extremely difficult to capture the city and advised Alexander accordingly. So the Termessians remained a proud and independent people.

The second event in the history of Termessos of which we have a fair amount of information was recounted by Diodorus Siculus. It happened in 319, four years after Alexander's death, at a time when his generals were bitterly fighting over the empire their king and leader had left. The struggle went on year after year, using foul play as well as straightforward fighting. Perdikkas had been murdered and Eumenes, formerly Alexander's secretary, was disputing the possession of southern Anatolia with Antigonos, another general. Alketas, a younger brother of Perdikkas and another of Alexander's former generals, was involved in this conflict against Antigonos. In a clash with him and his formidable army, Alketas and his forces, which included a strong contingent of Pisidian allies, were defeated. He escaped, however, to Termessos with his 6000 Pisidians, who were presumably Termessians. They were of outstanding prowess and 'bade Alketas to be of good courage, promising that they would in no way fail him for they were exceedingly well disposed to him for the following reasons.'

Diodorus goes on to explain how Alketas after the death of Perdikkas had favoured the Pisidians, distributing to them spoils and booty from hostile territories and honouring them in various ways, in order to secure their support.

'Therefore even at this time,' he continues, 'Alketas placed his hopes upon them, and they did not disappoint his hopes. For when Antigonos encamped near

Termessos with all his army and demanded Alketas, and even when the older men advised that he be surrendered, the younger, forming a compact group in opposition to their parents, voted to meet every danger in the interest of his safety.'[10]

The elders of Termessos greatly feared the enmity of Antigonos, which could lead to the city being captured. Having failed to persuade the younger men to surrender Alketas, they met in secret and decided on a stratagem which would enable them to deliver him to Antigonos alive or dead. They persuaded Antigonos to engage in a mock attack on the city which kept the young Termessians away in defensive skirmishes. As a result Alketas was left behind unprotected and the elders seized the opportunity to lay hands on him. But knowing that he would be put to death by Antigonos, Alketas committed suicide before they were able to take him. When the younger men returned and saw what had happened, they were enraged with the elders. They took full possession of part of the city and voted to burn all the buildings. With difficulty their parents persuaded them to desist, but they took up their arms and rushed to the mountains from where they devoted themselves to guerrilla warfare, ravaging and plundering the enemy's territory. Antigonos, delighted to have the body of Alketas which had been delivered to him by the elders, mutilated it for three days and then threw it out unburied to be torn to pieces by wolves and vultures. But the young Termessians succeeded in finding it, brought it back to their city and honoured it with splendid obsequies. They carved a magnificent tomb into the rock of the cliff overhanging the city in which they entombed him with all his arms and sculpted on the inner left side of the sepulchre an excellent image of him on horseback. It is still to be seen there and, though the head and right foot have suffered mutilation, it remains one of the most attractive reliefs in Anatolia (Pl. 33).

The third account we have from the Graeco-Roman past which relates to Termessos is a much briefer event. It occurred a little more than a hundred years later when Cnaeus Manlius Vulso, the Roman consul who had been sent to subdue the troublesome Galatians, was marching through southern Anatolia allegedly to establish order but actually to acquire money, supplies and booty. After obtaining these from the Kibyrites he was proceeding southward into Pisidia, as both Polybius and Livy relate, and on reaching Isinda he found the Termessians attacking the acropolis after they had occupied and pillaged the city. The site of Isinda, the Sinda mentioned by Artemidoros, is about 15 miles (24 km) west of Termessos at the village of Korkuteli, formerly called Istanoz, under whose houses the ancient ruins probably lie buried. Being in a desperate situation the Isindians sent envoys to Manlius begging for help. The Roman consul was able to relieve them of their danger by threatening the Termessians who had been plundering the whole neighbourhood. He agreed to grant them peace and friendship on payment of fifty talents, not an insignificant sum.

Though pugnacious by nature the Termessians had at the same time sufficient foresight to act diplomatically. They evidently realized the advantages of keeping on good terms with the Romans, whose power in Anatolia was rapidly increasing, and so from then on they cultivated this friendship and consolidated it by opposing Mithradates, the bitter enemy of Rome, who in the first century BC started to invade southern Anatolia.[11] They also maintained good relations with Attalos II, who founded Attaleia and who as a gift to them financed the construction of a stoa, the ruins of which are still visible.

As a result of their friendly relations with Rome the Termessians were able to retain complete independence: even when their city was officially incorporated in the Roman Province of Pamphylia their autonomy amounted to virtual independence, since they were allowed to enact their own laws and omit the image of the emperor from their coins. Of course they could no longer wage war, but this only favoured their prosperity.[12]

Termessos seems never to have been under the rule of a dynast, as Kibyra always was and as the Lycian cities were before their confederacy took shape. It is difficult to tell what the exact nature of its government might have been in its very early history, but when it became hellenized in the fourth century BC it started to develop a democratic government. The elders formed a council and would meet to decide matters of state interest, and perhaps the young men also had a council, or met at an assembly, since they would put their decisions to a vote as we gather from Diodorus. By the beginning of the second century BC, Termessos had definitely established a democratic city state constitution, in other words it had developed into a fully-fledged *polis*. This is confirmed by an inscription recording its alliance with the Pisidian city of Adada, in which reference is made to the democracy each of the two cities had established.

When the Roman empire started to decline Termessos, like the other cities of southern Anatolia, experienced conversion to Christianity followed by a period of Byzantine rule. This did not last long, however, since by then the city itself was in rapid decline, and there are scarcely any Byzantine ruins to be seen on the site. By the end of the seventh century it had probably ceased to be inhabited.

In the Hellenistic age Termessos went through a period of considerable prosperity during which a number of fine buildings were erected. A few of these have survived sufficiently well to be visually enjoyable. Then again in the first two centuries of the Roman principate the Termessians flourished and proceeded to build on a lavish scale. As elsewhere in Pisidia earthquakes have caused havoc, but there is still much to be seen that can give an idea of what the city was like. Most guidebooks to Turkey contain a full description of the site and the ruins, but so far the best is George Bean's even though his account dates back nearly 30 years.

Termessos is indeed a fascinating site for several reasons – the romantic natural beauty of its setting untarnished by the denuding requirements of

101

archaeological activity, its varied vegetation visually attractive and botanically noteworthy and its impressive remains, archaeologically, architecturally and historically of considerable interest, which have become an integral part of the landscape.

From a sheer visual point of view the splendid Hellenistic theatre (Pl. 32), its *cavea* forming more than a semi-circle in accordance with the Greek style but with its *skene* modified in the Roman age, is the most striking piece of architecture of the site. Its beauty is enhanced by the limestone hump of Mount Solymos towering behind.

Another Hellenistic edifice in a relatively good state of preservation and historically interesting is the handsome odeion, which may also have served as a bouleuterion. Built in fine ashlar masonry, with a row of pilasters in relief on the upper part of the façade, it is still standing to a height of over 30 feet (nearly 10 metres) and is indeed an impressive edifice. Inside the rows of seats are now covered with debris, the removal of which would not in the least affect the silvan setting of the building. The windows show that it must have had a roof, but how the wide area of the interior was spanned is still a mystery. On the north wall an inscription records the names of the victors in games.

Next to the odeion is situated the temple of Athena, a prostyle temple of which some fine ashlar walls are still standing with a splendid door. North-west of the odeion was the agora on the sides of which are the remains of two stoas, of historical and archeological interest rather than visual attractiveness. One was the Attalos portico, the other was built much later by a citizen called Osbaras, of whom we know nothing. Unfortunately these two buildings are in such a ruined condition that they can no longer play a notable part in the present setting. But a little further west embedded in thick vegetation rise the luminous remains of an elegant little Corinthian temple, which still form a living feature. Most imposing are the remains of the gymnasium (Pl. 34), in a remarkable state of preservation, which dates from the second century AD. It is a large building which stands amid decorative trees and is invaded by every sort of vegetation, so unless a little clearing is undertaken it will continue to be difficult to obtain a more complete idea of the whole edifice. The gabled structure of the upper part of the building visible from the nearby path is unusual and particularly interesting architecturally.

The necropolis extends over a wide area to the west of the site with hundreds of conspicuous tombs of the sarcophagus type, somewhat repetitive in character. Further up the hillside, carved in the overhanging cliff, are some rock tombs of which that of Alketas is by far the finest and most interesting.

About 50 miles (85 km) away to the north-east of Termessos is the site of another large city, Selge, on the summit of a mountain buttress at an altitude of 3000 feet (900 m). Although situated far inland, at about 35 miles from the sea, it should be regarded as a southern Pisidian city because of its close relations with the Pamphylian cities, which accounts for its early hellenization. It started to issue silver coins in the fifth century BC and by the fourth the coins had Greek legends.

Whereas very little is said by Strabo about Termessos he is much more informative with regard to Selge. He tells us that this city was first founded by Kalchas, the famous soothsayer, and subsequently settled by Spartans. Of course no serious credence should be given to this belief: several other Pisidian cities also claimed Spartan descent. They were indeed Pisidians of 'Pisidian blood' as Arrian would say, but when they began to feel true Hellenes, which in fact they had become in the sense Isocrates gave to the term, they needed a good explanation of their origins. Other Pisidian cities did the same for the sake of respectability in a hellenized world.

'Having waxed so powerful,' Strabo goes on to tell us, 'on account of the law-abiding manners in which its government was conducted, it once contained twenty thousand men.' If we are to interpret the term *dismyriandros* as meaning twenty thousand *men*, without women and children included, it would mean that the entire population was close on fifty thousand. Selge's warlike habits and frequent attacks on neighbouring cities were evidently not regarded by Strabo as incompatible with 'the law-abiding manners' of its government.

The geographer then describes the site of the city and the reasons for its prosperity. His account of its principal agricultural products is most interesting and worth quoting in full:

The nature of the region is wonderful, for among the summits of the Taurus there is a country which can support tens of thousands of inhabitants and is so very fertile that it is planted with the olive in many places, and with fine vineyards, and produces abundant pasture for cattle of all kinds; and above this country, all around it, lie forests of various kinds of timber. But it is the styrax-tree that is produced in greatest abundance there, a tree which is not large but grows straight up, the tree from which the styracine javelins are made, similar to those made of cornel-wood. And a species of wood-eating worm is bred in the trunk which eats through the wood of the tree to the surface, and at first pours out raspings like bran or saw-dust, which are piled up at the root of the tree; and then a liquid substance exudes which readily hardens into a substance like gum. But a part of this liquid flows down upon the raspings at the root of the tree and mixes with both them and the soil, except so much of it as condenses on the surface of the raspings and remains pure, and except the part which hardens on the surface of the trunk down which it flows, this too being pure. And the people make a kind of substance mixed with wood and earth from that which is not pure, this being more fragrant than the pure substance but otherwise inferior in strength to it (a fact unnoticed by most people), which is used in large quantities as frankincense by the worshippers of the gods. And people praise also the Selgis iris and the ointment made from it.

Strabo then describes the countryside round Selge and gives an account of the Selgians as people:

> The region round the city and the territory of the Selgians has only a few approaches, since their territory is mountainous and full of precipitous ravines, which are formed, among other rivers, by the Eurymedon and the Kestros, which flow from the Selge mountains and empty into the Pamphylian Sea. But they have bridges on their roads. Because of their fortifications, however, the Selgians have never even once, either in earlier or in later times, become subject to others, but unmolested have reaped the fruit of the whole country except the part situated below them in Pamphylia and inside the Taurus, for which they were always at war with the kings, but in their relations with the Romans, they occupied the part in question on certain stipulated conditions. They sent an embassy to Alexander and offered to receive his commands as a friendly country, but at the present time they are wholly subject to the Romans and are included in the territory that was formerly subject to Amyntas.[13]

So we can assume from what Strabo says that when Selge was incorporated in the Roman province of Pamphylia it lost its independence, which had already been impaired in the thirties of the first century BC, when Antony gave the city and its territory to Amyntas king of the Galatians, who for some years dominated over a large area of Isauria and Pisidia. In other words Selge could no longer wage war on its neighbours as it had been in the habit of doing, but none the less retained a degree of municipal autonomy which contributed to the prosperity it enjoyed in the world of peace established by the Roman emperors.

We have knowledge of only one of the warlike exploits of the Selgians. It turned out somewhat unsatisfactorily for them. Polybius has given us a long and detailed account of what happened in that part of Pisidia in the year 218 BC. Achaios, grandson of Antiochos I and rebellious general of Antiochos III, was at that time busy capturing for himself large parts of Asia Minor from the Attalids. The growing power of this ambitious man did not deter the warlike pursuits of the Selgians, who had set about besieging the city of Petnelissos. The hard-pressed Petnelissians sent messengers to Achaios asking for help, and he sent an officer of his, Garsyeris, with a force of 6000 infantry and 500 horse to relieve the city.

Polybius then relates how the Selgians continued to besiege Petnelissos in spite of all the efforts of Garsyeris and his forces. In their reckless daring, however, the Selgians went too far. In attacking the camp of Garsyeris, at first most successfully, when they were on the point of breaking in they left their rear undefended. So the enemy was able to surprise them from behind, thus getting the better of the fray with the help of the Petnelissians, who at that juncture sallied out from the walls of their city in support of Garsyeris. The Selgians fled, pursued by Garsyeris, lost many men and finally retreated within the walls of their own city. So they found themselves besieged in their turn and wished to come to terms with the enemy. They chose one of their citizens, Logbasis by name, who had been on close terms of friendship with the Seleucids, and sent him to negotiate terms of peace with Garsyeris. But Logbasis turned traitor. He urged Garsyeris to secure the immediate presence and help of Achaios himself, promising that he would then put the city into their hands. Achaios came and together they decided on a ruse.

Logbasis went back into the city and, on his strong advice, all the citizens gathered together in assembly to discuss the possible terms of a treaty. Meanwhile Logbasis himself stayed in his house, and armed himself and his sons for the impending fight. With the walls left undefended, Achaios and Garsyeris attacked the city from two different sides while the citizens were still debating at the assembly. A goatherd, however, having noticed what was going on, informed the assembly that the enemy was attacking. They all rushed to the walls and successfully defended the city; meanwhile a group of young men, enraged by the treachery of Logbasis, broke into his house killing him and all his family. The Selgians threw back the enemy, but fearing treason among themselves and alarmed at the presences of a hostile army encamped near the city, sent messengers to sue for peace. It was granted on condition of their paying 400 talents on the spot, releasing the Petnelissians they had taken prisoner and paying a further sum of 300 talents at a fixed date. Polybius concludes: 'Thus the Selgians neither disgraced their freedom nor their relationship to the Lacedaemonians.'[14]

Unfortunately there is no more about the Selgians in Polybius' history, but they certainly continued to be a proud, truculent and prosperous city pugnaciously inclined until they had to settle down to a more sedate life under the Romans.

The situation of Selge is undoubtedly fine; the ruins cover the spur of a lofty mountain, the Boz Buran Dag, and lie high above the Eurymedon river, in a scenery of wild beauty and grandeur. The site was first visited in the late thirties or early forties of the last century by Professor Schönborn who was able to establish from an inscription that the ruins were those of the ancient city of Selge. Shortly after the Revd E. T. Daniell, who for a while had joined Lieutenant Spratt's party, was able to reach the site in the course of an exploration of his own and described it with enthusiasm in a letter to Spratt before dying of malaria at Antalya. Spratt quoted this description in his book and also included a reproduction of a sketch Daniell had made of the site from which it can be seen that, apart from the theatre, Selge was already then extremely ruined although many columns were still standing.

Although the place was celebrated for its fertility, a certain aridity prevails there now and the little village of Zerk, which is situated up against the ruins and derives its name from that of the ancient city, ekes out only a meagre existence from tilling the ground owing to the shortage of water. Visited and admired by travellers in the past, and thirty years ago by George Bean who has left us a detailed description,[15] the remains are nevertheless disappointing from our point of view having suffered disastrously from earthquakes and to a lesser extent from farming encroachments by the villagers. Hardly any walls stand to an appreciable height. The only structure that survives as a visible building and as a more or less satisfactory, if incomplete, architectural unit in the landscape is the theatre. It is large and impressive, forming more than a semi-circle in the proper Greek style, so it may have been constructed in the Hellenistic age originally, but it was greatly modified in the Roman period. The stage building, which now lies in utter ruin, was attached to the *cavea*, a Roman feature.

The agora, the temples, the nymphaion and the other buildings of the city lie scattered on the ground and only the remains of a church are in part still standing.

The whole picture is one of grandeur, but at the same time one of chaotic desolation unrelieved by the mellowing presence of trees among the stones, except down by the stadium, poorly preserved, where the villagers have been farming. It is virtually impossible to obtain an idea of what Selge, the city, might have looked like, which is regrettable in view of its size and the part it played in the life of southern Anatolia.

In the very heart of mountainous Pisidia, about 30 miles (50 km) north of Selge, is the site of Kremna, which Artemidoros includes in his list of Pisidian cities. So it was already a noteworthy city in the Hellenistic age. Unfortunately Strabo does not tell us much. He only says that it was captured by Amyntas king of Galatia, in spite of its position which was considered impregnable, and that it was subsequently occupied by Roman colonists. These, however, were in the course of time absorbed by the hellenized population of the city since most of the inscriptions dating from the Roman age are in Greek. Kremna is not mentioned by any other ancient author whose writings have survived except Zosimos, so we know very little of its history.

Zosimos was a late Greek historian who lived in the first half of the sixth century AD. What he tells us of Kremna relates to events which took place in the days of the emperor Probus who ruled from AD 276 to 282. The Isaurians were still troublesome brigands. One of them, Lydios, a most enterprising and ruthless adventurer, was able to seize Kremna and proceeded, from this virtually unassailable base, to pillage Pamphylia and even Lycia. For a considerable time he held out against the Romans who strove to recapture the stronghold and was in the end defeated only as the result of treachery. One of his men, who had been trained by him as an excellent marksman, defected to the Romans who used him to shoot at and kill Lydios.[16]

The Greek name Kremna probably derived from the verb *kremannymi* – to hang or be suspended – for the city was indeed perched on a marble eminence or high promontory which ends abruptly and drops precipitously for a thousand feet or more into the valley below, from where the site high above looks, as it were, almost suspended in mid-air.

The ruins are extensive and interesting, but in a poor state of preservation on account of earthquakes and exposure generally, and moreover are now seriously affected by the farming activities of the village immediately below the site to the south-west. A track has been built leading to the top of the promontory up which the villagers drive their tractors right into the fields full of ancient remains. There is therefore a notable difference between the present condition of the site and the state in which it was when first discovered 150 years ago.

Kremna was visited by several travellers in the last century. The first to find his way there was probably F. V. J. Arundell in 1833 or 1834, who left a fairly vivid description of what he saw, 'immense masses of ruins, too much covered by trees and underwood, and in too deranged a state to enable one to form probable conjectures upon the original plan.'[17]

He saw a great gateway with massive arches and a couple of other gates still standing, a large wall with arched recesses walled up, numerous fluted columns, a great portico of enormous length and a much ruined theatre. These remains are still more or less visible though all in a deteriorated and prostrate condition, except for the large wall with walled-up recesses which is still conspicuously erect. He mentions also a temple with fourteen columns still standing, which have since collapsed. In fact at present there is very little to be seen that is upright.

Fellows, who visited Kremna a few years later and mistook it for Selge, was bowled over by the sight:

Upon this promontory stood one of the finest cities that probably ever existed, now presenting magnificent wrecks of grandeur. I rode for at least three miles through a part of the city which was one pile of temples, theatres and buildings, vying with each other in splendour; the elevated site of such a city is quite unaccountable to me. The material of these ruins, like those of Alaysoon, had suffered much from exposure to the elements, being grey with lichen which has eaten into the marble, and entirely destroyed the surface and inscriptions; but the scale, the simple grandeur and the uniform beauty of the style bespoke of its date to be early Greek. The sculptured cornices contain groups of figures fighting, wearing helmets and body-armour, with shields and long spears; from the ill proportioned figures and general appearance, they must rank in date with the Aegina marbles now in Munich. The ruins are so thickly strewn that little cultivation is practicable, but in the areas of theatres, cellas of temples and any space where a plough can be used, the wheat is springing up. The general style of the temples is Corinthian, but not so florid as in less ancient towns. The tombs are scattered for a mile from the town, and are of many kinds, some cut in chambers in the face of the rock, others sarcophagi of the heaviest form; they have had inscriptions, and the ornaments are almost all martial; several seats remain amongst the tombs. I can scarcely guess the number of temples or columned buildings in the town, but I certainly traced fifty or sixty; and in places where there were no remains above the surface I frequently saw vast arched vaults, similar to those forming the foundations of great public buildings. Although apparently unnecessary for defence, the town had strong walls, partly built with large stones of the Cyclopian mode. I never conceived so high an idea of the works of the ancients as from my visit to this place, standing as it does in a situation, as it were, above the world.[18]

In his enthusiastic description Fellows does not tell us how many of the buildings he saw were still standing, but from his mentioning 'temples, theatres and buildings vying with each other in splendour' as well as from his impression of their scale, grandeur and beauty, there must have been many more buildings in a good state of preservation still standing than there are now. At present the only structure in this condition is the wall with arched recesses mentioned by Arundell, although the main gateway is still standing and the location of the theatre is recognizable, but very little of the building remains. Several fine marble statues removed from the site are now in a room of the Burdur Museum. They represent various Greek goddesses and date from the second century AD, when evidently Kremna was extremely prosperous. What has happened to the reliefs Fellows saw which represented 'groups of figures fighting, wearing helmets and body-armour with shields and long spears'? Very curious is his finding them similar to the Aegina marbles, which he evidently did not appreciate. On the whole Fellows' taste was good and his perceptive appreciation well founded, but carried away with enthusiasm as he often was he could go hopelessly wrong in his assessment of the age of the buildings and sculptures he came across in his travels. He would frequently regard as 'purest Greek' or 'early Greek', in other words as belonging to the classical or Hellenistic periods, things that in fact dated from the Graeco-Roman age, the first two centuries AD, simply because they were not over-ornate, or were built with fine ashlar masonry and not mortar masonry.

In 1885, Count Lanckoronski made a thorough investigation of the whole site the result of which was included in his splendid publication 'The Cities of Pamphylia and Pisidia', and the American epigraphist J. R. S. Sterrett, who visited the site that same year, took copies of several interesting inscriptions none of which, however, throw any light on the history of the city.[19] Kremna certainly went on flourishing right into the late Roman age and early Byzantine period when it became a bishopric like other prominent Pisidian cities. The wall with its arched recesses was identified by Lanckoronski as the façade of an early church. The stairway leading up to the long stoa from the agora is still an impressive sight. But the temple mentioned by Arundell, still to a great extent erect in his days, had evidently fallen into ruin by the time Lanckoronski made his survey.

The picture we get of the site as it is at present is somewhat chaotic, but a great deal might meet the eye more prominently if some judicious excavation or at least clearing were carried out, which in this case could do no harm to the beauty of the setting as a whole since there are scarcely any trees left. Some remains of the earlier Hellenistic buildings might then emerge among the Graeco-Roman ruins which at present dominate.

Perhaps the most spectacular city site in the whole of Anatolia, rivalled only by that of Isaura, is that of Sagalassos, another important Pisidian town mentioned by Artemidoros. The scenery is of overwhelming grandeur and beauty. There are a few other sites of ancient cities which are superior, but in certain respects only, such as that of Termessos or Arykanda, inasmuch as the conspicuous remains of their ancient buildings happily blend with fine vegetation in a harmonious natural setting not lacking in grandeur. At Sagalassos there are no trees, everything is bare and the ruins are in a condition which can bear no comparison with those of either Termessos or Arykanda as far as preservation is concerned. But as for sheer grandeur, boldness of shapes and delicacy of colours, which its titanic limestone cliffs most generously provide, as well as quality of light effects in an ethereal air at an altitude of well over 5000 feet (1500 metres), no other natural scenery can beat the landscape of Sagalassos, awe-inspiring and sublime.

Even on the approach from the village of Aglasun, which derives its name from the ancient city, the view is quite breathtaking, looking up to the site backed by a range of sparkling white mountains 7000–8000 feet high, their jagged peaks cutting into the blue sky.

The site itself is raised up on terraces at different levels with, close behind, the grey-white cliffs rising precipitously to the north. Immediately in front and to the south the mountain declivity, to which the city clung, drops almost sheer, opening out beyond the sweeping surfaces of bare cone-like shapes into a wide prospect of green valleys, forested hills and lower ranges far away. The site of Sagalassos was made for rugged, bold people who would fight desperately for their freedom. This happened when Alexander came; his military genius and equal bravery were able to defeat them.

Whereas the capture of Termessos was not regarded by Alexander as essential to his ends, Sagalassos offered a challenge he could hardly disregard and no doubt he also felt that by its subjection his communications could be made secure. Arrian has left us a detailed account of what happened. 'The Pisidians,' he says, 'are all fine soldiers, but the Sagalassians were conspicuous even among a nation of fighters. On this occasion they occupied the high ground in front of the town, a position no less good for defensive action than the wall itself, and there awaited the Macedonian assault.'[20]

Arrian then goes on to tell us how Alexander deployed his forces, he himself taking command of the Macedonian infantry, the Longshields, which formed the right wing, with the footguards forming the centre of the line under the command of various officers, the left under the command of Amyntas, one of Alexander's companions. The Macedonian forces were screened in front by the archers and javelin throwers commanded by other officers. In the fierce battle that ensued the archers and javelin throwers were thrust back, but in the hand-to-hand struggle that followed, when the heavily-armed Macedonians came into action, the Sagalassians who were lightly armed suffered severe losses and had to yield. Five hundred of them were killed, but the rest fled and dispersed in the mountains where Alexander could not successfully pursue them. The city was then stormed and taken, but it seems that practically all the citizens had fled.

Given the nature of the terrain and the bravery of the defenders, who claimed to be of Spartan descent, it was undoubtedly a typical Alexandrian feat to get his heavily-armed infantry victoriously up the steep, and in parts precipitous, incline of the approach.

In spite of this defeat the Sagalassians rallied and recovered entirely. The city, by then to a great extent hellenized, was again a formidable stronghold and a prosperous owner of much fertile land covering a large area, when 130 years later Manlius Vulso arrived on his fund-grabbing campaign. He was not welcomed. Both Polybius and Livy tell us what happened. The account of Polybius is much shorter but in essence the same, presumably as the result of their having had the same source of information. Livy relates that as the Sagalassians were inclined to oppose Manlius, plundering parties were sent by the Roman consul into the countryside to pillage and ravage the crops of their fertile land. The alarmed Sagalassians obtained peace from Manlius, who was only interested in money and food supplies, on payment of fifty talents and the surrender of a certain quantity of wheat and barley.

After this event we hear very little of Sagalassos through the ages, but no doubt it continued to be a bellicose and independent city until the Roman age when, though no longer free to wage war, it flourished none the less in the first two centuries of the principate, as indeed its ruins show, since most of them date from that period.

The many public buildings of Sagalassos, temples, stoas, a gymnasium, a monumental nymphaion and other structures, have all been overthrown by earthquakes and lie broken on the ground but for a few pieces of doors and walls still standing here and there. It is therefore at first impossible to reconstruct a mental picture of the city such as it was. But the site can exert a gripping fascination on the mind when the ground as well as the layout is more carefully examined on which pieces of statuary rested until not many years ago. On the southernmost terrace stood the Corinthian peripteral temple of Zeus dedicated to Antoninus Pius. Although no longer standing, its position in the landscape is striking; the foundations and fallen stones and columns are no less impressive and the details of its carved cornices, weathered and worn though they are, still strike the eye most vividly (Pl. 35).

The first to discover this site was a Frenchman, Paul Lucas, who was travelling in Asia Minor in 1704. His enthusiasm had no bounds:

As soon as we had left Aglason we had still to climb one of the highest mountains, Aglason Bey, which derives its name from that of the village. It is divided into several branches, but has something even more wonderful than the mountains of Chenet and Biliere Ouvasi. On the edge of its cliffs you see several buildings covering a huge area. For a long time I kept contemplating these wonderful things which I could hardly believe existed, I mean an entire city the houses of which are built of huge stones, some even of marble. In spite of the place being quite delightful as well as magnificent it is entirely deserted, so it looks as though it belonged to a fairy tale world rather than like a real city.[21]

If this vision of an entire city reflected, as no doubt it did, an ensemble of conspicuous buildings still standing in Paul Lucas' days, Sagalassos must have suffered severely from earthquakes in the course of that century. However, when W. J. Hamilton visited the site in the mid-1830s the architecture of the city still survived to an impressive extent, for he too burst out with enthusiasm. 'I believe there is no ruined city in Asia Minor the situation and ruins of which are as astonishing as those of Sagalassos, where you are given such a complete picture of a stupendous setting of temples, palaces, porticoes, theatres, gymnasia, fountains and tombs with which ancient cities were adorned.'[22] Nor were F. V. J. Arundell's astonishment and delight less outspoken. He was travelling in Anatolia about the same time and described the ruins in greater detail than either Hamilton or Fellows, who followed him shortly after. Arundell included in his book a charming, though somewhat romanticized, sketch of the site. From this sketch as well as from his general description it would appear that the remains were in a far better state of preservation than they are today. The theatre was in an almost perfect condition and many other buildings were still partially standing. The remains of the basilica were still most impressive when Arundell saw them and the door, of which only the jambs are now erect, was in those days complete. The temple of Apollo Klaros near by has fared scarcely better: only some overturned column drums have survived.

On the uppermost part of the site, not far from the base of the cliffs which surge majestically into the sky, lies the theatre with its *cavea* measuring over 300 feet (90 metres) in diameter. This large structure dates from the first or second century AD and presents some architectural features characteristic of that age, though the *cavea* exceeds the semi-circle and the *skene* stands detached as a separate unit in accordance with the Greek mode. Of course the whole theatre has suffered from earthquakes, but not to the same disastrous extent as the other edifices on the site. It is still a magnificent building in a setting of striking grandeur and beauty.

Enthusiastic Fellows expressed himself as follows: 'On the side of a higher hill is one of the most beautiful and perfect theatres I ever saw or heard of; the seats and the greater part of the proscenium remain; the walls of the front have partly fallen, but the splendid cornices and statuary are but little broken. I walked almost round, in the arched lobby, entering as the people did above two thousand years ago.'[23]

Where is the splendid statuary observed by Fellows? There are no signs of it now. Evidently the whole theatre was in a better condition when he visited it, since the *parodoi* are now obstructed by fallen blocks of stone over which you have to clamber in order to get in. Moreover on one side of the upper part of the *cavea* the rows of seats have been badly dislodged. Hamilton wrote: 'The seats of the *cavea* are as perfect and level as the day they were placed.'[24]

When Lanckoronski made his scholarly survey in 1885, the remains of Sagalassos had already undergone much of the deterioration we now witness. For instance the upper rows of the theatre on the north-western side of the *cavea*, as they appear in the admirable illustration of his book, were dislodged to the same extent as they are today. But the stage building has suffered from further decay. The magnificent door lintels have collapsed.

Shaken, dilapidated and reduced such as it is today Sagalassos remains, nevertheless, one of the most wonderful sites of Anatolia, breathtakingly sublime.

Tucked away in an isolated nook of the Tauros folds at an altitude of nearly 5000 feet (1500 metres) is the site of Adada mentioned by Artemidoros as one of the thirteen cities of Pisidia. Its position is definitely not spectacular and so in this respect bears no comparison with that of Sagalassos; it has no view, being closed in on all sides, but some of its buildings are still standing in a far better state of preservation than any of the remains at Selge, Kremna or Sagalassos.

Although the city was once on the main route from Pisidian Antioch to Perge and the coast, along which Saint Paul travelled – he most likely halted at Adada for some time since the nearby village bears the name of Kara Baulo (Black Paul: why black?) – the site is now reachable only by a rough dirt road. It is hardly ever visited by travellers today and only by a very few in the past, for it lies more than 40 miles (65 km) from the main thoroughfares of Anatolia. Its seclusion and solitude may partly account for the remarkably good condition of some of its buildings, particularly of two prostyle temples (Pl. 37) whose ashlar masonry

△ **23** The odeion at Arykanda

△ **24** The theatre at Arykanda

△ **25** The stadium at Arykanda

◁ **26** An aqueduct at Phaselis

▽ **27** The temple door at Olympos

△ **28** The temple of Apollo at Side

▽ **29** The distyle-in-antis temple at Seleukeia

△ **30** Seleukeia

▽ **31** Seleukeia

△ **32** The theatre at Termessos

33 The tomb of Alketas at Termessos

35 (*overleaf*) Site of the temple of Zeus at Sagalassos

34 The gymnasium at Termessos

△ **36** The theatre at Sagalassos

▽ **37** A temple at Adada

△ **38** City gate of Isaura

▷ **39** City gate of
Isaura

▽ **40** Triumphal arch
at Isaura

△ **41** A tomb at Olba

△ **42** The tower of the Priestly Kings at Olba

▽ **43** The temple of Zeus at Olba

△ **44** The temple of Zeus at Aizanoi

◁ **45** The temple of
Artemis at Sardeis

▽ **46** A capital from a
temple at Sardeis

cannot fail to draw attention. Although their porches have collapsed these two temples, of which one was dedicated to the Augusti and Serapis and the other to the Augusti and Aphrodite, have stood up to earthquakes far better than a large building situated near by of which only a section of its fine walls is still standing.

The theatre is in a very poor condition, having greatly suffered from a landslide or earthquake, but partly also from the ploughing of a field on the edge of which it happens to be placed. No doubt some excavation could uncover the lower part of the *cavea*, perhaps less damaged.

In a much better state of preservation is the fascinating agora, placed in a pleasant wood of small holm oaks with, leading up from it, a flight of steps for the assembly to sit on at their meetings. The acropolis walls and other buildings stand shining in the sun, while the ashlar walls of the gymnasium recall the past in the shade of the ilex grove.

In spite of the absence of wide prospects the site of Adada is extremely attractive, for its remains are enhanced by overhanging trees in idyllic solitude undisturbed by the sheep that graze near by or sleep in the shade of the temple cellae. The level ground which forms the central part of the site is being farmed, however, and a road has been built through it; the consequences of these archaeologically damaging activities are bound to be unfortunate.

The buildings and walls still standing belong to the golden age of the Graeco-Roman world – the first two centuries of our era. Their simplicity, elegance and beauty would have again deceived Fellows who, had he seen Adada which he failed to reach, would have enthusiastically declared them as 'pure Greek' or 'early Greek'.

We know little of the history of Adada, but we can assume from the extent of its ruins that it was a prosperous town. We can also infer from the inscription recording its alliance with Termessos, where reference is made to the democracy established by both of them, that by the second century BC this remote Pisidian city, away in the Tauros mountains at a distance of more than fifty miles as the crow flies from the civilized Pamphylian coastland, was by then entirely hellenized.

Like the other main cities of Pisidia, Adada became a bishopric in the late Roman or early Byzantine age, but there are no ruins of buildings belonging to that period probably on account of the method of construction which came into use.

About 20 miles (32 km) north of Pamphylian Selekeia, near the village of Sirt and covering the steep slopes of a mountain, lie the ruins of a Pisidian city which in all probability was Etenna, not Petnelissos as one might assume. Whereas Petnelissos is listed by the geographers Artemidoros and Strabo as a Pisidian city, they make no mention of Etenna. Most of the information we have about this city comes from Polybius. In his account of the siege of Petnelissos by the Selgians, he says that Garsyeris on arriving with his army in an attempt to relieve the siege, was reinforced by 8000 hoplites from the Etennians 'who inhabit the highlands above Side'. This indication would indeed correspond with the location of the ruins at Sirt. Petnelissos, on the other hand, is placed by Strabo north of Aspendos and therefore much closer to Selge.

Compared with Seleukeia in the neighbourhood, Etenna must have been a much larger city if it could afford to lend 8000 hoplites to Garsyeris, in fact of a fair size as its extensive ruins indeed suggest. But unlike Seleukeia, none of its buildings are now standing. The theatre, no doubt as the result of an earthquake, is in a very poor condition, hardly recognizable, while the other remains, including a Byzantine church, lie scattered in a chaotic state on the slopes of the mountain. Sections of the city ashlar walls still stand to a considerable height, and a number of rock-cut tombs can be seen. The statue of a woman lies prostrate on the ground, but has lost its head. The whole position of the city is commanding and the remains, in spite of their dilapidated condition, are evocative.

Etenna began issuing its own coins as early as the middle of the fourth century BC[25] and survived as a city right into the early Byzantine age when it became the seat of a bishop, for it is mentioned in the Notitiae Episcoporum of the early sixth century AD.

The site was surveyed by members of the Lanckoronski expedition in 1885 and then visited by Hirschfeld, Jüthner[26] and in more recent years by George Bean. The sites of two other Pisidian cities, Kotenna and Erymna, have been located some 20 miles (32 km) north-east of Sirt, but the ruins found there are very scanty.

ISAURIA & CILICIA

THE TAUROS IS NOT A SINGLE CHAIN OF MOUNTAINS BUT A WHOLE complex of ranges covering a vast area of southern Asia Minor. In Lycia, where its westernmost reaches stretch, the mountains attain altitudes of over 10,000 feet (3000 metres) and again in the far eastern region centring round the Cilician Gates, through which the road from Cappadocia and the north leads to the plains of Cilicia Pedias, there are peaks that rise well over 11,000 feet. Lying in between, the central area of the Tauros includes the regions of Pisidia, Isauria and Cilicia Tracheia, or Rough Cilicia, where the mountain summits are not quite so high, but where the land is even more rugged.

The Pisidian tribes were renowned in antiquity for their warlike nature and plundering propensities. But little by little they organized themselves into city states by adopting the *polis* constitution as well as the Greek language and way of life. In other words they became civilized, though hardly less warlike. Their close neighbours to the east, on the other hand, the Isaurian tribes, scarcely ever became civilized, at any rate most of them. They remained wilder than the unruly Pisidians had ever been. They were robbers and most of them remained robbers. Well embattled in their strongholds they would sally forth on their predatory pursuits. Some of them lived in villages, but few of these developed into cities, their tribal life continuing to prevail right into the Roman age.

If the Isaurians were troublesome brigands, their close neighbours to the east, the Cilicians, were ruthless pirates who infested the seas. They became rich and in a way more civilized than the Isaurians, perhaps, ironically enough, as the result of the slave trade they engaged in and their consequent dealings with the Hellenic world.

The Isaurians, who were divided into three main tribes, the Homonadeis, the Oroandeis and the Isaurians proper, or Isauri, remained isolated in their mountainous country and for a long time impervious to the influence of Hellenism. Under the very loose control of the Seleucid and Attalid hegemonies their tribal life continued unaffected. Only when they were subdued by force of arms in the Roman age did they start to build in a manner indicating adoption of the Hellenic way of life. They remained troublesome and were never softened; indeed they provided the Byzantines with two hardy emperors, (Zeno and Leo III) and excellent troops as well.

With Pisidia to the west, Galatia and Lykaonia to the north, and Cilicia Tracheia to the east, the exact boundaries of Isauria remained vague nevertheless, for sometimes it became part of Lykaonia, sometimes of Galatia, and sometimes of Cilicia Tracheia. Not far beyond its border with Pisidia stood the three Pisidian cities, Etenna, Kotenna and Erymna. Immediately to the north-east of these came the region where the Homonadeis dwelt, the toughest and most unruly tribe of Isauria. Their strongholds and pastures were situated to the south and west of Lake Trogitis (Lake Sŭgla of today). Not until the Roman age did their villages approach city status and even then, when their tribal structure was broken up, it is doubtful whether Homana, their main centre of habitation mentioned by Hierokles in the days of the emperor Justinian, ever achieved municipal status. No remains of buildings have survived.

Somewhere north-east of the Homonadeis came a curious enclave of Pisidia in which lay the city of Amblada mentioned by Artemidoros as one of the main cities of Pisidia, which was a proper *polis* issuing its own coins and therefore hellenized long before the other inhabitants of the region. It was famous for its vineyards and excellent wine.[1] Unfortunately the remains of Amblada have vanished. In the neighbourhood touching this enclave dwelt the Oroandeis, a scarcely less unruly tribe of Isauria.

The Isauri proper occupied a region somewhat further east on an elevated and very rugged plateau, barren in parts but well wooded in others, which from the northern foothills of the Tauros bordering Cappadocia and Lykaonia stretched almost as far south as the sea. At the heart of it stood Isaura Palaia, their main stronghold. The whole region is intersected by lofty ridges through which the rushing waters of the two main branches of the Kalykadnos, the river in which Frederic Barbarossa was drowned, have carved out canyons on an awe-inspiring scale.

Though scarcely less addicted to brigandage than the other two tribes of the country, the Isauri developed into a more organized or at least centralized community, for their main centre of habitation achieved city status in course of time. They too had several strongholds, but their principal one was not a mere fort: it emerged in the days of Alexander as a fortified, populous town which crowned a rocky hill. Isaura Palaia – Old Isaura, as it was called, to differentiate it from a lesser stronghold known as New Isaura – stood well protected by the precipitous sides of its hill at an altitude of nearly 5000 feet (1500 metres) above the sea from which it could carry on its plundering activities. Persian rule had been lax and before Alexander's conquest no serious effort had been made to bring the tribes of the region under control. Their reduction was felt to be desirable, however, when the satrapies of Asia Minor were reorganized by Alexander.

The first event in the history of Isaura of which information has survived occurred in 323 BC. Thanks to Diodorus Siculus, Isaura and its people suddenly spring into the light of history. Alexander was dead and the Isaurians had rebelled and killed Balakros, the Macedonian satrap of Cilicia. Perdikkas, who was endeavouring to establish himself as Alexander's successor, set about the task of subduing the tribes and besieged their main stronghold, Isaura. Diodorus Siculus' account of what happened is worth quoting:

> The city of the Isaurians was strongly fortified and large and moreover was filled with stout warriors; so when they had besieged it vigorously for two days and had lost many of their own men, they withdrew; for the inhabitants, who were well provided with missiles and other things needed for withstanding a siege and were enduring the dreadful ordeal with desperate courage in their hearts, were readily giving their lives to preserve their freedom. On the third day, when many had been slain and the walls had few defenders because of lack of men, the citizens performed a heroic and memorable deed. Seeing that the punishment that hung over them could not be averted, and not having a force that would be adequate to stave the enemy off, they determined not to surrender the city and place their fate in the hands of the enemy, since in that way their punishment combined with outrage was certain; but at night all with one accord, seeking the noble kind of death, shut up their children, wives and parents in their houses, and set the houses on fire, choosing by means of the fire a common death and burial. As the blaze suddenly flared aloft, the Isaurians cast into the fire their goods and everything that could be of use to the victors; Perdikkas and his officers, astounded at what was taking place, stationed their troops about the city and made a strong effort to break into the city on all sides. When now the inhabitants defended themselves from the walls and struck down many of the Macedonians, Perdikkas was even more astonished and sought the reason why men who had given their homes and all else to the flames should be so intent upon defending the walls. Finally Perdikkas and the Macedonians withdrew from the city, and the Isaurians, throwing themselves into the fire, found burial in their homes along with their families. When the night was over Perdikkas gave the city to his soldiers for booty. They, when they had put out the fire, found an abundance of silver and gold, as was natural in a city that had been prosperous for a great many years.[2]

It is perhaps worth noting how often in history this form of self-annihilation has occurred – a beleagured city or fastness in which the inhabitants hold out until resistance is no longer possible and then opt for dying in combat after having destroyed their families, houses and belongings, rather than surrendering to the enemy with all the consequences that would follow. It happened at Xanthos twice, at Masada in Israel, at Zalongos in Epirus more recently in history and doubtless on several other occasions.

The picture we get of Isaura from Diodorus Siculus is of a prosperous and populous town. Throughout his account he refers to it as a *polis*, but at the end of the fourth century BC it could not have been a real city state for in those days Isaura was entirely barbarian, scarcely affected by Hellenism. No doubt it was a populous town, but not yet a city with buildings appropriate to the Greek way of life. We cannot help wondering what sort of buildings they could have been, when it was set on fire by the inhabitants and then pillaged by Perdikkas and his men. Probably they were all timber houses, for the whole neighbourhood was at the time well wooded.

There followed more than two hundred years of Seleucid and Attalid rule which proved even looser and even more indirect than the Persian dominion had been, during which the Isaurian tribes were left to themselves, free to pursue their predatory activities. Some elements of Hellenism may have begun to seep in, but to what extent and in what form we are unable to tell owing to the paucity of the surviving records. They continued to be aggressive and when they started associating themselves with the pirates of Cilicia in various unlawful pursuits at the beginning of the first century BC Publius Servilius Vatia, who had been sent by the Roman senate to quell the power of the pirates, found it necessary to reduce the Isaurians. So he pushed inland with an army in 76 BC, subdued the Homonadeis and Oroandeis, and then besieged and captured Nea Isaura by cutting off its water supply. This stronghold of the Isauri was situated some 17 miles (27 km) north-east of Isaura Palaia, possibly at the present village of Dorla, in territory that had been captured from the Lykaonians. But its exact location has not yet been established with certainty, no remains of its buildings having survived nor any definitely clarifying inscriptions. Isaura Palaia was also reduced and according to Strabo demolished.[3]

Servilius earned the title Isauricus from this campaign, but whether he was able to quell the brigandage of the Isaurian tribes is more than doubtful. The territory could be invaded by an army and a few fastnesses could be captured, about 43 in all according to Pliny;[4] but these predatory tribes could hardly be brought under lasting control in this manner, certainly not the Homonadeis who remained virtually unsubdued and continued to cause trouble. 'In the midst of the heights of the Tauros, which are very steep and for the most part impassable,' so Strabo tells us, 'there is a hollow and fertile plain which is divided into several valleys. But though the people tilled this plain, they lived on the overhanging brows of the mountains or in caves. They were for the most part armed and were wont to overrun the country of others, having mountains that served as walls about their country.'[5] Indeed the precipitous ranges of the territory occupied by the Homonadeis rise to heights of more than 9000 feet (2700 metres).

A question now arises to which there is as yet no answer. What happened to Isaura, the main centre of habitation which had been virtually left to itself for nearly two and a half centuries, from when Perdikkas brought about its destruction to when it was demolished again by Servilius? The town was presumably reconstructed, but to what extent and in what manner? Were the buildings at all Hellenistic in character as the result of some penetration of Hellenism under the loose suzerainty of the Seleucid and Attalid kings? Since none of the ruins on the site nor any of the inscriptions date back to that period, the question must remain unanswered until some excavation is undertaken which might bring to light informative material. In any case the official language of the city most probably became Greek in the course of those two and half centuries.

We hear nothing of Isaura again until about forty years later when Antony made Amyntas king not only of Galatia, his native country, but also of Lycaonia, Isauria and parts of Pisidia and Pamphylia. He was a hellenized Galatian as well as an ambitious and energetic man. Since the days of Publius Servilius unrest was again rife in Lykaonia and Isauria. In Lykaonia a brigand by the name of Antipater had set himself up as tyrant of two towns, Derbe and Laranda. Not far to the south Isauria was again a stronghold of bandits, and the Homonadeis were again marauding beyond their confines. So Amyntas attacked Antipater, whom he killed, and then proceeded to invest Isaura, which he occupied. From Strabo we learn that he destroyed whatever buildings he found there and 'built for himself a royal residence',[6] indeed a proper city judging by the extent of the walls the circuit of which is more than two and a half miles (4 km), which he built but was unable to complete before his untimely death. He was killed by the Homonadeis whose territory he had begun to invade. Strabo says that 'he was caught by treachery through the artifice of the tyrant's wife',[7] an intriguing statement, which makes us want to know more. Did his capture and death occur as the result of an incautious love affair? In any case the thorough hellenization of Isaura can be said to have started with his reconstruction of the city.

After the death of Amyntas the whole region of Isauria and western Cilicia Tracheia reverted to an unsettled condition for another thirty years. At last, under the reign of Augustus, the consul Sulpicius Quirinius, governor of Syria, was sent to bring the tribes into disciplined subjection. He undertook this assignment in the year 12 BC and carried it out with greater thoroughness than Servilius had been able to do. Strabo tells us that he subjugated the Homonadeis 'by starving them, and capturing alive four thousand men whom he settled in the neighbouring cities, leaving the country destitute of all its men who were in the prime of life.'⁸ We gather that Quirinius accomplished this feat by surrounding and blockading the fastnesses to which the Homonadeis had retreated. Since they were dependent for food supplies on their valleys and plains which they could no longer farm and gather crops from, they were soon starved into surrender. As for Quirinius, when he returned to Rome he obtained triumphal honours in recognition of this victory, so Tacitus tells us.⁹

The period of relative tranquillity that followed may to some extent have been due to the Roman colonies which Augustus settled on the outer fringe of the region for the purpose of keeping some degree of order, in particular at Lystra and Parlais in Lykaonia, at Antioch in Phrygia, near the Pisidian border, and at Kremna. Strangely enough, no Roman colony was established at Isaura Palaia, the main city of the region.

If we look at the map of Isauria drawn by that indefatigable topographer and cartographer R. Kiepert, and printed at the beginning of this century, we cannot help being struck by the number of ancient sites localized there and well marked with their names. In addition to Isaura are Kolybrassos, Astra, Adrassos, Artanada, Lauzados, Liassos, Domitiopolis, Zenopolis, Germanicopolis, Kestros, Eirenopolis, Philadelphia and others.¹⁰ Six of these are mentioned by Hierokles in his list of cities. Some are marked on the map with a sign indicating ruins as well as their names, others are not: their location was probably conjectural. Kiepert marks the ruins of many sites without their names, probably because he could not identify them. W. M. Ramsay, in his *Historical Geography of Asia Minor* published in 1890, is of no help because he did not travel extensively in that particular region. But the epigraphist J. R. S. Sterrett was able to identify some sites at the end of the last century, and more recently George Bean and T. B. Mitford established the location of others.¹¹ It may well be that some were at first those very bandit strongholds which caused so much trouble in the days of Publius Servilius. In the course of time even these may have attained municipal status probably by the beginning of the second century AD as Isaura had done, notwithstanding the state of unrest and revolt which continued to predominate in the whole region right into the Byzantine age. Astra, for instance, crowning the top of a high mountain, became sophisticated enough to have a theatre as well as temples though the position was hardly convenient for a city. It was extremely well placed as a stronghold for banditry.

When under the Roman principate urbanization spread far afield, hellenization proceeded alongside it and Isauria became filled with *poleis*. The fundamental part played by the *boule* and the *demos*, as well as the importance of the gymnasia, is ubiquitously reflected in the inscriptions. The language, customs and culture of these cities were Greek, and likewise the festivals and games with their all-pervasive agonistic spirit characteristic of Hellenism. Of course the system of government was no longer strictly speaking democratic. The *demos*, usually mentioned in the inscriptions side by side with the *boule*, had no power.

The assembly was simply expected to accept the decisions taken by the council
and by the magistrates who were usually chosen by the councillors from among
themselves. The office of councillor had become hereditary, held by the rich
citizens, usually landowners. This state of affairs did not apply to a specific area
of cities any more than to others; it prevailed throughout the whole hellenized
world of the Roman empire. Of outstanding importance was the rich donor on
whom the services and amenities of the city, as well as the splendour of its public
buildings, depended to a great extent. But however civilized the cities were or
aimed to be, in the rural and mountainous area of Isauria, beyond the city walls,
the people never ceased to be barbarian, speaking their indigenous language and
remaining addicted to banditry.

Partly on account of earthquakes but also as the result of the endemic
unrest throughout the whole territory, the ruins of these Isaurian cities are most
inconspicuous compared with the remains of Isaura, which by the beginning of
our era had developed into a fully-fledged *polis*, with a council and an assembly
of the people as the Greek inscriptions and coins attest.

Crowning a lofty, rocky hill of light-coloured limestone speckled with
black junipers, the remains of Isaura occupy one of the most striking sites of
Anatolia rivalled only by that of Sagalassos. The clarity of the air at that altitude,
the varied configuration of the ground, the undulating ridges which one after
another sink further and further away in every direction, and the delicacy of the
modulating colours enhanced by the quality of the ashlar masonry of the ruins,
all combine to provide an unbelievably beautiful site.

Even the main access to the site is alluring, up a steep path from the
village below which, flanked by a succession of rock tombs, leads to the city walls
and towers built by Amyntas. The tombs surmounted by lions belong to the
Roman age and though basically Hellenic in character are somewhat barbarous
in proportions and taste as one might expect, being the work of such a rugged
and isolated people as the Isaurians. They are, none the less, not without a
degree of grandeur.

The first modern discoverer of Isaura was the traveller and geologist
W. J. Hamilton, who visited the site in 1836 and identified it from an inscription. He wrote a thorough description of it, the main part of which is
worth quoting, though not all he says still applies to the present condition of the
ruins.

Without the walls of the town to the S.S.E. are the remains of several small
buildings constructed of well-hewn blocks of marble, and put together without
cement, and which appear to be tombs of a superior character. Some of the
stones are enriched with lions' claws, others with carved medallions, roses and
flowers. The buildings themselves, which have all been thrown down, appear
to have stood upon substantial bases, approached by three or four steps, still

for the most part perfect, and having the front part of the upper step scooped out like the seats of the ancient theatres . . .

Isaura was encompassed by strong and massive walls which may be traced all round, except along the steep and precipitous cliffs to the N.W. and N. They are undoubtedly ancient, and of very beautiful workmanship, but in a style which I never saw before applied to this description of building; they are moreover strengthened by numerous lofty towers, which, on the S.W. side, where the hill is less precipitous, are placed very close together; the principal gateway to the south, represented in the accompanying drawing, has been defended by two of these towers, now fallen to ruins. They are built in the same style as the wall itself, which consists of alternating courses of thick and then thin blocks of marble, each long stone being separated by a very short one [the architectural term for this type of ashlar masonry is 'pseudo-isodomic']; their combination has a singular appearance, the former courses being nearly four feet, the others scarcely a foot in thickness. I saw no square or round towers; they are all either hexagons or octagons. The arch over the gateway is still standing, in apparent defiance of the rude convulsions which have overturned everything around it [Pls. 38, 39]. Two medallions representing shields are sculptured, or rather left in relief, on one of the courses of stone in the western tower of the gateway, within which several roads or streets may be traced branching off in various directions; one on the right leading to quarries and the citadel, another on the left to a large substantial building, apparently the foundation or cella of a temple, about one hundred yards from the gateway. Built in the same style as the walls, and all the other buildings, it stands on a rocky eminence commanding an extensive view, and is 142 feet by 87: there is an entrance at the south west end between two gigantic door-posts, 12 or 14 feet high; a large stone near the S.E. corner measured 13 feet 3 inches in length.

A few hundred yards to the north of this edifice the ground is covered with a confused mass of buildings, of different sizes and characters, amongst which the remains of a forum or agora may be distinctly traced, with a row of columns along a third street leading to the principal gateway . . .

A short distance to the N.E. of the forum, and nearly a quarter of a mile north by west from the gateway, was the most interesting monument of this ancient city, viz., a triumphal arch built of red and yellow marble, in the same style as the walls, standing by itself in an almost perfect state amongst junipers and ilex bushes, and erected by the inhabitants of Isaura (the council and the people) in honour of the emperor Hadrian, as appears from the inscription which I copied from the architrave, and which leaves no doubt as to the name of the city.

The height from the ground to the top of this building is 24 feet, and its width 18 feet and 10 inches, and total depth 12 feet . . .

To the N.W. of this triumphal arch were also remains of steps leading to a terrace, on which, from the number of large and deeply fluted columns lying near, a large temple probably once stood. Near it I found a well executed bas-relief representing men and animals fighting and hunting . . .

To the S.E. of the arch of Hadrian, and above the street of columns, were some slight indications of a small theatre.[12]

The present city walls and towers, though impressive, are in a worse state of preservation than they were when Hamilton saw them. The arched gateway still spans intact the two sides of the entrance to the city from the south-west, but the way under the arch is now obstructed by fallen blocks of stone from the walls that led to it. The way in was clear of such encumbrance when Hamilton visited the site, as the sketch he made of the gateway suggests. It shows the partly ruined tower on the left in more or less the same condition as now, but the wall leading to it bearing the medallions he describes has collapsed. The medallions may now lie buried under the present heap of stones. They were still to be seen *in situ* a generation later when the traveller E. J. Davis visited the site. He says: 'On the left side of the passage leading to the gateway, shields are sculpted in relief, some quite plain, others with a boss and spear.'[13]

The streets Hamilton observed 'branching off in various directions' are no longer easy to trace and not much of the 'substantial' remains of the temple he describes is still visible nor of the row of columns leading to the agora except for their bases, while 'the confused mass of buildings covering the ground' is in an even more chaotic state than it apparently was. But the agora and what might have been a stoa are still easily identifiable. Still standing most conspicuously and in a good state of preservation is Hadrian's triumphal arch (Pl. 40) built in his honour by the council and the people of Isaura, which once bore the inscription Hamilton was able to copy but which has now fallen off. The relief representing men and animals has disappeared and lies perhaps under the stones and debris. Likewise the traces of the theatre he saw are now difficult to find.

The deterioration which the remains of Isaura have suffered in the last 150 years is doubtless due to earthquakes, but most probably also to spoliation. E. J. Davis, who visited the site in the 1870s, observed that much damage had been done by the inhabitants of the village at the foot of the hill who had been 'pulling down the stones in order to extract the iron bolts with which they had been secured'. Many blocks of stone may have also been taken away for building purposes. However, the site has never been excavated and much could come to light if this task were undertaken. What still strikes the eye and can still be enjoyed vindicates Charles Texier's exclamation of delight on beholding the walls and towers when he visited the site shortly after Hamilton: '*La beauté des matériaux étonne après tant de siècles, et ces ruines ont encore un aspect de fraîcheur extraordinaire.*'

In spite of its decay Isaura, with some of its beautiful walls and towers still standing, its elegant gateway, its imposing trumphal arch and its stupendous position, cannot fail to impress any visitor as one of the most fascinating sites of Anatolia where once a splendid city took shape in the wake of Hellenism.[14]

The northern branch of the Kalykadnos as far downstream as Ninika-Klaudiopolis, the site of which is now occupied by modern Mut, may be regarded as the eastern boundary of Isauria. Ninika, renamed Klaudiopolis by Antiochos IV of Commagene in the days of the emperor Claudius, was for a time the capital of an important tribe, not Isaurian but Cilician, the Lalasseis. Unfortunately only very scanty traces of the ancient city have survived. The region east of the river, no less broken up by deep gorges, is to be regarded as Cilicia Tracheia proper. In the area south of Klaudiopolis, almost as far as the sea, dwelt a turbulent Cilician tribe, the Ketai, who broke into open rebellion against the Romans in AD 36 and again in 52. 'A wild and savage race inured to plunder and sudden commotions,' so Tacitus describes them. 'From their fastnesses they came rushing down on the plain, and advancing along the coast attacked the neighbouring cities.'[15]

Cutting off Isauria to the north, this part of Cilicia stretches along the coast as far west as the promontory of Korakesion which in the first century BC became the westernmost stronghold of the pirates, the easternmost being the ancient city of Soloi on the threshold of Cilicia Pedias. This whole coastal land was contested for over two centuries by the Seleucid and Ptolemaic kings. First it was ruled by the Seleucids, then by Egypt and then again by the Seleucids, but always more loosely and ineffectively, until the Romans were able to establish uniform order.

In describing this coast and enumerating its cities Strabo says that Cilicia Tracheia begins at Korakesion, though Artemidoros, less plausibly, regarded the beginning to be at Kelenderis which was situated considerably further east. We learn from Strabo that a Syrian rebel, Diodotos Tryphon, was able to seize Korakesion the city, which crowned a precipitous rock of the promontory above the sea, and that there he organized the famous gangs of pirates. He held it for some years dominating the coast and finally, besieged by Antiochos VII, committed suicide in 138 BC. The site of the ancient city is now occupied by Alanya, a thriving little town full of fine Seljuk buildings and more recent houses, including monstrous concrete blocks, which have obliterated the ancient edifices. The worst possible type of modern architecture has totally disfigured the beauty and charm Alanya could boast of up to the 1960s.

Of the origin of Korakesion we know nothing, but the hellenization of the city and of the entire Cilician coast probably started more or less at the same time as the hellenization of Pamphylia, with Mopsos settling his horde of immigrants from the west in the eleventh century BC. Some of the cities were founded or re-peopled by colonies from Greece, some others were Seleucid foundations and a couple were founded by Antiochos IV of Commagene. As the result of the progressive enfeeblement of the Seleucid and Ptolemaic hold they became virtually independent, issuing their own coinage, while the tribes of the hinterland, the Ketai in particular but no doubt also the Kennatai who dwelt further east, could pursue their plundering activities virtually unhindered. So towards the end of the second century BC the more ruthless elements of the country resorted to piracy as an easy source of wealth, the slave trade being particularly profitable, and proceeded to use the cities on the coast, either with their connivance or by force, as harbours from which to operate. The forests of the country provided timber in abundance for their ships.

The principal cities Strabo mentions, proceeding in succession eastward from Korakesion, are: Hamaxia, 'where ship-building timber was brought down', Selinous, Anemurion, Arsinoe, Kelenderis and Holmoi. Selinous was founded by the Seleucid King Antiochos IV and was subsequently called Selinous Traiano-polis because the emperor Trajan died there in AD 117. Kelenderis was said to have been founded by Phoenicians, but received a colony from Samos in the fifth century BC. Iotape, situated a few miles north-west of Selinous, is not mentioned by Strabo because it did not yet exist in his days; it was founded some years after his death by Antiochos IV of Commagene who named it after his daughter. He also founded Antioch ad Cragum on the coast further east. There were other lesser cities Strabo does not mention. As regards Holmoi, which was situated not far from the outlet of the Kalykadnos river, he says it was the main Seleucid residence before Seleukeia on the Kalykadnos was founded.[16]

Of all these coastal cities only a few inconspicuous ruins survive. At Anemurion, for instance, the theatre is hardly recognizable; only the odeion is in a good state having been cleared and restored in recent years. But most of the ancient city is buried under medieval remains which impart a ghostly character to the whole site.

Many more substantial remains were to be seen on the coast in the last century, but they have now disappeared mainly as the result of urban develop-ment. So from the point of view of ancient architecture still reflecting the history of those days, this coastal area of Cilicia west of the Kalykadnos is disappointing compared with the eastern part and its uplands. This is one of the most fascinating regions of southern Anatolia, where still many ancient remains eloquently illustrate the penetration of Hellenism as well as the power and wealth of the pirates.

Seleukeia on the Kalykadnos was founded by Seleukos Nikator about 300 BC and rapidly grew into a prosperous city whose hellenizing influence on the native population of the neighbourhood must have been considerable, particularly on the Kennatai tribe with their capital, Olba, situated a little further east at no great distance. The citizens of Seleukeia, however, 'stood aloof from the Cilician and Pamphylian usages,' says Strabo, probably meaning that they would have nothing to do with piracy.[17] He moreover tells us that Seleukeia produced two distinguished Peripatetic philosophers, Athenaios and Xenarchos, who were active in his own days. Athenaios was also active in politics, whereas Xenarchos, whose pupil Strabo had been, was entirely dedicated to teaching in Alexandria, Athens and finally Rome.

Unfortunately the buildings of this important ancient city have been almost entirely wiped out by modern Selefke after having suffered the vicissitudes of the Middle Ages when it changed hands many a time.

Pirates and priests lived, perhaps not always happily together, only a little further east where the limestone land, rent by deep gorges and rocky ravines, was studded with towers, fortresses, fortified cities and splendid mausolea. In the centre of this region stood a fine Corinthian temple, the revered sanctuary of Olbian Zeus, and a magnificent tower in which the high priest, lord of the country, dwelt.

The penetration of Hellenism, which occurred some centuries before it made itself felt in Isauria, did not apparently affect the tribal structure of the inhabitants for a long time in spite of a certain degree of urbanization. The Kennatai and the Lalasseis were the two dominant tribes whose language became Greek under the influence of the Seleucid overlords and the coastal cities. In fact they were virtually independent, the Kennatai occupying the heart of the region where Olba, the capital, was situated, and the Lalasseis a region somewhat further west in the Kalykadnos valley. As we see from coins inscribed in Greek, Olba would regard itself as the capital of both the Kennatai and the Lalasseis, but it would also issue coins with the legend 'Olba metropolis of the Ketai' although this tribe was in historical times no longer occupying that part of Cilicia. In earlier days, however, the entire population of Cilicia Tracheia seem to have been Ketai. Subsequently the more civilized branches of the tribe, the Kennatai and the Lalasseis, broke away, occupying the area east of the Kalykadnos, while the more primitive Ketai were left to dominate exclusively in the region south-west of the Kalykadnos. The difference in the level of development is apparent in the buildings the Kennatai constructed, so many of which have withstood the worst effects of time and exposure, as against the total absence of buildings of any kind in the Ketai region. Although the tribal nature of the Kennatai community lasted until the Roman age, they built several cities and were ruled by a dynasty of kings who were at the same time the high priests of the sanctuary of Olbian Zeus.

When hellenization began to penetrate towards the end of the fourth century BC Zeus was the Greek name given to the indigenous god worshipped there, an ancient Asiatic deity, probably the Hittite Tark or Tarku. This name was also borne by the priestly dynast who represented the god and embodied the cult. There came a time when he felt the need to establish a plausible Greek pedigree of heroic origin. So from Tark or Tarku the name became Teucer, the name of the ancient Greek hero who after the death of Ajax, his brother, was exiled from Salamis and emigrated to Cyprus where he founded a city to which he gave the same name as that of his native town. Subsequently, according to a local tradition, he settled in Cilicia Tracheia. The island of Cyprus being opposite Cilicia to the south and not far off, we can assume that the dynast of Olba found it expedient to have recourse to this tradition and to claim to be a descendant of the Greek hero with some degree of plausibility, no matter how legendary the story was. So the priestly kings called themselves Teucer or Ajax from father to son.

Strabo, describing the region, says: 'Above Soli is a mountainous country in which is a city Olbe, with a temple of Zeus founded by Ajax son of Teucer. The priest of this temple became the dynast of Cilicia Tracheia; and then the country was beset by numerous tyrants, and the gangs of pirates were organized.'

So there can be little doubt that the Kennatai and to some extent also the Lalasseis were the very people who about the middle of the second century BC resorted to piracy as a means of enrichment. They were more deeply involved than the wild Ketai seem to have been, which is demonstrated by the wealth they derived from these pursuits embodied in the buildings that sprang up in their country. The extent to which the priestly dynasts of Olba were themselves involved in this lucrative business is difficult for us to assess, but it would appear from what Strabo says[18] that their hold on the country declined for a while towards the middle or end of the second century BC and that their power was contested by local chieftains or warlords directly connected with the outburst of piracy.

In his account of Pompey's crushing victory over the pirates and the leniency with which he treated all those who surrendered before the final battle in 67 BC, Plutarch tells us:

He continued to pardon all that came in, because by them he might make discovery of those who fled from his justice, as conscious that their crimes were beyond an act of indemnity. The most numerous and important part of these conveyed their families and treasures, with all their people that were unfit for war, into castles and strong forts about Mount Tauros; but they themselves, having well manned their galleys, embarked for Korakesion in Cilicia, where they received Pompey and gave him battle. Here they had their final overthrow, and retired to the land, where they were besieged. At last, having despatched their heralds to him with a submission, they delivered up to his mercy themselves, their towns, islands and strongholds, all of which they had so fortified that they were almost impregnable, and scarcely even accessible.[19]

Given the nature of this total surrender, which resulted from the pirates realizing the hopelessness of their situation, blockaded and cut off from the sea as they were, and the impossibility of their resuming their former activities, it proved unnecessary for the Romans to occupy Cilicia Tracheia with an army, or to undertake a punitive expedition as a few years earlier Publius Servilius had done in Isauria. So the Cilician strongholds and fortresses were not destroyed, but remained standing undiminished, though useless under the Pax Romana, and so only subject to the limited decay of time and exposure.

After the collapse of the pirates the dynasts of Olba could rapidly resume their ascendancy over the country, new blood and energy being instilled into them by Ada, the daughter of Zenophanes, one of the former chieftains of the buccaneers. She came into the family of the high priests and kings by marriage and took over the power herself, initially 'in the guise of a guardian'. But having gained favour with Cleopatra, her rule was confirmed by Antony who was 'moved by her courteous entreaties'. She was evidently a woman of great charm as well as of ambitious determination. Later she suffered a severe reverse, the exact nature of which we do not know; but the rule of the country remained with her descendants, the priestly kings, until Cilicia Tracheia lost its independence in the days of the emperor Vespasian, after having passed under the more or less nominal suzerainty of Archaelaos of Cappadocia, Polemon II of Pontus and Antiochos IV of Commagene.

The Olbian Zeus sanctuary is still an impressive building, its columns rising loftily into the blue sky to a height of 42 feet (12.6 metres) (Pl. 43). All but two are still standing, though many have lost their uppermost part. It is worth noting that the lower third of the shafts is not fluted but faceted, the earliest surviving example of this columnar style. This peripteral temple, which is hexastyle and has twelve columns on its flanks, was built at the very beginning of the third century BC with funds donated by Seleukos Nikator. It is therefore the earliest Corinthian temple ever built, or at any rate the earliest we know of. Particularly interesting are the capitals, somewhat experimental in form. Having been conceived in the incipient Hellenistic age they have not yet reached the full development which we can see exemplified in the Corinthian capitals of the Roman age on the pillars of the colonnaded street situated near by.[20]

A few hundred yards away the magnificent tower of the priestly kings still stands to a height of over 60 feet (22.5 metres), made of fine ashlar masonry (Pl. 42). The structure is not entirely square, the dimensions being 39 feet 3 inches by 37 feet 6 inches (15.7x12.5 metres). It dates from the second century BC and an inscription observed by travellers in the last century records that it was built by Teucer, the name borne in succession by the dynasts. There is also a later inscription referring to a repair project in the Roman age.

Overlooking the site about a mile to the west stands a building which looks like a tower but is in fact a square tomb about 50 feet (16 metres) high (Pl. 41), with a pyramidal top, built in perfect ashlar masonry. It may have been the sepulchre of one of the priestly dynasts. This piece of architecture, most probably

Hellenistic since its encircling frieze is decorated with triglyphs and metopes in the Doric style (unusual in the Graeco-Roman age), is of great beauty and in an almost complete state of preservation.

Apart from the temple, the tower and this tomb, practically all the other ruins on the site belong to the Roman age. Many of these still stand conspicuously, namely the colonnaded street, the Tychaion, which according to the inscription on the architrave was a structure dedicated to the goddess Fortune, the city gateway, the theatre and other lesser ruins.

Before the buildings of the Roman period came into existence, in other words before a whole city sprang up, the ancient sanctuary, temple and tower stood alone. The capital lay about three miles (5 km) to the east, where a few remains survive on the site known as Oura. But in the early Roman age the sanctuary grew into a considerable centre of habitation and eventually became, under the emperor Vespasian, a city in its own right with the new name of Diokaisarea, detached from Oura and issuing its own coins.[21]

At Oura the remains are far less conspicuous. In fact little has survived apart from a nymphaion, a theatre of the Roman age in very poor condition, walls of the acropolis scarcely emerging above thick undergrowth, the arches of a grand Roman aqueduct built about AD 200 which spans a fine ravine and some rock tombs. But of course more would come to light if the site were cleared and some excavation undertaken.

J. Theodore Bent, although not the first to visit the region, was the first to make a proper survey of it, in the spring of 1890, and write an account of what he found and saw. The epigraphist Heberdey followed the next year.[22] Now that a tarmac road has been built from Selefke to Uzumcaburç, the Turkish village at Diokaisarea, this site and that of Oura are visited by tourists in the summer, but luckily have not yet become commercialized.

The existence and power of the pirates two thousand years ago are more manifest in various places of the neighbourhood, which are somewhat arduous to reach, than at either Diokaisarea or Oura. The nomadic Yuruks are still to be seen with their flocks and black tents, but not nearly so many nor so frequently as some years ago as the result of an agricultural and resettlement policy. Nowadays some roads intersect the region where formerly only paths and a few rough tracks were available to locals as well as travellers. However, the country retains much of the character it had when Bent visited it and a few years later J. G. Frazer, who described it as follows:

Great indeed is the contrast between the bleak windy uplands of Western or Rugged Cilicia, as the ancients called it, and the soft luxuriant lowlands of Eastern Cilicia, where winter is almost unknown and summer annually drives the population to seek in the cool air of the mountains a refuge from the intolerable heat and deadly fevers of the plains. In Western Cilicia, on the other hand, a lofty tableland, ending in a high sharp edge on the coast, rises steadly inland till it passes gradually into the chain of heights which divide it from the interior. Looked at from the sea it resembles a great blue wave swelling in one uniform sweep till its crest breaks into foam in the distant snows of the Tauros. The surface of the tableland is almost everywhere rocky and overgrown, in the intervals of the rocks, with dense, thorny, almost impenetrable scrub. Only here and there in a hollow or a glen the niggardly soil allows a patch of cultivation; and here and there fine oaks and planes, towering over the brushwood, clothe with a richer foliage the depth of the valleys. None but wandering herdmen with their flocks maintain a precarious existence in this rocky wilderness. Yet the ruined towns which stud the country prove that a dense population lived and throve here in antiquity, while numerous remains of wine-presses and wine-vats bear witness to the successful cultivation of the grape. The chief cause of the present desolation is lack of water; for wells are few and brackish, perennial streams hardly exist, and the ancient aqueducts, which once brought life and fertility to the land, have long been suffered to fall into disrepair.

But for ages together the ancient inhabitants of these uplands earned their bread by less reputable means than the toil of the husbandman and the vinedresser. They were buccaneers and slavers, scouring the high sea with their galleys and retiring with their booty to the inaccessible fastenesses of their mountains. In the decline of Greek power all over the East the pirate communities of Cilicia grew into a formidable state, recruited by gangs of desperadoes and broken men who flocked to it from all sides. The holds of these robbers may still be seen perched on the profound ravines which cleave the tableland at frequent intervals. With their walls of massive masonry, their towers and battlements, overhanging dizzy depths, they are admirably adapted to bid defiance to the pursuit of justice. In antiquity the dark forests of cedar, which clothed much of the country and supplied the pirates with timber for their ships, must have rendered access to these fastnesses still more difficult. The great gorge of the Lamas River, which eats its way like a sheet of forked lightning into the heart of the mountains, is dotted every few miles with fortified towns, some of them still magnificent in their ruins, dominating sheer cliffs high above the stream. They are now the haunt only of the ibex and the bear. Each of these communities had its own crest or badge, which may still be seen carved on the corners of the mouldering towers. No doubt, too, it blazoned the same crest on the hull, the sails, or the streamers of the galley which, manned with a crew of ruffians, it sent out to prey upon the rich merchantmen in the Golden Sea, as the corsairs called the highway of commerce between Crete and Africa.

A staircase cut in the rock connects one of these ruined castles with the river in the glen, a thousand feet below. But the steps are worn and dangerous, indeed impassable. You may go for miles along the edge of these stupendous cliffs before you find a way down. The paths keep on the heights, for in many of its reaches the gully affords no foothold even to the agile nomads who alone roam these solitudes. At evening the winding course of the river may be traced for a long distance by a mist which, as the heat of the day declines, rises like steam from the deep gorge and hangs suspended in a wavy line of fleecy cloud above it. But even more imposing than the ravine of the Lamas is the terrific gorge known as the *Sheitan dere* or the Devil's Glen near the Corycian cave. Prodigious walls of rock, glowing in the intense sunlight, black in the shadow, and spanned by a summer sky of the deepest blue, hem in the dry bed of a winter torrent, choked with rocks and tangled with thickets of evergreens, among which the oleanders with their slim stalks, delicate taper leaves, and branches of crimson blossom stand out conspicuous.[23]

The Lamas Gorge is one of the most spectacular canyons of the world. Its interest as well as its impressive scenic character is enhanced by the remains of the fortresses and cities the pirates built on the edge of its precipitous cliffs. J. Theodore Bent's description of the gorge and of the ruins he visited on both its sides is more concise than Frazer's, though not so evocative. In addition, however, Bent mentions a site near the village of Tapureli on the eastern side of the gorge: 'At a spot now called Tapureli the ruins are exceedingly extensive. The hills are covered with large buildings of both regular and polygonal masonry, several fortresses, temples and a theatre.'

The site is indeed impressive not only because of the abundance of the city remains, many in a fair state of preservation, but also because of their situation. They extend to the very edge of the gorge, where the buildings, overhanging the drop of sheer rock, dominate a breathtaking prospect of the canyon. The ruins lie in a confused medley with fine ashlar walls still standing, splendid doors, arches, tombs with sculptures and the remains of early Byzantine churches. They await a systematic archaeological survey which could determine the layout of the city and the exact nature of many buildings at present difficult to identify owing to the accumulation of vegetation, debris and earth. But there can be no doubt that the city, perhaps Benisos by name, was large and flourished in the Graeco-Roman and early Byzantine ages. Was it a city founded by the pirates, which continued to prosper for several centuries? There is a disconcerting absence of any references to it by ancient authors.

The fortresses of the pirates still stand on the edge of the gorge, with their huge stone walls and turrets dominating the approach. But there are several other strongholds and fortress cities away from the Lamas to the west, on the edge of lesser gorges. For instance at the site called Takkaden today, situated about 10 miles (16 km) inland from the coast, the walls of a Byzantine castle stand high up on the edge of a gorge, overlooking a Hellenistic fortress on the other side. They rest on older foundations and the remarkable ruins that spread immediately below are doubtless those of a pirate city, rough, uncouth and some cut out of the rock at an early stage of the settlement. Others more sophisticated probably belong to a somewhat later period.

A characteristic feature of Cilicia Tracheia is the remarkable number of mausolea, many of which have survived in a good state of preservation, inland as well as along the coast. Several of them are sumptuous, reflecting the degree of wealth and refinement the Ketai inhabitants achieved in the Graeco-Roman age. These tombs are buildings, not mere sarcophagi, of which basically two types can be distinguished: (a) the lean rectangular mausoleum with two pediments on opposite sides, but no columns though usually furnished with Corinthian capitals at the four corners; (b) the columnar mausoleum, sometimes with two superimposed rows of columns, somewhat pompous in appearance, which tends to give an impression of opulence if not ostentation, unlike the dignity and restraint of the pyramidal tomb at Olba, which belongs to the first type. Nevertheless, these tombs are not without a certain baroque beauty in their setting amongst limestone outcrops and thick kermes brushwood or in the middle of an empty field basking in the delicate light of the plateau's altitude.

Along the coast east of Seleukeia lie scattered the ruins of several ancient cities which were most probably founded by Greek settlers from the hordes of Mopsos or by later settlers from the Greek mainland or islands. Korikos, on the site of present-day Kizkalesi, was said to have been founded by a Cypriot prince, Korikos by name. Korasium was a much later foundation of the Roman age, but Eleussa, further east, came to life in the Hellenistic age and flourished from the time when Archelaos king of Cappadocia, who had received possession of the territory from Augustus in 20 BC, established his residence there.

The ruins of these cities are plentiful but do not come within the field of our survey since the inhabitants were not of indigenous stock subsequently hellenized, at any rate not the original settlers and citizens. There are also many remains from the Byzantine age and the medieval Armenian kingdom, including two picturesque castles. Further east still, on the border with Cilicia Pedias, stood the ancient city of Soloi founded by Rhodian colonists in about 700 BC. Like Korikos and other cities of the coast, Soloi frequently changed hands between the Seleucid and Ptolemaic dynasts in the Hellenistic age, retaining however some degree of local autonomy. Later on Pompey repeopled the city with many of the pirates he had vanquished at the naval battle of 64 BC and renamed it Pompeiopolis.

Most of the remains of these cities were far more conspicuous and in a much better state of preservation until about half a century ago. They have suffered a great deal since the completion of the coastal road, which has become an important asphalt highway with countless lorries tearing noisily by. The road has also encouraged intensive commercialization and tourism, which has led to the construction of many ugly buildings.

Nowadays the main centre of attraction for package tours and groups of visitors in buses is the famous Corycian Cave, about a mile inland from the coast, in which the monster Typhon, begotten by Earth and Tartaros, mentioned by Homer and described by Hesiod, was born and reared before he challenged the gods in the battle of the giants. Vanquished in the end by Zeus he was imprisoned in the bowels of Mount Aetna.[24]

This impressive chasm was described by Strabo: 'It is a great circular hollow, with a rocky brow situated all round it that is everywhere quite high. Going down into it, one comes to a floor that is uneven and mostly rocky, but full of trees of the shrub kind, both the evergreen and those that are cultivated. Among these trees are also the plots of ground which produce the crocus. There is also a cave here, with a great spring which sends forth a river of pure and transparent water; the river forthwith empties beneath the earth, and then running invisible underground, issues forth into the sea.'[25]

Frazer's description of the chasm in *The Golden Bough* is similar to Strabo's though somewhat more colourful. As the result of earthquakes and natural disruptions, he explains, the stream nowadays is invisible and can only be heard underground at the bottom of the cave. On the upper edge of the cave stand the considerable remains of a Byzantine church resting on the foundations of a pagan sanctuary dedicated to Zeus. There can be no doubt that a very ancient indigenous deity was worshipped here, who later became hellenized while the story of the local monster was subsumed into Greek mythology.

Of particular interest from our point of view are the remains of an ancient city situated close to the south-western edge of the chasm. The fine ashlar walls of its temple of Zeus are remarkable, still standing to a considerable height. The building is Hellenistic, of the third or second century BC. Also noteworthy is the fine polygonal masonry of the walls that enclosed the sanctuary, sections of which are still in a fair condition. J. Theodore Bent discovered here an inscription with names, probably of the presiding priests, many of them barbarous-sounding. 'Zas' appears frequently, no doubt relating to the cult of Zeus.

Although we know nothing of this city's history it was most probably a hellenized centre of habitation dating back to the pre-Roman age. The ruins show that the site continued to be inhabited right into the early Byzantine period when the temple was converted into a basilica.

Among the many interesting sites of Cilicia Tracheia where the penetration of Hellenism is manifest, Kanytelis not least deserves attention. Situated inland a few miles from the coast the remains of this city encircle a precipitous depression not unlike the chasm of the Corycian cave, about 190 feet (60 metres) deep, its bottom covered with vegetation. Although most of the ruins belong to the Byzantine era and include some fine basilicas of which considerable parts are still standing, some other ruins show that the city came into being in a much earlier age. According to a Greek inscription found by Bent[26] it was a dependency or deme of Olba, though later it belonged to Eleussa on the coast. Of the pagan age the conspicuous remains of a polygonal tower or fortress can be seen on the edge of the chasm, parts of which still rise to a considerable height. There is also a very fine mausoleum in an excellent state of preservation, of the lean, restrained type, which may date from the pre-Christian era.

Cilicia Pedias, or Level Cilicia, extends eastward from Soloi, or from the Lamas Gorge, as far as what used to be the Syrian border in ancient times and is bounded on the north by the Tauros range. It consists of a great plain which has always been extremely fertile, for it is well irrigated by three rivers, the Kydnos, Saros and Pyramos.

Strabo mentions several cities of the region, some of them ancient Greek settlements such as Mallos, founded by the legendary Mopsos, others of native origin subsequently hellenized. But they were all eclipsed by Tarsus to which Strabo devotes three long paragraphs. Among other things he says:

> The people of Tarsus have devoted themselves so eagerly not only to philosophy, but also to the whole subject of education in general, that they have surpassed Athens, Alexandria or any other place that can be named where there have been schools and lectures of philosophers. But it is so different from other cities that there the men who are fond of learning are all natives, and foreigners are not inclined to sojourn there; neither do these natives stay there, but they complete their education abroad; and when they have completed it they are pleased to live abroad, and but a few go back home ... Further, the city of Tarsus has all kinds of schools of rhetoric; and in general it not only has a flourishing population but also is most powerful, thus keeping up the reputation of the mother-city.[27]

Strabo might have added, 'in spite of the fact that such able men leave the city and never return.' He then carries on his account by enumerating the many philosophers and distinguished citizens of Tarsus.

Now although Tarsus claimed to have been founded by Argives under Triptolemos, there can be little doubt that in origin it was an indigenous town. The very name suggests some connection with the god Tarku. However, partly as the result of an influx of Argive settlers in the eighth or seventh century BC, and partly under the influence of nearby ancient Greek cities such as Soloi and Mallos, Tarsus became fully hellenized certainly more than a century before the advent of Alexander and his hellenizing thrust. But notwithstanding its remarkable history and its importance as a prominent city of the Greek world, practically nothing has survived of its ancient buildings which now lie buried under the houses of modern Tarsus.

The same sort of obliteration has affected nearly all the other ancient cities of Cilicia Pedias including Mallos, scarcely anything of which can be seen today.

The remains of only two cities, Anazarba and Kastabala, which were originally indigenous, have to some extent survived.

Situated inland near a tributary of the Pyrammos river, Anazarba, according to Suidas, was first called Kyinda, which Strabo says was a fortress 'at one time used as a treasury by the Macedonians'. Be this as it may Anazarba began to flourish as a Greek city in the second century BC under the cultural influence of Tarsus and the thoroughly hellenized coast. It was favoured by Augustus and Tiberius and for a while renamed Caesarea ad Anazarbum. Having greatly suffered from an earthquake early in the sixth century AD, it was rebuilt in 525 by the emperor Justin who renamed it Justinopolis.[28]

Though the remains of this city are by no means in a remarkable state of preservation, the natural position of Anazarba provides one of the most spectacular sights of Anatolia. A great cliff, russet, golden or pink according to the time of the day and the light, rises sheer from the plain to a height of a little over 500 feet (170 metres). Its crest is crowned by a magnificent medieval castle built by the Byzantines and the Armenians, its walls and towers still standing undaunted. The ancient city lay at the foot of this rock to the south where its side is most perpendicular. So the fortification walls, long stretches of which are still standing, formed a horseshoe, the open side being closed and naturally protected by the great rock. A mass of ruins lies within the wall including a large Byzantine church. The courses of the main streets can be traced, where many columns lie fallen, and the gymnasium can be identified. The theatre is carved into the eastern side of the rock but is in a poor state of preservation probably on account of spoliation. Splendid, on the other hand, is one of the gateways which dates from the Roman age and still stands lke a triumphal arch. Close outside the city walls, to the south, are the remains of a large stadium which would repay excavating.

The position of Kastabala in the neighbourhood of Anazarba, though attractive, is not nearly so impressive. The ancient city began to flourish in the first century BC, when it became the capital of a local ruler, Tarkondimotos. It lay on a slope overlooked by the acropolis, a rocky eminence on which a mediaeval fortress now stands.[29]

Strabo reports: 'At Kastabala is the temple of Perasian Artemis, where the priestesses, it is said, walk with their naked feet over hot embers without pain. And here, too, some tell over and over the same story of Orestes and the Tuaropolos, asserting that she was called "Perasian" because she was brought from the other side.'[30]

So evidently the citizens of Kastabala would claim that theirs was the site of Artemis Tuaropolos since it was actually at the foot of the Tauros range, and therefore was not in remote Tauric Scythia, now the Crimea, which is the site usually accepted for the location of the sanctuary. Euripides merely says: 'Tauric land'.[31] In mythological days the sea no doubt came as far as the slopes of

Kastabala before it was silted up into the present plain by the Pyramos river. The belief that the sanctuary of Artemis Tauropolos was at Kastabala would conform, though not entirely, with what Strabo says earlier on,[32] where he describes the priestly town of Komana in eastern Cappadocia. He states that there Orestes and Iphigenia brought the rites of Artemis Tauropolos to the priests at the temple of the goddess Ma 'from Scythia'; but the Crimea would have been very remote compared with the location of Kastabala barely a hundred miles south of Komana as the crow flies.

As well as being the goddess of the priestly city of Komana, Ma may have also been the goddess of Kastabala before she was hellenized or ousted by Artemis coming from 'the other side', or in other words from the world of Greece.

Of her temple only the foundations remain. But a fine street running from south to north, of which eight columns still stand, is impressive. (There were originally 78 columns of red conglomerate, of which 30 were standing in Bent's day.) Parts of an attractive building, probably baths, are also still standing and a delightful small theatre nestles in the hillside a little further north, its seats still *in situ* except for the upper rows. Most of the ruins here belong to the Graeco-Roman age, but the theatre may be Hellenistic in origin with some modifications at a later date.

We have now come to the easternmost confines of Cilicia Pedias, beyond which it is tempting to proceed into the former kingdom of Commagene. Its main city, Samosata, was the home town of Lucian, Syrian by birth, who spoke Aramaic as a child and yet became not only thoroughly hellenized but also one of the most polished, prolific and brilliant writers of the ancient world. Indeed he proved to be the very embodiment of the Hellene to whom Isocrates' pronouncement refers: 'The name Hellene no longer suggests a race but an intelligence, and the title Hellene is applied rather to those who share our culture than to those who share our blood.'

We must refrain, however, from going further east, for what used to be the territory of Commagene, though now situated in Turkey, was historically part of Syria, a very different world from that of Anatolia.

VI

NORTH OF THE TAUROS & THE MAEANDER

AWAY TO THE NORTH, OVER THE CRESTS OF THE TAUROS HEIGHTS, THE deeply rutted uplands of Isauria sink into the uniform surface of a vast plateau.

From a lofty crag the eyes of an eagle would perceive, beyond the distant reaches of the steppe, the level waste becoming furrowed with ravines and gorges and then crinkling with a crust of tufa, white cones and ash-coloured escarpments, into which dwellings, monasteries and churches were carved in the early centuries of our era. Towering above this volcanic region of Cappadocia the snow-capped peak of Mount Argaeus glistens in the ethereal light of its altitude. The extinct volcano rises in a pyramidal shape to a height of 13,000 feet (3900 metres), a mighty landmark over a vast distance around. 'The highest mountain of all,' says Strabo, 'where the summit never fails to have snow upon it.'[1]

Further still to the north extends a region of mountains and valleys which was known as Pontus, and then *thalatta, thalatta*, the Euxine Sea which Xenophon and his men finally reached some miles to the east.

Away to the west as far as the Propontis and the Aegean the various regions of central and northern Anatolia touch and overlap, Phrygia, Galatia, Lydia, Mysia and Bithynia. At the very heart of this extensive territory, where the great River Halys flows, the Hittites rose to power more than three thousand years ago, long before the age with which we are here concerned.

In the whole of this vast area north of the Tauros range and the River Maeander there were once more than 150 cities, in other words *poleis*, that sprang up and flourished for a number of centuries.

In addition to the cities proper, that is the new foundations by the Seleucid and Attalid kings and the indigenous towns or villages raised to city status through hellenization, there flourished, north of the Tauros and the Maeander divide, about a dozen temple states or priestly princedoms based on the cult of ancient Anatolian deities, particularly Men, Ma, Anaitis and Cybele. Men and Ma were indigenous deities; Anaitis was of Persian origin and Cybele Thracian, but the worship of both goddesses had taken root in Asia Minor centuries before the expansion of Hellenism.

Some of these centres of religious cult were little independent states governed by a high priest, not unlike Teucer or Ajax at Olba. The great temple of Komana in Cappadocia had 6000 serfs or *hierodouloi* attending the cult, as well as several thousand prostitutes. These attracted the pilgrims and constituted a source of considerable revenue for the priests who ruled over a territory of some size. A similar situation prevailed at Komana in Pontus with no fewer priests and serfs as well as prostitutes. Moreover there was a fervent cult of the goddess Anaitis at Zela, a thriving centre ruled by a high priest with a similar set-up, of Men at Kabeira, of Cybele at Pessinus and similarly at other places. Eventually these sacerdotal princedoms under the nominal suzerainty of a king, who ruled over the whole country, were affected by the great wave of Hellenism that spread from the west after Alexander the Great. The wealthier ones, such as Komana in Pontus, survived somewhat longer than others as virtually independent priestly states. But in the end they were all converted into cities with a municipal administration either by Pompey, who overthrew the ruling Mithridatic dynasty, or by the subsequent Roman emperors. By then Hellenization had become complete. The temple would be reconstructed as a Hellenistic or Graeco-Roman building, as for instance at Aizanoi in Phrygia where the goddess Meter Steunene, or in other words Cybele, was worshipped before Zeus came to predominate. The need was then felt for a theatre, a stadium and a gymnasium, the hallmarks of the *polis*. The smaller centres of indigenous cult would tend to decline and in the course of time fade away, as the cult of Men did near Pisidian Antioch.

Of all these cities and hellenized centres of religious cult barely a dozen have left any remains that stand prominently above the ground. The rest have practically vanished, leaving only a few scattered stones to be seen. By contrast, out of not quite so many cities that came into existence south of the Maeander river and of the uppermost ridges of the Tauros range, the remains of nearly fifty still stand conspicuously enough in the landscape to conjure up a picture of their past life.

Why is it that the buildings of most of the cities north of this divide have endured the test of time so poorly? The frequent destructive earthquakes to which Asia Minor is subject affect the south no less than the north and cannot therefore account for the difference. We must look for an explanation elsewhere.

To some extent the causes lie in the nature of the ground which in the south tends to be extremely mountainous, except for a few not very extensive plains by the sea, and therefore more suited to pasture for nomads than to farming by settled communities. After the cities were deserted and the land captured by the Turks not many villages sprang up near the site of the cities, whose inhabitants would despoil the ancient buildings for the construction of their houses. Most of the cities, Alinda, Kaunos, Pinara, Tlos, Arykanda, Termessos, Sagalassos, Adada and several others, were left to themselves and scarcely touched by intruders until relatively recently. By contrast in the central and northern regions of Anatolia, except of course in the more mountainous parts, there are vast stretches of land suited to agriculture which went on being farmed through the ages giving rise to many villages whose inhabitants, in the natural course of events, would remove the stones from the nearby ancient site for their own houses. In reading the descriptions of sites in Phrygia and Lydia left to us by travellers of the last century, such as Arundell, Hamilton or Ramsay, one cannot help being struck by the contrast between what was still prominently visible in those days and the present-day vestiges.

Moreover not only have Turkish villages proliferated in the course of centuries but large centres of habitation have also emerged, towns such as Bursa on the site of ancient Prusa, Manisa on the site of Magnesia ad Sypilum, Alaşehir on the site of Philadelphia, Dinar on the site of Apameia, Kayseri on the site of Caesarea, Konya on the site of Ikonion and so on; in these places not surprisingly, hardly any trace of the ancient buildings has survived. In several of these towns fine Seljuk and Ottoman mosques, medresses, khans and turbes, as well as other structures of more recent date and less architectural value, have come into existence at the expense of the ancient buildings many parts of which were cannibalized, a process which had already started in the Byzantine age.

Another factor should be taken into account. Whereas the south and the south-west suffered only from periodic incursions by the Arabs, who for a few centuries after the rule of Justinian would swiftly come, pillage and leave without much destruction, the cities north of the Maeander and the Tauros after the decline of the ancient world and a period of Byzantine stability were subject to repeated invasions, waves and waves of various strains of Turkish tribes as well as Mongols who eventually settled in the conquered country. Particularly devastating were the Tatars under Timur at the beginning of the fifteenth century. The wars that went on for some centuries not only between the invaders and the Byzantines but also between the various Seljuk and Ottoman dynasties were not conducive to the survival of ancient remains.

Finally we should bear in mind that most of the cities founded or established by the Romans in the northern regions of Anatolia in order to further the expansion of Hellenism and consolidate the empire came into existence relatively late. Often they were mere villages or practically extinct ancient indigenous centres raised to city status by the Roman emperors with the infusion of some hellenized settlers, but in an age when the *polis* as an institution was in decline. These cities never developed that individuality, civic pride and mutual rivalry which characterized the ancient cities of Caria, Lycia and Pisidia. Nor did they ever enjoy rich patrons such as Opramoas of Rhodiapolis, Jason of Kyaneai, or Licinius of Oineoanda, eager to lavish funds on their city for the construction of magnificent monuments. The age of private donors was over. So the buildings of cities such as Hadrianopolis, Germanicopolis, Traianopolis, Neoclaudiopolis, Pompeiopolis, Nicopolis, Flaviopolis and other similar foundations were in all likelihood fairly modest from an architectural point of view. This may partly account for the paucity or absence of remains where their presence could be expected.

So for all these reasons it is perhaps not surprising that relatively little has survived of the buildings pertaining to the ancient world which for several centuries was scarcely less flourishing in central and northern Anatolia than it was in the southern regions so rich still today in eloquent tokens. Nevertheless, comparatively few though the remains are, a number of sites are indeed remarkable and worth recording in this survey because, apart from their archaeological interest, their evocative power reaching back to a memorable past lingers on in the landscape.

As we proceed from the Tauros foothills of Isauria into the plain that stretches to the north we first come to a region known in the past as Lykaonia. With Cappadocia to the east and north, Galatia to the north-west, Phrygia to the west, Pisidia to the south-west, Isauria and Cilicia Tracheia to the south, its boundaries repeatedly changed according to the power or ruler it would come under. At one time its territory came to include parts of Phrygia and the whole of Isauria. When the energetic king of Galatia, Amyntas, ruled over the entire area he incorporated Lykaonia with Galatia in the thirties of the first century BC, but later it reverted to within approximately the former vague boundaries.

The scenery, predominantly flat, is tame compared with the dramatic configuration, deeply cut and precipitous, of the region to the south. But in the plain that stretches beyond the eroded foothills of the Tauros fine outlines of mountains that rise like islands relieve the prevailing monotony, bleak in unfavourable weather, and impart an element of grandeur to the landscape in the delicate light and rarefied air of its altitude. Strabo describes it as a treeless and waterless region, which no doubt it still is except for a few oases, but full of wild asses and sheep for which the steppe-like nature of the land, endowed with deep wells as Strabo says, provided sufficient pastures.[2] Here indeed we are in Lykaonia.

The land is first mentioned by Xenophon in his *Anabasis*,[3] but only fleetingly as a territory east of Phrygia through which Cyrus the Younger marched. It was a wild country which was to some extent subdued by Perdikkas a few years after

Alexander's death, but remained backward for centuries being remotely situated and therefore scarcely affected by the civilizing influences of the coastal regions. Hellenism and the Greek language made only little penetration before the Roman age, tribal life prevailing over city life in spite of there being four main centres of habitation, Laranda, Lystra, Derbe and Ikonion. The last-named where Konya of today is situated, was originally inhabited by Phrygians and referred to as a Phrygian city by Xenophon,[4] but it was subsequently incorporated within the territory of Lykaonia of which it was regarded in Roman times as the principal city or capital. Strabo refers to it as a 'well settled town', and Pliny as 'a most famous city'.[5] It certainly grew in size and was flourishing by the middle of the first century AD when Saint Paul visited it. There were then many Jews in Ikonion as well as a predominant population of hellenized gentiles and a multitude of Lykaonians who spoke their own indigenous language.

Derbe was the town where in the first century BC the notorious Antipater set himself up as tyrant, dominating and terrorizing much of Lykaonia with brigandage until he was killed by Amyntas,[6] who was then able to bring the country under some degree of control. At Lystra, another notable Lykaonian town though not mentioned by Strabo, Augustus established a Roman colony, and another at Parlais which could have hardly been more than a village. Laranda, the present Karaman, was another stronghold Antipater held, which after the death of Amyntas passed to Augustus.

It is worth noting that the Seleucids, who ruled over the whole area from the very beginning of the third century BC until 189 BC, never founded any cities in Lykaonia, great hellenizers though they were; nor did their successors, the Attalids, likewise great hellenizers and founders of cities, who held the land for about another fifty years. So it is perhaps not surprising that Lykaonia remained primitive until the Roman age and that the penetration of Hellenism was slow. It is unlikely that any of the four main towns, Ikonion, Derbe, Lystra and Laranda, achieved full city status until well into the Roman age when they started to issue their own coins. While the Seleucids were rulers the official language had to be Greek, of course, and doubtless a proportion of the urban population was hellenized, but many people spoke their own indigenous language and went on doing so, even in the towns, as late as the first century AD when Paul was preaching in that region. It is significant that no remains of theatres or gymnasia, hallmarks of Hellenism, or of any ancient monument for that matter, are to be seen on Lykaonian sites, though of course they may have been more subject to destruction than in certain other parts of Anatolia. By the end of the second century AD Laranda must have been a fully-fledged city with appropriate buildings reflecting the Hellenic way of life since it produced two prominent Greek epic poets, Nestor and Peisander.[7] Similarly at Ikonion there must, of course, have been all the appropriate *polis* buildings for it grew into a large Hellenized city, but there also everything belonging to that period has been wiped out by the

Turkish town that has developed on the site. Hellenism had indeed penetrated to the extent of the citizens forgetting about their remoter past and claiming Perseus as their founder rather than their native Phrygian hero Nanakos.

With the encouragement the Romans gave to urbanization, city life in the Greek sense, *diaita*, spread easily when the time was ripe among the more well-to-do inhabitants of these cities. A native backlash, as in Syria or Egypt, could never take place since unlike Syriac or Coptic the local language never reflected an indigenous culture or historical past. To become educated could only mean to become hellenized. The picture of Ikonion which the Apocryphal Acts of Paul give us in the account of Saint Thekla's conversion is that of a Greek or Hellenized city under Roman rule in the second century AD.

Lykaonia has withstood the effacement time and oblivion bring about not because of the testimony left by any ancient monuments or ruins, since none have survived, but because of the vivid account of Paul's and Barnabas' activities at Ikonion, Derbe and Lystra which we find in the Acts of the Apostles. To this picture we may add the story of Saint Thekla of Ikonion, passionately in love with virginity – or was it Saint Paul? This proto-feminist, against whom Tertullian vented his spleen for presuming, as a woman, to teach and baptize,[8] brings back to us, whether she actually existed or not, the whole world of Lykaonia.

To the east and north a much larger region of Anatolia opens out – Cappadocia. In the east it rises abruptly and descends over the sharp-edged crests of the Antitauros; in the north it sweeps across the great upland plateau, a steppe as flat as the sea which then rising and sinking in waves is intersected with gullies and ravines that modulate into the white tufa zone where the outlines of Mount Argaeus loom majestically ethereal.

Cappadocia is a very ancient region of Anatolia over which Hittites, Phrygians, Lydians and Persians ruled in succession before Hellenism started to penetrate, relatively late as in Lykaonia. Although several civilizations had come and gone it was inhabited by rural tribes who remained unaffected and primitive even longer than in Lykaonia, the centres of habitation being few. But here too, these towns became civilized little by little as the result of being hellenized; some indeed flourished. The language of all educated people became Greek and remained Greek for a millennium. But the rural population of the vast outlying areas remained practically untouched and in certain parts of the country people continued to speak the indigenous tongue until their conversion to Christianity.

Like Lykaonia, the boundaries of Cappadocia were never very definite, 'a country of many parts which has undergone many changes', says Strabo. But roughly speaking it can be said that the region was encompassed by Pontus on the north, Galatia on the north-west, Phrygia on the west, Lykaonia on the south-west, Cilicia on the south and Armenia on the east. The Cappadocians proper were the tribe who lived in the whole region north of Lykaonia. Those who occupied the eastern part were known as the Kataonians, but Strabo says that in his days, as far as language and customs were concerned, they were indistinguishable, all differences having by then disappeared.[9]

After the Persian domination and the reorganization that followed Alexander's death, Cappadocia was for more than two centuries ruled by a dynasty of kings of mixed Persian and Greek descent. Most of them were called Ariarathes and followed each other from father to son. They were not only thoroughly hellenized but some of them were also men of outstanding culture, dedicated to Hellenism, particularly Ariarathes V, Eusebes as he liked to call himself – the Pious. Under the encouragement and patronage of this king, whose mother and paternal grandmother were Seleucid princesses, the indigenous towns began to be hellenized.[10] As in Lykaonia no Greek cities had been founded by the Seleucids or Attalids in this part of Asia Minor.

The main towns of Cappadocia were Mazaka, Tyana, Kybistra and Komana. Mazaka was the metropolis of Cappadocia, as Strabo tells us, 'situated below Mount Argaeus'. He then goes on to great lengths in describing its unfavourable situation, 'waterless and unfortified by nature'. It was nevertheless chosen by the kings of Cappadocia as their residence because of its central position in the country and close to fertile regions. So the town flourished and became hellenized to a considerable extent, in other words it developed into a *polis* when it was given a gymnasium and granted autonomy under Greek city constitution by Ariarathes V, who changed its name to Eusebia. Under his enlightened policy the Mazakeni adopted the laws of Charondas, the Sicilian law-giver. Apparently the king was keenly interested in constitutional law.

In the days of the emperor Tiberius, Cappadocia was made into a Roman province after the death of its last king, Archelaos. Towards the end of his reign he had changed the name of Mazaka to Caesarea which it kept through the ages and still retains in the slightly modified form of Kayseri. The city became a centre of Christian activity with Saint Basil the Great, a native of Caesarea, as its bishop. Unfortunately the intolerance of the Christians brought about the destruction of the temples of Zeus Poliouchos and Apollon Patröos as well as probably other buildings such as the gymnasium and theatre. So Caesarea ceased to be a city in the *polis* sense of the term and no doubt the vicissitudes of time have since then brought about further destruction so that virtually nothing of ancient Mazaka remains.

Tyana was situated about a hunded miles south of Mazaka near the Tauros range in that region of Cappadocia which Strabo says was inhabited by the Kataonian tribe. The town was no doubt very ancient, being already mentioned in Hittite records, but remained more or less barbarian until Ariarathes V in the second century BC gave it a Greek constitution as well as a gymnasium, the institution essential to anyone wanting to become, and lead the life of, a citizen. So the transformation took place and Tyana became a Greek *polis*, a thriving city in the Roman age where Apollonios was born, the neopythagorean sage, wanderer and teacher with miraculous powers who lived in the first century of our era. His fame has reached us thanks to the full account of his life and deeds Philostratos wrote. The author refers to Tyana as a 'Greek city'. Strabo describes it as follows: 'It is called Eusebeia near the Taurus (to distinguish it from Eusebeia below Mount Argaeus), and its territory is for the most part fertile and level. Tyana is situated upon a mound of Semiramis, which is beautifully fortified.'[11]

The mound is still there and on it is the present-day village of Kisli-Hissar, but nothing of the ancient buildings has survived.

There was another Kataonian town, Kybistra, mentioned by Strabo, not far off to the north which probably achieved city-status. But again there are no remains of this city to be seen.

Komana, situated further east in the Kataonian district, is worth remembering because of its exceptional nature as a town ruled by high priests who worshipped the goddess Ma, in fact a highly organized centre of habitation but on a totally different basis from that of the *polis*. It was a sacerdotal principality centred in a religious cult which had a strong oriental stamp and which none the less was eventually hellenized, at any rate to some extent, when Ma, an earth goddess personifying fruitfulness and closely connected with the Persian Anaitis, became Artemis Tauropolos. The town was probably converted into a city by Archelaos, the last king of Cappadocia, when its name became Hierapolis. The city status conferred must of course have implied the establishment of a council, but in Strabo's days the high priest seems still to have had overriding power.

There were two centres of the Ma cult bearing the same name and ruled by high priests with thousands of serfs at their service, Komana in Pontus and Komana in Cappadocia. Each of them had, like Corinth, a multitude of prostitutes dedicated to the goddess and attached to the temple, the cult being orgiastic. Strabo describes the Cappadocian Komana as follows:

In the Antitauros are deep and narrow valleys in which are situated Komana and the temple of Enyo whom the people call Ma. It is a considerable city; its inhabitants, however, consist mostly of divinely inspired people and the temple slaves who live in it. Its inhabitants are Kataonians who, though in a general way classed as subject to the king, are in many respects subject to the priest. The priest is master of the temple, and also of the temple slaves, who, on my sojourn there, were more than six thousand in number, men and women together. Also considerable territory belongs to the temple and the revenue is enjoyed by the priest. He is second in rank in Cappadocia after the king and in general the priests belong to the same family as the kings.[12]

So in Strabo's days the high priest appears to have still been a sort of dynast whose government could hardly have been compatible with that of a *polis* constitution. However city status may have been conferred or imposed upon Komana after the days in which Strabo was writing, that is to say after the end of the first century BC or the very beginning of the following century when Archelaos was still ruling. With the change that then occurred the administration probably became less centred in the affairs of the temple, the serfs having been enfranchised.

Unlike the Cappadocian sites mentioned earlier, Komana still retains some interesting vestiges which, few though they are, can act on the imagination and stir up a vivid image of the hellenized past mainly thanks to the still unspoilt situation untouched by the modern concrete blocks of offices and flats which obliterate important ancient sites such as Kayseri. Komana lies in a nook of the Antitauros where the present-day village of Shahr thrives in a verdant little valley of the river Saros. In its upper reaches it is a delightful stream which cuts its way southward under bare and awe-inspiring ridges. The scenery of the whole neighbourhood is one of the most exhilarating and impressive of Asia Minor.

Until barely a hundred years ago the *cavea* of the theatre was complete, but now only a few sections of the rows of seats are to be seen, the stones having been removed probably for the construction of village houses. The same fate has befallen a large ancient building which stood with a fine front towards the river on the left bank: many of the blocks of stone and pieces of marble can be seen in the walls of the village houses. This form of cannibalization, as one might call it, is a familiar sight in Anatolian villages. But a little beyond the houses of Shahr up a small valley an interesting building still survives from the ancient world in most of its parts. It is an early church built into, or rather on to, the walls of a pagan tomb the lower structure of which supports it. This curious, rather attractive building is a considerable size for it measures 60 feet in length and nearly 32 feet in width (18 x 9.25 metres). It still stands to its full height and somewhat resembles a temple-like tomb such as those we have seen, for instance, at Arykanda. It was already converted into a church most probably in the fifth century, but the actual tomb dates back to the first half of the fourth according to R. P. Harper who with I. Bayburtluöglu undertook excavations on the site in 1967.[13] They found in the building an inscription with the name of Aurelius Claudius Hermodoros for whom the sepulchre was made and who seems to have been governor of the region.

Near by sections of large columns lie in a heap with other stones and fragments which belong to a prostyle temple of the end of the second century AD. No traces of the great temple of Ma, to which Strabo refers, have been found. The building may have been erased as soon as Christianity abolished the cult.

In addition to the three or four major cities of Cappadocia there were some smaller towns, such as Garsura, which were granted municipal autonomy in the course of time, especially by Pompey. In the late Roman age a few more towns received city status such as Nazianzos, the home town of Saint Gregory.

Even in the early Byzantine period a number of cities were founded or rather villages raised to city status. But what did city status really mean in those later days? Certainly no longer the original *polis* organization with its autonomous administration based on the existence of an assembly and a council with magistrates appointed by them, promoting pride in civic life and with patrons lavishing funds on the construction and upkeep of monuments befitting the city. In backward Cappadocia, with its vast rural areas inhabited by primitive indigenous tribes scarcely affected by Hellenism and speaking their own language until their conversion to Christianity, city status could only have meant that some degree of administrative freedom was allowed locally to a number of imperial government officials residing in the so-called city. Justinian bemoaned the fact that there were hardly any councils left in the empire. So perhaps it is not surprising that on the sites of all these cities virtually no remains of ancient buildings such as the bouleuterion, the gymnasium, the theatre, the stadium, the odeion, stoas and the like are to be seen. Regrettably, therefore, this region of Anatolia, full of natural beauty and rich in fine buildings of a more recent past, especially the Seljuk period, is disappointing from the point of view of our present pursuit.

Phrygia – a word resonant with a number of evocative derivations familiar to our ear or vision, a word which conjures up a whole world now part of our cultural heritage: the Phrygian mode in music; Midas the Phrygian king who turned everything he touched to gold; the Phrygian cap, symbol of liberty, under which Midas tried to hide when he had grown the ears of an ass; Marsyas the Phrygian satyr, who dared to challenge Apollo in a flute contest and having lost was flayed alive by the god; the Phrygian mother goddess Cybele whose cult spread throughout Greece and the west; the daring, heroic Tantalus, a Phrygian, and Niobe, also a Phrygian according to Strabo, and so on. The myths, stories and cults of Phrygia became integrated into the whole landscape of the Greek world. Except for Lycia, this was not the case with the other regions of Anatolia: Cappadocian, Lykaonian, Paphlagonian, Bithynian are attributes much less familiar than Phrygian. These mysterious immigrants from Thrace created a remarkable civilization of their own, with their religion, language and script remotely related to Greek, with their centres of Cybelian cult and their strikingly original monuments of which unfortunately relatively little survives. Their civilization, whose echo still rings so vividly, did not last long, at its height barely a century or two, having been first reduced by Kimmerian hordes and then, after a brief revival, totally crushed by the Lydians in the sixth century BC. Was it because in battle the Phrygians would trust too much in their flutes that they finally succumbed? And yet Marsyas succeeded in repulsing an invading army by playing the flute the music of which mesmerized the enemy.[14] Musical as they were, the Lydians must have learnt to play even better and not only the flute, for they added pipes and harps to their musical equipment – a most civilized way of overcoming an enemy.[15]

At an early stage of the country's history Phrygia included the whole of Lydia as far as Mount Ida in Mysia. Later its confines varied, but its territory was more or less limited to an area encompassed by Lydia and Mysia on the west, Bithynia and Paphlagonia on the north, Cappadocia and Lykaonia on the east, Pisidia and Caria on the south.

Although the Phrygian language survived in the remoter rural regions until the early Byzantine age, the towns were all hellenized in the wake of the great cultural impact of Alexander and his successors. There were very many cities, if we take into account the villages which in the later Roman and early Byzantine periods were raised to city status. Several cities were Seleucid and Pergamenian foundations with Greek or Macedonian settlers, but the majority were Phrygian in origin. Unfortunately of all these many cities very few ruins are still standing for the reasons already touched upon. Compared with Caria, Lycia, Pamphylia, Pisidia and even Rough Cilicia, Phrygia is disappointingly poor in conspicuous survivals of its Hellenistic and Graeco-Roman past. Apart from Hierapolis and Aizanoi scarcely any other sites are to be found with ruins prominent enough in the landscape to recall the past visually, though several are of archaeological interest.

Moving westward from Lykaonia we first come to the interesting site of Antioch. It is usually referred to as Pisidian Antioch to distinguish it from the homonymous Syrian city, but in fact it is situated in Phrygia: Strabo quite clearly states 'near' not 'in' Pisidia. Antioch was strictly speaking not Phrygian in origin, however, nor did its citizens ever speak Phrygian let alone Pisidian, the city having come into existence as a colony of Greek settlers from Magnesia on the Maeander. It was named Antiocheia by Seleukos Nikator, after his mother, a name he gave to several of the cites he founded or brought under his dominion. The inhabitants were not necessarily all of Greek origin, however, for in the neighbourhood there stood, Strabo tells us,[16] a Phrygian temple of the moon-god Men with, no doubt, many priests attending the cult and a local indigenous or Phrygian community. Nearly three centuries later Augustus established a Roman colony in the city which consequently became Romanized, to some extent at any rate, with Latin as the official language, the purpose of the colony being to bring under orderly control the whole area badly affected by brigandage. The main square was called Augusta Platea and the adjoining square Tiberia Platea. There were various quarters, or *vici*, adjoining the square. Nevertheless, as the inscriptions confirm (many of which can be seen in the local museum), by the end of the second century AD Greek had again become the overriding language spoken even by those of Roman origin who in the course of two centuries had forgotten Latin.[17] The Roman colonists had been absorbed.

Interesting remains of the Hellenistic city have come to light in the neighbourhood, but at present the more evident ones belong to the Roman period, for during the first two centuries of our era Antioch enjoyed considerable prosperity and importance as an administrative centre of the region. In the days of the emperor Claudius it was visited by Paul and Barnabas and so, because mentioned in the Acts, the city has retained a certain fame.

The remains lie near the present-day village of Yalvaç, on a hillside overlooking the river Anthios which flows in a lovely valley rich in vegetation. The scenery is gentle and extremely attractive with rolling hills, bare and smooth, and with verdant dells full of poplars. From the uppermost slopes of the site the prospect opens out far and wide. But Antioch near Pisidia, though not lacking in historical and archaeological interest, today presents a sight of utter desolation as far as its architecture is concerned – a few stones barely emerging above the ground except parts of the fine Roman aqueduct which still stand about a mile beyond the site of the city. This display of total ruin, or rather obliteration, seems a far cry from what can be seen on a truly Pisidian site not so far to the south – Adada, which is far less renowned simply because Saint Paul only passed through it. However, Antioch has the site of a temple occupying the centre of a remarkable rock-cutting which rises like a wall from a semi-circular platform. This was cleared by a team of archaeologists from the University of Michigan some years ago, so that the stylobate of a temple built in honour of the emperor Augustus is now distinctly in view with the remains of a rock-cut cella in the centre; but the building itself has not survived. A couple of fine bulls' heads in marble have fallen from the structure and now lie musing on the ground.

About forty miles west of Antioch and also near the Pisidian border is the site of Apollonia, which was a Seleucid or Attalid foundation, whose settlers were hellenized Lycians and Thracians. The city was never Romanized and so retained its Greek character throughout. But its name changed to Sozopolis in the Byzantine age, the City of the Saviour or the Saving City, for indeed it held out against the Seljuks until 1180. Of its buildings, however, nothing survives.

Nor does anything remain of a much more important city, a great city in ancient times, Apameia, which stood on the site of present-day Dinar, nor of the older town it superseded, Kelainai, situated close by at the source of the Maeander. This very ancient centre of habitation was a Phrygian town, large and prosperous according to Xenophon, which on account of its favourable situation at the conjunction of important highways, flourished for some centuries. It had a virtually impregnable acropolis on a precipitous hill. The market-place lay below and also a palace king Cyrus built with a large park full of wild animals where Cyrus the Younger would hunt on horseback 'whenever he wished to give himself and his horse exercise'. Xenophon adds: 'Through the middle of the park flows the Maeander river; its sources are beneath the palace, and it flows through the city of Kelainai also.'[18]

Long before Cyrus the Younger dallied there, enjoying his time hunting, the town was visited by Xerxes and his army who in 481 BC were on their way to Sardis. Herodotus tells us:

> They marched through Phrygian country to Kelainai, where is the source of the river Maeander and another as great as the Maeander which is called Kataraktes; it rises in the very market place of Kelainai and issues into the Maeander. There also hangs the skin of Marsyas the Silenus, of which the Phrygian story tells that it was flayed off him and hung up by Apollo.[19]

Pliny says that the city was 'situated at the foot of Mount Signia, with the rivers Marsyas, Obrima and Orba, tributaries of the Maeander, flowing round it.'[20] But Pliny's topography is never entirely accurate.

Kelainai had probably decayed by the time of the Seleucids, under whom it underwent a great change which Strabo relates: 'It was from Kelainai that Antiochus Soter made the inhabitants move to the present Apameia, the city which he named after his mother Apama who was the daughter of Artabazus and was given in marriage to Seleukos Nikator.'

The new foundation flourished. 'Apameia is a great emporium of Asia Minor,' the geographer tells us, 'and ranks second only to Ephesus, for it is a common entrepôt for the merchandise from both Italy and Greece. It is situated near the outlets of the Marsyas river, which flows through the middle of the city.'[21]

There is no evidence that any Macedonians or Greeks ever settled at Apameia as a colony. All its citizens were most probably of indigenous origin, descendants of the Phrygian inhabitants of Kelainai. But these Phrygians were rapidly hellenized, since at the beginning of the second century BC Apameia had a proper Greek city constitution.[22]

Not only has Kelainai disappeared but nothing also remains of neighbouring Apameia, this great city which replaced the older one. The present little Turkish town of Dinar has grown out of its ruins. On the banks of the stream that runs through it Marsyas' skin flayed off by Apollo might have hung from a willow, but wafted away by time and the wind it has been replaced by dangling rubbish bags from off the unswept streets.

Nor has the actual spring of the Marsyas, less than a mile north-east of Dinar, fared any better. At the foot of a sheer cliff the stream emerges fully-grown. Once the traveller would halt there spellbound by the beauty of the spot. Nature untouched by man and mythology would harmoniously mingle. Now a large, pretentious-looking hotel, which stands ostentatiously up against the cliff a few yards away from an asphalt road, dominates the situation unredeemed by a few ducks and a pelican in an artificial pool.

Away to the west beyond the inland plateau and under the peaks of lofty Mount Kadmos a valley broadens out where the Lykos flows. Before the river joins the Maeander three important ancient cities were situated in its vicinity: Kolossai, Laodikeia and Hierapolis.

Kolossai was an old Phrygian town. Referring to Xerxes' march through Asia Minor, Herodotus says: 'Passing by the Phrygian town called Anaue and the lake from which salt is obtained, he came to Kolossai, a great city in Phrygia; the river Lykos plunges into a chasm of the earth and disappears, reappearing again about five stadia away and issuing like another river into the Maeander.'[23]

Nowadays there is no underground passage at Kolossai through which the Lykos flows. But since those days the ground may have undergone an upheaval. Strabo says that the whole region 'is full of holes and subject to earthquakes'.[24]

Xenophon says more or less the same thing about Kolossai: 'An inhabited city, prosperous and large.'[25] It is worth noting his use of the attribute 'inhabited', also when referring to Kelainai, from which it can be deduced that in those days Phrygia was already in decline, many of its towns being deserted.

After Xenophon we hear nothing more of Kolossai until we come to Strabo who states that Apameia and Laodikeia were the largest cities of Phrygia and only mentions Kolossai in his enumeration of 'small' Phrygian towns. It had apparently suffered from the prosperity of neighbouring Laodikeia, its rival in business. This city kept flooding the market with its own wool, a trade from which Kolossai, famous for its black sheep, had always derived great profit. However, in the first century AD it was still a notable city. Pliny mentions it as one of the famous cities of Phrygia[26] and in the days of Saint Paul it was still very much alive, with a community of Christians large enough for the apostle to address one of his epistles to it. As the result the name Kolossai, or rather Colossae in its Latinized form, has remained familiar through the ages as that of a city possessing an important seat of the early Christian Church.

The name is Phrygian in origin and endured without change throughout the Graeco-Roman age until the early Byzantine era when the site was deserted. But although originally Phrygian, Kolossai had become an entirely Greek city by the time Saint Paul wrote his epistle, and yet it had never been colonized or refounded by the Seleucids as Kelainai had been. The impact of Hellenism brought about by Alexander the Great was such that by the second century BC Kolossai was enjoying a normal Greek city constitution.

Unfortunately nothing has survived of the city apart from mere traces of the theatre and a few stones emerging from the ground. Many travellers went there in the last century expecting to find some significant vestiges of the city to whose Christian community Saint Paul had addressed his epistle. But they were all disappointed.

Laodikeia has proved somewhat luckier, though situated in the same earthquake belt. Some of its ruins are still to be seen.

This city was not Phrygian in origin as Kolossai was. It came into existence as a Seleucid stronghold which was subsequently rebuilt by Antiochos

II and renamed after his wife Laodike in about 260 BC. Pliny mentions it in his perfunctory manner and says merely: 'The actual town of Kibyra belongs to Phrygia and is the centre of 25 city-states, the most famous being Laodikeia. The city is on the river Lykos, its side being washed by the Asopus and the Caprus. Its original name was "the City of God", and it was afterwards called Rhoas.'[27]

In fact the 25 cities referred to by Pliny, which included Laodikeia, were situated well away to the north of Kibyra whose territory formed an enclave bordering on Caria, Lycia and Pisidia. Strabo is more explicit and provides us with greater details about Laodikeia:

> Though formerly a small town, Laodikeia grew large in our time and in that of our fathers, even though it had been damaged by siege in the time of Mithridates Eupator. However it was the fertility of its territory and the prosperity of certain of its citizens that made it great: at first Hieron who left to the people an inheritance of more than two thousand talents and adorned the city with many dedicated offerings, and later Zeno the rhetorician and his son Polemon, the latter of whom, because of his bravery and honesty, was thought worthy even of a kingdom at first by Antony and later by Augustus. The country round Laodikeia provides sheep that are excellent, not only for the softness of their wool, but also for its raven-black colour, so that the Laodikeians derive splendid revenue from it, as do their neighbouring Kolosseni from the colour which bears the same name. And here the Kapros river joins the Maeander, as does the Lykos, a river of good size, after which the city is called 'Laodikeia near the Lykos'.[28]

Shortly before Strabo's days Laodikeia produced a famous school of physicians which flourished at a nearby sanctuary of Men and specialized in the practice of dissection.[29] The most notable physicians who established and ran the school were Zeuxis and Alexander Philalethes. Another distinguished physician of Laodikeia, who belonged to the Erostrateian school, was Hikesios. Laodikeia produced also a famous pharmaceutical chemist, Zeno by name, a distinguished rhetorician likewise called Zeno, another rhetorician famous in the third century AD called Menandros, a celebrated sophist called Polemon and a sculptor of note, Charinos. (See Appendix A.)

Like Kolossai, Laodikeia received the attention of Saint Paul, for its inhabitants included numerous Jews busy in the wool trade and also a growing community of Christians who constituted one of the Seven Churches to which Saint Paul addressed letters in his Revelation.

The city suffered not only from the Mithradatic wars but also from earthquakes, and yet it was always able to recover. One catastrophic earthquake which virtually wiped it out occurred in the reign of Nero. Nevertheless its citizens, without outside help, rebuilt it. So it continued to flourish for several centuries until it started to decline in the Byzantine age. It was ravaged first by the Turks and then by Timur, its final destruction being probably brought about by earthquakes.

The ruins of Laodikeia are interesting from an archaeological point of view, but few of them rise sufficiently above the ground to strike the eye in the landscape. Practically nothing of the Hellenistic age has survived, probably as the result of the great earthquake in Nero's days. A few walls of the gymnasium are to be seen and close by is the long hollow of the stadium, an interesting structure because built, or rebuilt, with both its extremities closed so as to form an amphitheatre like the stadium at Aphrodisias. This was presumably in order to provide for gladiatorial contests and shows of wild beasts, fashionable in the Roman age. The two theatres of Laodikeia, the most striking features of the landscape, were not designed or modified to provide for that sort of spectacle. They lie at the far end of the site, on the north-eastern slope of the plateau on which the city was built. The larger one of the two, probably Hellenistic, if properly excavated and somewhat restored would be practically complete. Almost all the seats survive, but badly disarranged. The theatre looks out over the valley of the Lykos towards the hills of Hierapolis, a magnificent view.

The smaller theatre, which is of Roman date, seems at first sight in a better state of preservation. It faces north-west with a fine view over the Asopos river. All the upper rows of the *cavea* are in a good condition, the lower ones in disarray and partly missing.

There is a nymphaion, parts of which are still standing, a building of the early third century AD which was excavated about twenty five years ago. It has an interesting and unusual plan consisting of a basin, a colonnade on two sides and two semi-circular fountains. As you look over the denuded plateau of the site where desolation and natural beauty nostalgically mingle, the eye can catch the outlines of several other inconspicuous ruins of unidentified buildings.

The third city of the Lykos region was Hierapolis, magnificently situated overlooking the valley on a broad terrace formed by white calcareous deposits from abundantly flowing springs. The temperature of the water is slightly below human blood heat, so that bathing in the many pools and standing under the waterfalls are a delight in every season of the year. This is the main reason why Pamukale, meaning 'Cotton Castle' in Turkish, has become extremely popular in recent years as a holiday resort for well-to-do middle-class Turks no less than a Mecca for package tours of foreign tourists. The great attraction the site used to have until about a generation ago, largely on account of its natural position, the ruins resting on the ledge of spectacular limestone deposits and commanding a vast view across the Lykos valley as far as the majestic outlines of Mount Kadmos and Salbakos, has inevitably been marred by commercialization. The view of the theatre has been blocked by a huge hotel, while other hotels line the edge of the petrified waterfalls and shamelessly hug the ruins from south to north.

It might be thought that Hierapolis means 'Holy City', as it does in the case of other places bearing the name. But the name of this Hierapolis is said to have derived from Hiera, the wife of Telephos, son of Herakles, who was the legendary founder of Pergamon. The name was given by Eumenes king of Pergamon, when he founded or refounded Hierapolis. Before then it was probably an old Phrygian sanctuary, a centre of the Cybelian cult, so that 'holy' could apply just as well. In 133 BC the city was ceded to Rome as the result of the bequest Attalus III made of his kingdom. By then the constitution of the city was entirely Greek, and so of course was the language and *diaita* of the citizens, though many if not most of the inhabitants were of Phrygian descent, as no doubt the philosopher Epictetus was, a native of Hierapolis.

The patron deity was Apollo, a hellenized indigenous sun-god. Other gods were of course worshipped, especially Pluto, ruler of the underworld, who played an important part in the life of the city on account of the Plutonium. Strabo describes it in detail:

> The Plutonium, below a small brow of the mountainous country that lies above it, is an opening of only moderate size, large enough to admit a man, but it reaches to a considerable depth, and it is enclosed by a quadrilateral handrail, about half a plethron in circumference [50 feet or 15 metres], and this space is full of vapour so misty and so dense that one can scarcely see the ground. Now to those who approach the handrail anywhere round the enclosure the air is harmless since the outside is free from that vapour in calm weather, for the vapour stays then inside the enclosure, but any animal that passes inside meets instant death. But the Galli, who are eunuchs, pass inside with such immunity that they even approach the opening, bend over it, and descend into it to a certain depth, though not without holding their breath.[30]

It is not surprising that this vent in a deep hollow of the earth emitting poisonous gas should have aroused wonder and awe in those days. It became the centre of a sanctuary with eunuch priests to which pilgrims flocked. When the city declined and the site was finally deserted the Plutonium vanished from sight under the ruins. But it may have already been filled in and covered over in the Byzantine age when it would have been regarded as the dwelling-place of Satan. In recent years, as the result of some clearing undertaken by archaeologists, the Plutonium has come to light again as well as the remains of the temple of Apollo built up against it in the second century AD, of which scarcely anything was previously visible. The site, as it is at present, is interesting but visually unimpressive, with only foundations of buildings and low-lying blocks of stone above the ground.

The large theatre, on the other hand, situated near by is a magnificent structure of the second century AD in an excellent state of preservation. Most of the stage building is now standing to its full height after having been successfully restored by Italian archaeologists. Charming marble niches adorn its base on the level of the orchestra, with a row of fine reliefs on the stage above representing mythical scenes. Although the *cavea* slightly exceeds the semi-circle the building is very Roman in character. It probably replaced an older Hellenistic theatre.

In addition to the theatre there are two huge baths, or thermae, standing sturdily at each end of the site which stretches along a horizontal axis from south to north. The baths at the south end, near the entrance to the site, have been converted into a museum. The adjustment involved has not embellished the interior of the building. The other baths, situated beyond the northern limit of the city walls and converted into a basilica in the early Byzantine age, are an impressive structure. But the most attractive surviving piece of architecture is the triple triumphal arch of Domitian still standing to its full height at the far end of the colonnaded street which is in ruin.

Like Laodikeia, Hierapolis suffered catastrophically from the earthquake which occurred in the days of Nero and was thereafter entirely rebuilt, so there is nothing Hellenistic to be seen on the site. What survives from the Roman age is large and conspicuous, no doubt as the result of the prosperity the city enjoyed from the wool trade and the crowds of pilgrims and tourists the Plutonium kept drawing. The size and quality of the Roman masonry exude an atmosphere of opulence verging on ostentation which Aphrodisias, for example, and other cities that flourished in the Roman age, do not inflict upon us. Links with the Hellenistic world seem to have remained closer.

The inscriptions show that festivals, games and competitions were held at Hierapolis in traditional Greek fashion, but the lack of even traces of a stadium, a bouleuterion or an odeion, and the abundance of opulent tombs of the Roman period in an extensive necropolis make us regret the obliteration of the Hellenistic city. We are brought face to face with a picture of bygone prosperity ageing and sinking into the Byzantine world, a picture glamorized by commercialization.

The articulated valleys and mountains of Phrygia, with forests, pasture land, cultivation and bare stretches, were full of ancient Greek cities. But of the approximately three dozen sites where these cities stood, that of Aizanoi is the only one where the greater part of a temple is still standing. In fact, apart from Hierapolis and to some extent Laodikeia, Aizanoi is the only Phrygian site where the remains stand sufficiently above the ground to convey a visual impression of the hellenized past. Situated in a little green valley, the position is not spectacular but the architecture is most impressive.

Aizanoi was an ancient Phrygian centre of religious cult where Meter Steunene, the Standing and Promising Mother, or in other words the goddess Cybele, was worshipped, a sanctuary whose priests ruled over the surrounding area. When it became a hellenized city the need arose for appropriate buildings.

The present temple, dedicated to Zeus (Pl. 44), was built in the early days of the emperor Hadrian's reign and bears those purist elements characteristic of the Anatolian architecture of that age with several Hellenistic features still persisting. It rests on an elevated rectangular terrace to which six steps give access. The peristasis is pseudo-dipteral and has fifteen columns of the Ionic order on the long side and eight on the short, many of which are still standing to their full height. The cella is in a fair state of preservation placed at a distance from the peristasis of two intercolumnations, a characteristic pseudo-dipteral feature, with a pronaos of four columns of the composite order and with a distyle-in-antis opisthodomos.

There is a very fine barrel-vaulted substructure, the equivalent of a Christian crypt, which if not unique of its kind survives in an unusually good state of preservation. Here evidence has been found of the continuing worship of Cybele alongside that of Zeus. The splendid effigy of the goddess, in workmanship somewhat barbaric, stands conspicuously on the ground in front of the temple like a fallen acroterion.

The well-preserved theatre was also built in the reign of Hadrian, but most of its features are definitely Hellenistic, with its *cavea* originally detached from the stage building and exceeding the semi-circle. It may have been built on the site and plan of a much earlier theatre.

The stadium is rather unusual inasmuch as its extremity is placed right up against the back of the stage building. This curious arrangement is not Hellenistic, devised probably to provide for gladiatorial contests and shows of wild beasts which became fashionable in Anatolia from the second century onwards.

The remains of a gymnasium, a palaestra and an agora are additional evidence of the city life Aizanoi enjoyed in the Graeco-Roman age. It is a pity we know so little of its history.

Hierapolis, Laodikeia, Aizanoi and then? If we scour the whole of Phrygia, up hills and mountains, down valleys and gorges, in search of architectural remains, what do we find? A few scattered stones, a few inscriptions, some traces of a theatre perhaps, but no more. The rock tombs fail to be remarkable or conspicuous enough to compare favourably with the impressive sanctuaries and sepulchral monuments of the Phrygians. Whether we linger at Peltai, Synnada, Eumeneia, Brouzon, Dokimion, Lunda, Metropolis and so on, whether it be the site of a hellenized Phrygian town, as most of them are, or that of a Seleucid or Attalid foundation, the remains, if at all visible, are so meagre as to be invariably disappointing. Take for instance Akmonia, a rich and prosperous city of Phrygian origin, but so thoroughly hellenized as to have erected all the buildings necessary to a *polis*. The remains of many were still in a fair state of preservation when the site was visited in the last century by Hamilton, Ramsay and other travellers. A theatre, an odeion, two temples and other conspicuous pieces of architecture were still to be seen at that time, but virtually nothing remains now. For even in those days the stones were being removed, some to be used in the nearby village, some sent to 'the masons and stone-cutters of Uşak'. In the course of time much damage has also been done by local farming activities.

Blaundos, further west and close to the border with Lydia, has fared somewhat better than Akmonia, the site being situated on a narrow ridge between two deep ravines well away from the nearest village. Like Akmonia it was an old Phrygian town in decline when the Seleucids refounded it as a city with Macedonian settlers.

The fine situation and surrounding scenery of Blaundos immensely enhance the quality as well as the sheer presence of the remains now greatly reduced. The buildings have suffered more from shattering earthquakes than from human spoliation as at Akmonia. The arch of an aqueduct still stands, surging from the ground and spanning a stretch of the sky like a rainbow, as it greets the visitor who approaches the site along the crest of the limestone ridge. Broken columns and pediments, fractured cornices and dentils lie in heaps where the temples have fallen, speckled with lichen and shining in the luminous light of the high altitude which pervades the rarefied air, earth and rock.

The theatre, carved into the side of the ridge below the acropolis, is now in a state of utter disarray, worse than the poor condition in which Hamilton saw it a century and a half ago. On the acropolis only a few pillars are still standing among a mass of ruins. But the gateway of the acropolis, which spans the narrow neck of the ridge about 170 feet (50 metres) across still stands to a considerable height and width, a splendid edifice of limestone ashlar masonry erected some time in the first or second century of our era.

The site was first visited and described by Arundell in the 1830s and shortly after by Hamilton whose account is somewhat critical of Arundell's deductions: 'Notwithstanding the opinion of a recent traveller, who says the gateway belongs to the Lower Empire, there can, I think, be little doubt that it is Roman, even if it cannot claim to still greater antiquity. He says it was originally arched, and the top has been since filled in and squared off. But it is evident from the accompanying sketch that it must have been square from the very first.'[31]

Hamilton then proceeds into detail to prove his point and says, among other things, that a massive tower stood on each side of the door of the gate 'surmounted by a Doric frieze with triglyphs, part of which still remaining'. In fact the sketch he made shows what the gate looked like in his days, with a section of the frieze still *in situ*. Considerable spoliation must have taken place since then, the towers having virtually disappeared. Nevertheless the entire structure is still an imposing sight in the landscape.

In 1908 a proper archaeological survey of the site was carried out by

J. Keil[32] which, however, failed to disclose any interesting information regarding the history of the city, which must have enjoyed considerable prosperity in the first centuries of our era and possibly in the late Hellenistic age as well. The site is seldom visited by travellers nowadays and as no excavations have been undertaken so far its scenic sublimity has scarcely changed since the last century.

Goddesses of motherhood and fertility held a prominent position in the religious life of central and northern Anatolia, where sanctuaries and priests devoted to their cult proliferated. A Phrygian sanctuary of greater importance than Aizanoi, in fact of pivotal importance for the ancient kingdom of Phrygia, not only as a seat of religious cult but also as a centre of trade, prosperity and wealth, was Pessinus. It was the kingdom's chief sanctuary of Cybele, the Great Mother goddess protectress of people, mistress of wild animals, goddess of mountains, wild nature and fertility. She was worshipped there in a splendid temple, attended by many priests called Galli who were rulers of what became eventually a city and governed also the surrounding territory. Pessinus was therefore a theocracy like the two Komanas and the other priestly states of Anatolia. The priests flagellated themselves in orgiastic rites with other worshippers which often led to self-castration. This practice was presumably connected with the ancient myth of Cybele, who at Pessinus was called Agdistis, the name of the original hermaphroditic deity before its male parts were amputated by the gods. Having thus become entirely female she fell in love with Attis her son, who went mad as a result and cut off his own genitals.[33]

This eastern part of Phrygia was invaded and occupied by the Gauls in the third century BC and so became incorporated in the territory subsequently known as the province of Galatia. However the Pessinian priests were able to come to terms with the Galatians, and when the Roman consul Manlius Vulso and his army succeeded in bringing these wild Celtic tribes under some degree of control in 189 BC, Pessinus under the suzerainty of the Attalid kings regained much of its prosperity with a considerable degree of local autonomy. It was in this period that Hellenism began to penetrate. Pessinus continued to flourish under the Romans with whom it had kept on the closest of terms ever since it had donated its statue of Cybele to them in 204 BC. So the cult of the goddess spread throughout the Graeco-Roman world.

According to Strabo:

Pessinus is the greatest of the emporiums in that part of the world, containing a sanctuary of the Mother of gods, which is an object of great veneration. They call her Agdistis. The priests were in ancient time potentates who reaped the fruits of a great priesthood, but at present their prerogatives have been much reduced, although the emporium still endures. The precinct has been built up by the Attalid kings in a manner befitting a holy place, with a temple and also with stoas of white marble. The Romans made the sanctuary famous when, in accordance with the oracle of the Sibyl, they sent for the goddess there.[34]

The veneration the sanctuary enjoyed continued until the emperor Theodosius put an end to the worship of pagan divinities at the close of the fourth century AD. Thereafter Pessinus was deserted and fell rapidly into ruin. For a long time the site was used as a quarry by the villages in the neighbourhood, so apart from a few ruins of the temple practically nothing of the ancient city could be seen until recently. But as the result of excavations, which were started by a team of Belgian archaeologists in 1967, the remains of the temple, of porticoes and an odeion have come to light.

The Graeco-Roman architectural features of the peripteral temple and of the porticoes would seem to indicate that these structures were erected at the outset of the first century AD. If so, they must have replaced the Attalid buildings referred to by Strabo. In any case the hellenization of Pessinus started under the Attalids and was probably complete by the first century AD, as the presence of the theatre and odeion suggest. The large *cavea* of the theatre has lost its rows of seats, but the steps which lead up to the temple and which are regarded as belonging to the odeion still survive in a fairly good condition. But rather than being part of an odeion they may have served as steps or seats for the assembly or for the members of the council to sit on and deliberate like the steps of the agora at Adada. The lower structure of the large temple which has been excavated is impressive but nothing above it stands erect. So the landscape of the site now lacks what once must have constituted its most important feature.

Gordion: the mere sound of the word brings to mind Alexander the Great cutting the famous knot with a stroke of his sword. Situated not far from Pessinus on the banks of the river Sangarios, Gordion was the ancient capital of the kingdom of Phrygia. It flourished until the centre of gravity of the Phrygian world gravitated westward after the devastation of the country by the Kimmerians and the conquests of the Lydian king Alyattes. So when Manlius Vulso at the head of his army reached the site in the course of his campaign against the Gauls, who had occupied most of Phrygia, he found it deserted.[35] The inhabitants had fled and only a few returned, for in Strabo's days it was no more than a little village.[36]

The various popular stories about Midas, the wealthy king of Phrygia, belong entirely to a myth of relatively late date which was essentially Greek in character and origin. The various writers who relate them or refer to them are of the late Hellenistic or of the Roman age. There was more than one king of Phrygia by the name of Midas, the most historical one being the last who was overthrown by the Cimmerians about 700 BC. On account of this disaster he was said to have drunk the lethal blood of a bull to end his life. But he has little if anything to do with the great king Midas of mythology.

The mound where Gordion once stood has been excavated in recent years by an American expedition. A conspicuous gateway has come to light and many interesting Phrygian finds have been recovered which are now in the Ankara museum. In the course of these excavations some thirty years ago a sepulchre was found which, according to recent conjectures, may have been that of the historical king Midas.

Although most of Phrygia came under the transforming influence of Greek civilization in the course of centuries, Gordion, the ancient capital, was never hellenized, its life having virtually come to an end before the age in which such a development could have taken place.

As we move westward out of Phrygia into the territory that was once the kingdom of Lydia, the configuration of the land scarcely changes except for the gradual descent to a level lower than the uplands. The scenery varies little. Poplars abound in the valleys where water collects and streams flow, kermes oak and pines cover the rugged hills, while mountains and escarpments continue to mark the landscape. But unlike the Tauros region and the whole of southern Turkey, where pine forests often constitute an important part of the scenery, few conifers are to be seen in central Asia Minor today. The dominant tree, where vegetation breaks the sweep of bare undulating expanses of land, is the poplar followed by the willow.

Ancient sites are not lacking in Lydia but as in Phrygia there are few where the buildings have withstood the vicissitudes of time and where any conspicuous remains are to be found. As far as history is concerned, however, we move from a world like a sea of myth, where only a few islands of recorded events emerge, into the closely knit history of a famous nation whose kings stand out as clear-cut personalities. The records are plentiful by comparison. Herodotus, who gives us an outline of the kingdom's history, provides us with the following information about the people:

> The customs of the Lydians are like those of the Greeks, save that they make prostitutes of their female children. They were the first men known to us who coined and used gold and silver currency; and they were the first to have shops. And according to what they themselves say the pastimes now in use among them and the Greeks were invented by the Lydians.[37]

By pastimes Herodotus does not mean athletic games; he specifies *pegniá* as dice, knuckle-bones and other such games. In fact the Lydians differed very markedly by not engaging in athletics, running and racing, as the Greeks did. Nor did they go in for theatrical performances. By the time Herodotus was writing, about a century after the Persian conquest, contact in the field of culture as well as trade between the Greeks of the coastal cities and the Lydian people was no doubt fairly close, but whatever customs they had in common by then, the differences remained profound. Neither Croesus, culturally hellenized though he was, nor any of his predecessors on the throne would have ever envisaged decentralization by founding cities with a democratic constitution in the far-flung kingdom covering a vast area of Anatolia. Sardeis was not in those days a *polis* but the capital of a centralized monarchy under an autocratic king like any other oriental monarchy, which remained centralized and autocratic until the end when Cyrus conquered the whole country in 546 BC. Lydia then came under the administration of a satrap in no wise inclined to adopt the form of hellenization the satrap Mausolos undertook in Caria in the fourth century BC. Although there were in Sardeis many Greeks engaged in various activities, whatever influence they may have had no town or village in Lydia evolved into a city as Carian Alabanda or Alinda did, with buildings befitting the life of a *polis*. This form of develoment failed to take place before Alexander's conquest even though Sardeis by the first half of the fifth century BC was already deeply penetrated by Greek culture and produced a famous historian, Xanthos, who wrote in Greek a history of the Lydian people. With the coming of Alexander and under his successors Lydia became so thoroughly hellenized that by the time Strabo was writing no one spoke Lydian any more. It had become a dead language.[38]

Apart from their aptitude for commerce which led them to be the first to invent minting and introduce coinage, the Lydians were brave and excellent warriors,[39] but they also knew how to enjoy life and love. At Sardeis they had a park of pleasure, 'a place of sweet embracing called the coming together of women'[40] or '*le Bon Coin*', as Georges Radet calls it in his book on the Lydians,[41] adding: '*La prostitution s'étalait ouvertement, naturellement et avec une sérénité ardie et une joyeuse candeur*,' a statement corroborated by Herodotus who indeed tells us that the daughters of the Lydian people plied the trade of prostitution to collect their dowries.[42]

It was evidently a happy, joy-giving trade carried out in harmony with the existing code of morals. In the park, the '*Bon Coin*', under the leafy boughs of oak, plane and poplar trees with the gold-bearing Paktolos stream rippling alongside, there was merrymaking and music. The girls danced, played the flute and sang, accompanying themselves on the cithera, and some no doubt also played the harp, the *magadis* invented by the Lydians[43] – very seductive music which the strict moralist Plato had banished from his undemocratic Republic.[44]

Sardeis under the Lydian kings, particularly Croesus, was renowned for its wealth and its prosperity which were due to its commerce and the gold that was carried down in minute particles from Mount Tmolos by the waters of the river Paktolos. It was indeed a great city, but not a *polis* and therefore virtually nothing survives of its buildings. It had no public edifices of stone, only houses of an ephemeral structure. 'The greater part of the houses of Sardeis were of reeds and as many as were of brick, even they had roofs of reeds.'[45] Consequently the city went up in flames, including the ancient temple of Cybele which must have consisted chiefly of timber, when the Ionians in revolt against the Persians took the city and set fire to it in 498 BC.

The palace of the Lydian kings may have been more substantial but was not constructed in stone masonry to withstand fires and earthquakes, and the perishable nature of the buildings persisted throughout the Persian period. So what we see today emerging above ground belongs to the age in which the city had become a fully fledged *polis*, a process that started from the time of Alexander under the lax control first of the Seleucid and then of the Attalid kings. Already in the middle of the third century BC Sardeis had a council and an assembly electing magistrates and issuing coins. It was recognized as a Greek city by Delphi and it was then that the citizens sent envoys to Delphi to renew their ancient ties with the seat of the great oracle.[46]

On this site of ancient renown and great natural beauty almost nothing could be seen standing above the ground at the beginning of the present century. The friable soil of the overlooking hills had been for centuries eroded and washed down over the ruins, particularly from the acropolis, carving it into the sharp-edged cliffs we now see. So until a few generations ago only two columns of the great temple of Artemis, built to replace the temple of Cybele which had been destroyed by fire, stood above the ground. A century earlier several columns could still be seen bearing part of the architrave. In 1914, American archaeologists started excavating and after an interruption work was resumed in 1958 by Professor Hanfmann and his team.

What we can now see and enjoy are the remains of a pseudo-dipteral temple of the Ionic order which cannot fail to strike the eye with an impressive image of the whole building, even though the same two columns are still the only ones that stand to their full height. But considerable sections of several other columns help to complete the picture. The temple had a peristasis of twenty columns on the long side and eight on the short side. The pronaos, or the porch in front of the cella, and the opisthodomos, the porch at the rear, each had six columns, another fourteen being inside the cella. The two columns that have survived complete and substantial parts of several other columns stand on a magnificent stylobate (Pls. 45, 46). Only the four columns of the opisthodomos are fluted. Building had started about 300 BC on a plan for a dipteros of which only the cella was finished. In a subsequent phase during the second century BC work was resumed, the original plan being changed to that of a pseudo-dipteral temple. The peristasis, however, was left unfinished and only completed in the reign of Antoninus Pius, while the fluting of most of the columns was never carried out.

In the hellenized city of Sardeis, Artemis had replaced Cybele without any fundamental change. In most centres of Anatolian religious cult the ancient female deity, whether Ma, Anaitis, Astarte or Cybele, would in due course be worshipped in hellenized form, usually that of Artemis.

The other buildings pertaining to the hellenized life of the city have suffered even more than the temple, from earthquakes, wars, invasions, plunderings and fires as well as from the embedding earth washed down from the foothills of Mount Tmolos. Scarcely anything, therefore, remains of the theatre and stadium. The gymnasium has fared better, being situated further away from the foothills. It was built in the early third century AD and has been virtually reconstructed in recent years – a huge, imposing edifice, architecturally very Roman in character and somewhat pompous. More attractive is the successfully restored synagogue, a splendid structure close to the gymnasium, displaying an interesting mixture of Jewish and Graeco-Roman features.

Hellenized Sardeis was remarkably prolific in producing celebrated Greek historians, philosophers, rhetoricians and poets. The names of at least eight have come down to us (see Appendix A), though relatively little of their writings has survived. Pausanias, whose invaluable description of Greece survives, was a Lydian, a fact which transpires from his referring to 'the dwelling among us of Pelops and Sipylos'. [47] We may assume that he came from Sardeis, since it was the largest and most important city of Lydia not far from Mount Sipylos. Also noteworthy is Xanthos the historian, whose 'History of the Lydians' was an important source of information for both Herodotus and Strabo. Another distinguished historian followed Xanthos a couple of centuries later – Xenophilos, who also wrote a historical work about the Lydians. Unfortunately the writings of both these historians have failed to reach us except for a few fragments.[48]

Sardeis continued to be a prosperous city throughout the Graeco-Roman and early Byzantine ages when it became one of the Seven Churches of Asia mentioned in the Revelation. Thereafter it declined, like most other cities of Anatolia, and was finally wiped out by Timur and his horde of Tatar invaders.

The remains of the other Lydian cities are scanty, inconspicuous or by now obliterated. Philadelphia, for instance, founded by Attalos II Philadelphos, was a flourishing city throughout the Graeco-Roman age. It was called 'Little Athens' on account of its temples and festivals, and it was one of the Seven Churches mentioned in Revelation. Today nothing remains of its buildings apart from fragments in the walls of Alaşehir, the Turkish town which has sprung up on the site. The same applies to Thyateira, a Seleucid foundation and another of the Seven Churches, where modern Akhisar has wiped out the ancient remains.

In the Hellenistic age Lydia and Phrygia were already teeming with Greek cities, some founded by Alexander's successors, many others indigenous in origin though no less Hellenic in character and culture, city status having been achieved by them. But if we look at the territories that lie contiguously to the north, namely Bithynia, Paphlagonia and Pontus, we cannot help being struck by the paucity and in many parts virtual absence of centres of habitation belonging to that period which could be regarded as cities except for the old Greek colonies strung along the Propontis and Euxine coasts, Kalchedon, Herakleia, Sinope and several others.

Alexander's successors were scarcely interested in the north of Asia Minor and appear to have been content with nominal suzerainty over the territories of that region, which developed into centralized monarchies after the collapse of the Persian empire. Powerful dynasties emerged, the Mithridatic dynasty of Pontus being the boldest, most ambitious and aggressive, though the Nicomedian kings of Bithynia were scarcely less tenacious and enterprising.

Most of these monarchs were hellenized, or at any rate professed Hellenism by adopting the language and culture for themselves and the personnel of their courts, though not to the extent of feeling impelled or inclined to pursue a policy of founding cities or transforming indigenous centres into cities, as was the hellenizing policy of the Seleucid and Attalid kings. As long as these dynasties lasted, roughly from two to three centuries, the government of each respective territory remained highly centralized so that the native tribes, which constituted the bulk of the population, were but little affected by Hellenism. However, in Bithynia, a fertile country whose inhabitants were of Thracian stock, the dynasty of kings established by Zipotes in 297 BC not only endured for over two centuries but also came to understand the economic as well as political advantages of urbanization. Notable in this respect were Nicomedes I and II and Prusias I, who indeed founded a few cities, an activity, however, which consisted mostly in renaming and revitalizing older foundations or colonies.

The principal cities of Bithynia were Nikomedeia, Nicaea and Prusa. Nikomedeia, established on the shores of Propontis where the Turkish town of Izmit now flourishes, was founded by the Bithynian king Nikomedes I in 264 BC and settled with inhabitants from Astakos, a city in the neighbourhood which had been founded by Megarians and Athenians and which had been razed to the ground by Lysimachos. Therefore Nikomedeia, the capital of Bithynia and residence of the kings, can hardly be regarded as having been hellenized: it was Greek from the start. It grew into a great city with splendid buildings, of which unfortunately nothing survives above ground. In the course of centuries they have been obliterated by the turbulent events to which the whole region was subject and by more recent constructions on the site.

Nicaea, situated on the edge of the Askanian lake, was founded by Antigonus who called the city Antigoneia. After his death it was occupied in 301 BC by Lysimachus who renamed it Nikaia, commonly known in its Latinized form as Nicaea, after his wife.

The layout of this famous city was in accordance with the classical Hippodamian plan. Strabo describes it as having its streets cut at right angles so that its four gates could be seen from a stone which was set in the middle of the gymnasium.[49] This gymnasium was evidently the one the Nicaeans reconstructed on a grander scale involving architectural problems and an expense which proved a source of worry to Pliny the Younger, whom the emperor Trajan had sent to Bithynia as his legate to overhaul the finances of the province. Trajan's reply to Pliny's letter asking for advice is amusing because of the emperor's somewhat scathing remark about the passion the Greeks had for gymnasia. The theatre which was being rebuilt on a grand scale was likewise a source of worry to Pliny.[50] Unfortunately nothing survives of either the gymnasium or the theatre, nor for that matter of ancient Nicaea as a whole. The only conspicuous structures today are the late Byzantine walls, parts of which are still standing remarkably well preserved. The name of the city, however, has survived with the resonance of its illustrious past culminating in the great council the Christian Church held there in AD 325.

Prusa was situated further inland at the foot of a lofty mountain, the Mysian Mount Olympus, where abundant brooks and springs converge to irrigate the fertile land. It was said to have been founded by Prusias, a Bithynian king. It was a prosperous and important city in the Hellenistic and Graeco-Roman age, but nothing visible of its buildings has survived, the site being occupied by the thriving Turkish town of Bursa, nowadays a magnet for tourism on account of its splendid Ottoman buildings of the fourteenth and fifteenth centuries.

The other cities of Bithynia which emerged under the inducement of the kings were of much lesser importance and size, apparently with restricted autonomy since none issued coins until the Roman age. Their vestiges are insignificant. By contrast in the adjacent territory of Troad, which after the collapse of the Persian empire came first under the sway of the Seleucids, then the Attalids and finally the Romans, a great city came into existence under the impact of the Alexandrian Hellenic expansion – Alexandreia Troas. It was founded by Antigonus who called it Antigoneia, but of course as in the case of Nicaea, Lysimachus did not like the name and changed it to Alexandreia. It grew into a large city with imposing buildings and achieved prosperity as well as considerable importance, especially in the Graeco-Roman age. It was from there that Saint Paul sailed to carry the gospel from Asia to Europe and it was there that he raised Eutychus from the dead,[51] or perhaps just from a state of coma.

In the course of centuries the stones of the city walls and buildings have been plundered and carried away to Constantinople, the site being close to the sea; little remains standing, therefore.

In neighbouring Mysia, enjoying the splendour of Pergamon, we might expect to find conspicuous remains of several cities founded by such a dynamic dynasty as the Attalid kings who, no less than the Seleucids, were foremost in promoting the penetration and diffusion of Hellenism in Asia Minor. But perhaps because this small territory was in any case under their immediate surveillance and its rural population, of Thracian origin like the Bithynians, was being hellenized simply by a process of osmosis, there was no need for any outstanding colonizing efforts. The cities that emerged east of the ancient Greek coastal settlements such as Assos and Antandros were not many. Little remains of Apollonia a few miles east of Pergamon. There are still some walls at Apollonis founded by Eumenes II, to the south-east, but here we are already in Lydia.

Further north, in the mountainous, rugged and wooded territory of Paphlagonia which bordered Bithynia and extended eastward between the Euxine Sea and Phrygia, the absence of urbanization is even more striking. Until the Romans took over control Paphlagonia retained a tribal structure with no cities at all: perhaps its hellenized and fairly stable dynasty of kings was of too short a duration for any change to take place. Moreover parts of its territory were being constantly fought over by the rival kings of Bithynia and Pontus, and large tracts bordering on Phrygia were being overrun and occupied by the Galatians. The Paphlagonian kings had their residence at Gangra, a fortress, scarcely a town, which did not achieve city status until it came under the Romans in AD 6. It was subsequently renamed Germanicopolis.

The people of Paphlagonia went on leading their tribal life in the mountainous hinterland, speaking their own language and adhering to their customs without contact with the Greeks of the coastal cities to whom they remained alien and remote, even though they had played a noteworthy part in the *Iliad* as allies of the Trojans. By 121 BC Paphlagonia had lost its political identity; the last of its kings, Pylaimenes II, who died that year, had bequeathed his kingdom to Mithradates V of Pontus.

The geographical picture we get of these three northern countries of Anatolia – Bithynia, Paphlagonia and Pontus – tends to be confused not only because of their constant mutual territorial encroachments and conflicts that kept modifying the borders, but also because of the invasion of the Gauls at the beginning of the third century BC and their sprawling occupation of large tracts of Phrygian and Paphlagonian territory within ill-defined frontiers.

These wild tribes had crossed the Hellespont into Asia Minor in 278 BC at the invitation or with the encouragement of Nikomedes I of Bithynia in order to bolster his forces in his war with Ziboetes who held part of Bithynia. During the following years they raided and plundered vast areas of Lydia and Phrygia until they were to some extent subdued by Attalus I of Pergamon and made to settle in northern Phrygia. But they continued to harass their neighbours so that the consul Manlius Vulso was sent by the Roman senate to bring them under control. This he achieved by the campaign he undertook against them in 189 BC, vividly described by Livy,[52] after his memorable fund-grabbing expedition south of the Tauros, where we found him engaged on the outskirts of Lycia, in Pisidia and in Pamphylia (see Chapter V, above).

We are lucky to have from Strabo a clear and detailed description of the social structure of the Galatians, as the Gauls were called. He tells us that they were divided into three tribes, the Trokmi, the Tolistobogli and the Teknosages, who all three spoke the same language and had the same customs. They were ruled by four tetrarchs who each had a judge and a military commander under him, with subordinate commanders. There was also a council which passed judgement on murder cases.[53]

This tribal structure proved enduring and therefore the conception of a city with its own constitution and local autonomy remained totally alien to the Galatians. Each of the three tribes, however, had a centre of administration, a sort of capital, for which they chose the most conveniently situated place, an old Phrygian town or village in the area occupied by the tribe. The Tolistobogli chose Pessinus, the Teknosages had Ankyra and the Trokmi Tavion, situated some miles further east where a colossal statue of Zeus stood, perhaps originally of Men.

Strabo refers to Ankyra, the present-day Ankara, as a fortress, which no doubt it was. However, at the end of the first century BC, when Augustus made Galatia a Roman province, Ankyra grew rapidly into a considerable town, the centre of administration. It was then, about 20 BC, that the temple of Augustus was built, an imposing structure of which the cella survives in much of its parts. The splendid door stands unusually high, perhaps because it provided the only opening through which the windowless cella received light. The temple was built on the site of the sanctuary of Men and Cybele, and stood on an elevated podium like the temple of Aizanoi for which it may have served as model. It was at first a prostyle structure with a porch consisting of four Corinthian columns, parts of which lie now on the ground in front of the cella. In the second century AD a peristasis of Ionic columns was erected round the original building which thereby became a pseudo-dipteral temple. This part of the building has not survived. In the Byzantine age the temple was converted into a church.

A particularly interesting feature of the temple is the long inscription relating the deeds of Augustus, the *index rerum gestarum* of his will, which is to be seen carved on the walls of the cella. On the walls inside the cella the inscription is in Latin, while a Greek version is carved on the exterior of the south-west wall. It is noteworthy that, although Latin was presumably the official language of the administration, a Greek translation was needed, suggesting that the people of Ankyra spoke Greek in those days. But whether the town ever obtained municipal status and developed a *polis* constitution as the towns Pompey converted into 'cities' may have done, remains uncertain.

In the course of time strong individuals emerged from among the Galatians who were able to establish themselves as dynasts and sometimes rule over all three tribes. Noteworthy was Deiotaros, a tetrarch of the Tolistobogli, who became king of Galatia. He was a hellenized potentate, extremely able, who reaped the advantages he sought by cultivating contact with Pompey and giving him his full support in the third Mithradatic war. Amyntas, his secretary and after his death his successor, proved another enterprising hellenized dynast. Antony granted him the rule of a huge territory which comprised not only the area occupied by the Galatian tribes but also vast tracts of Lycaonia, Pisidia, Pamphylia and Isauria. There he rebuilt the ancient city of Isaura before being killed by the wild Homonadeis (see Chapter V above).

When Amyntas died in 25 BC Galatia proper and much of these other territories were formed into a single Roman province. But within their more restricted confines the Galatian tribes continued to retain their customs and their language right into the Christian age wherever urbanization had not developed.

Pontus, famous for its intrepid kings, was the region that extended eastward from the river Halys, which formed an approximate border with Paphlagonia. The kingdom covered an area between the Euxine Sea on the north and Cappadocia on the south as far as the confines of Armenia on the east. After being a mere satrapy under the Persians it came first into prominence with Mithradates I of Kios, who claimed descent from one of the companions of Darius the Great. He founded the Mithradatic dynasty which ruled the country for about two and a half centuries. The greatest and most ambitious of these monarchs was Mithradates VI, the last king of Pontus of that dynasty. In the three successive wars he conducted with the Romans and other opponents his fortunes fluctuated and at times rose to spectacular heights with the conquest of most of Asia Minor and even Greece, from where, however, he was expelled by Sulla. Finally the military genius of Pompey proved too formidable for him to overcome. In 66 BC he escaped to the Crimea where, having failed to raise sufficient forces to redress his fortunes, he committed suicide. His son Pharnakes II attempted to reconstitute the kingdom but failed. He was defeated at Zela by Caesar who announced his success with the famous words 'Veni, vidi, vici.'

Mithradates VI, Eupator as he was surnamed, was an extremely bold and ambitious monarch of mixed Persian and Macedonian descent who affected Hellenism and copied Alexander's personal appearance as his portraits show. But he ruled like an eastern potentate and like his predecessors was not interested in founding cities, though finally he started to have one built, Eupatoria. The mixed population of Pontus remained scarcely affected by Hellenism under the Mithradatic dynasty, the social structure continuing to consist of an Iranized nobility, the villagers and the primitive tribes. There were only four large clusters of habitation which could be regarded as towns, albeit not as *poleis*: Komana, Kabeira, Zela and Amaseia. The first three of these were great religious centres ruled by priests with thousands of slaves and prostitutes. Amaseia was the capital where the king resided with his court and where many Greeks lived engaged in business and the administration of the country. Greek was the official language, but given the centralized nature of the government headed by the king, Amaseia had no scope for becoming a city in the specific sense of the term, a *polis*, until the Roman age. It was Pompey who proved to be the great hellenizer of Pontus by founding several new cities and converting old native centres into cities, this policy being the most effective way of breaking up the cohesion of the Mithradatic monarchy. He completed Eupatoria and renamed it Magnopolis. Kabeira became Diospolis, Dasteira became Nicopolis, Karana Sebastopolis. Zela retained its name and so did Amaseia. Megalopolis, Neapolis and Pompeiopolis in Paphlagonia were new foundations. Komana, however, was allowed to carry on as a sacerdotal principality until AD 34.[54] But unlike its homonymous site in Cappadocia it has little more than a mound of rubble to show today. Likewise virtually nothing survives on the sites of the above-mentioned cities except Amaseia. A medieval fortress crowns the acropolis of Kabeira, nowadays Niksar, of which only the substructure dates back to the Roman age. The same applies to the acropolis of Zela situated on a hill which Strabo calls the mound of Semiramis, where the walls of a medieval fortress are now all that can be seen.

Still evocative of a golden past is beautiful Amaseia, the native city of Strabo, our companion and guide throughout Anatolia. 'My city,' he tells us,

> is situated in a large deep valley, through which flows the Iris river. Both by human foresight and by nature it is an admirably devised city, since it can at the same time afford the advantages of both a city and a fortress; for it is a high and precipitous rock which descends abruptly to the river, which has on one side the wall on the edge of the river where the city is settled and on the other the wall that runs up on either side to the peaks. These peaks are two in number, united with one another by nature and are magnificently towered. Within this circuit are both the palaces and the monuments of the kings.[55]

Amaseia was the capital of the Pontic kings until the father of Mithradates VI Eupator transferred the court to Sinope. Several of their tombs, to which Strabo refers, were carved into the face of the cliff overlooking the city. These great sepulchres probably belong to the 2nd century BC and their features are vaguely Hellenic in character with elements, however, of Persian influence. Of the palace or palaces of the kings nothing survives except substructure, mighty walls which have been restored in more recent times but whose lower courses of ashlar masonry date from antiquity. On the towering crag a thousand feet above the town, which Strabo describes, stands a medieval fortress but with some remains that date back to earlier times. There are still two fine Hellenistic towers.

Besides these remains nothing survives of ancient Amaseia. Although the Pontic kings were hellenized they were so culturally, not politically. There were many Greeks settled in Amaseia, active in business, participating in the administration of the kingdom and intermarrying with the indigenous people. Strabo himself was of mixed descent. The official language was Greek and probably by Strabo's time everybody spoke Greek, perhaps only Greek. But the Pontic kings ruled as absolute monarchs and would do nothing to encourage local city constitutions and administrative autonomy. Therefore there cannot have been an assembly, council and gymnasium at Amaseia with their appropriate buildings until Pompey made it a free city in 65 BC. By the time Strabo was living, a couple of generations later, this development may have taken place. But unfortunately no ruins reflecting *polis* life at that time have survived, probably because of the fertility of the region and for the very reasons relating to the situation which Strabo points out: the site was ideal for both a town and a fortress. So Amaseia continued to be inhabited through the ages, each period and prevailing culture building anew and destroying the earlier buildings. At present what survives most conspicuously in the town itself are splendid Seljuk and early Ottoman edifices.

With the death of Mithradates VI and his son Pharnakes II the Mithradatic dynasty came to an end. Pontus survived as a kingdom, though much reduced territorially, for about another century under the rule of various dynasts appointed by Rome, the most prominent of whom was Pythodoris, 'a wise woman qualified to preside over affairs of state.'[56] She ruled as queen for over half a century with her residence and court at Kabeira, not Amaseia.

East of Pontus and Cappadocia lay the ancient kingdom of Armenia which had been preceded by the Urartu civilization. The Armenians had not only their own language but also their own remarkable culture that produced, in a period later than the one covered by this survey, outstanding pieces of architecture of which there are still notable remains. This civilization, however, was only remotely affected by Hellenism and therefore no ruins reflecting the process of Hellenic penetration are to be found in Armenia proper.

Leaving aside the enclave of Trebizond, or Trapezos as it was called, on the far eastern coast of Pontus, a borderline from a point on the Mediterranean coast a few miles east of the Pyramos river can be drawn northward as far as the Euxine sea with a couple of slight curves to include Melitene in the south and Komana of Pontus in the north. Westward of this confine, which roughly corresponds to the dividing line Strabo makes, there stretches as far as the Aegean sea and the Propontis the large peninsula known as Anatolia, the 'Land of the Rising Sun', or in other words Asia Minor proper, which was hellenized. East of this confine extends the region of Armenia, which geographically is also part of Turkey today and which could be regarded as part of Asia Minor in a wide sense, but, never having been hellenized, not of Anatolia.

From the south-west to the south-east, from the centre west to the centre east and from the north-west to the north-east of the great peninsula we have scanned the land of hellenized Anatolia and brought this survey, highlighted by the architectural remains, to its conclusion.

The diffusion of Hellenism in the Middle East was uneven. In Egypt under the Ptolemies and even throughout the Graeco-Roman age the majority of the indigenous population went on speaking, and to some extent writing, Egyptian and later Coptic. Hellenism was the world of the dominant élite; it penetrated the Egyptian native elements only to a limited degree.⁵⁷ In Syria the indigenous language and culture were never wiped out by Hellenism; not only did they survive but they flourished again in the early Christian period.

By contrast the hellenization of Asia Minor was not merely widespread but of a radical nature, wiping out or totally supplanting earlier cultures, absorbing and integrating indigenous religious cults. If a native language and way of life survived for any length of time, it was only in remote tribal areas among illiterate people. If any of them acquired some education, it could only be Greek.

The council and the people – this is the formula which heads many of the inscriptions on every site where an ancient city stood all over Anatolia. Even in the remotest corners of the vast territory, wherever the eye catches sight of the familiar wording we can be sure a Greek city flourished in which the administration of the *polis* would take effect. The council and the people would be issuing ordinances and enacting municipal laws in accordance with the constitution of the *polis*. The *demos* may no longer have had the power it once possessed, it may have only acclaimed or confirmed the decisions of an oligarchy embodied in the council. No matter. The complete formula was of essential importance, the seal of the *polis* as it were, the hallmark of Hellenism, even more so than the language itself, the language of civilized life. It was Aristotle who said: 'The city was invented to preserve life; it exists to preserve the good life.'⁵⁸

NOTES

hovels among the ruins of the foot of the hill.

9 47 The best archaeological survey of Herakleia is to be found in Wiegand's *Milet, Latmos III* (Berlin, 1925); see also Bean, *Aegean Turkey* (London, 1984).

10 53 Xenophon, *Hellenica*, 2.1.15
11 53 Strabo, 14.2.25; Polybius, 31.7; Livy, 33.30; Ptolemy, 5.2.15
12 55 Herodotus, I.172
13 55 Strabo, 14.2.3

CHAPTER III
LYCIA

1 61 Artemidoros of Ephesus, geographer, flourished in the first half of the first century BC. His works, 'Ionikà Ypomnemata' and 'Geographoumena', have not survived.
2 62 Strabo 14.3.3
3 63 Plutarch, *Marcus Brutus*, xxx.xxxi
4 67 Bryce, *The Lycians* (Copenhagen, 1987), p. 184
5 67 E. Akurgal, *The Birth of Greek Art*, pp. 187–8
6 67 *Iliad*, VI.179–83; Hesiod, 319ff
7 68 Pauly, *Realencyclopädie*, sv. Leto
8 69 Hornblower, *Mausolos* (Oxford, 1982), pp. 47–8
9 71 De Bernardi-Ferrero, *Teatri classici in Asia Minore* (Milan, 1969)
10 72 Strabo 14.3.5
11 73 Texier, *Description de l'Asie Mineure* (Paris, 1849), vol. 2, p. 187
12 74 Fellows, *Travels and Researches in Asia Minor* (London, 1852) on Kadyanda, p. 306
13 75 Strabo, 13.4.17
14 76 Detersen & von Luschan, *Reisen in Sudwest Kleinasien* (Vienna, 1888), vol 2, pp. 189f
15 83 Fellows, op.cit., (London, 1852), on Arykanda, p. 373f
16 84 *F.H.G.* 194; *J.A.* 210
17 84 Athenaios, *Deipnosophistai*, XII.528
18 86 Spratt and Forbes, *Travels in Lycia* (London, 1842), vol. 1, pp. 181, 182
19 87 Plutarch, *Pompeius* 24
20 87 Strabo, 14.5.7; Ormerod, *Piracy in the Ancient World* (Liverpool, 1978), p. 216
21 88 Bean, *Turkey's Southern Shore*
22 89 Plutarch, *Alexander*, 17

CHAPTER IV
PAMPHYLIA & PISIDIA

1 91 Herodotus, VII.91; Strabo, 14.4.3 (C.668), 14.5.16 (C.675–6)
2 94 Arrian, 1.26.4
3 94 Strabo, 14.4.2
4 96 The epigraphist Heberdey saw the ruins in 1891 and so did Felix von Luschan a few years previously, as a member of the Lanckoronski expedition, but neither surveyed them or even described them.
5 96 Bean, *Turkey's Southern Shore*, pp. 88, 89
6 97 Strabo, 12.7.2
7 97 *Princeton Encyclopedia of Ancient Sites*; Bean, *Turkey's Southern Shore*, pp. 112–13
8 98 Plutarch, *Alexander*, 328f
9 99 Arrian, I.27.6
10 100 Diodorus Siculus, XVIII.46–7
11 101 Polybius, 21.35; Livy, 38.15
12 101 The considerable degree of freedom accorded by Rome to the citizens of Termessos, 'friends and allies of the Roman People', was confirmed by a law enacted by the tribunes of the plebs in accordance with a decision of the Senate in about 72 B.C. Much of the text of this law survives inscribed on a bronze tablet in Rome. CIL I²589; ILS 38.
13 104 Strabo, 12.7.3
14 105 Polybius, V.72–7
15 106 Bean, *Turkey's Southern Shore*, pp. 110–18
16 107 Zosimos, I.69–70s
17 107 Arundell, *Discoveries in Asia Minor* (London, 1834), vol. 2, p. 74
18 108 Fellows, *Travels and Researches in Asia Minor*, (London, 1852), on Kremna, p. 130f
19 108 Sterrett, *The Wolfe Expedition in Asia Minor*, (Boston, 1884–5), p. 320

20   110   Arrian, *The Life of Alexander the Great*, I.28.2

21   111   Lucas, *Voyage en Grèce* (Paris, 1712), vol. 2, p. 182

22   111   Hamilton, *Researches in Asia Minor* (London, 1842), vol.I, p. 487f

23   112   Fellows, op.cit., on Sagalassos theatre, p. 124

24   112   Hamilton, op.cit., vol. 1, pp. 488–9

25   114   Bean, in the *Princeton Encyclopedia of Ancient Sites*

26   114   Jüthner, *Denkmäler aus Lykaonien, Pamphylien und Isaurien* (Prague 1935)

CHAPTER V

ISAURIA & CILICIA

1   116   Strabo 12.7.2. The site has been located a few miles south of Lake Karalitis (Beyşehr): Hall, *A.S.* IX, p.121; XVIII, p.75

2   117   Diodorus Siculus, XVIII.22.2–8

3   118   Strabo, 12.6.2; Sallust, *Historiae*, II.870–85

4   118   Pliny, *Naturalis Historia*, V.97

5   119   Strabo, 12.6.5

6   119   *Ibid.*, 12.6.3

7   119   *Ibid.*, 12.6.5

8   120   *Ibid.*

9   120   Tacitus, *Annals*, III.48.2

10   120   Germanicopolis, on the site of the present-day Ermenek, Eirenopolis and Philadelphia were all founded by Antiochos IV of Commagene in the days of the emperors Caligula and Claudius.

11   120   The ruins of Kolybrassos at Ayasofia, 20km inland from Alanya; Laertes, 15 km east of Alanya; Syedra, modern Demitras, 15 km from Alanya; Lamos near the coast, etc: Bean and Mitford, 'Journeys in rough Cilicia, 1962'; *Denkschriften der Akademie den Wissenschaften in Wien*, Bände 102, 1970; 'Sites Old and New', *A.S.* XII, 1962.

12   123   Hamilton, *Researches in Asia Minor* (London, 1842), vol.2, pp. 331ff

13   123   Davis, *Life in Asiatic Turkey* (London, 1879), p. 415

14   124   At the end of the last century Isaura was visited by the epigraphist T. R. S. Sterrett, who travelled in 1895, and shortly after by Hirschfeld (*Denkmäler aus Lykaonien*). More recently, in 1931, the site was surveyed by J. Jüthner (*Denkmäler aus Lycaonien, Pamphylien und Isaurien*), who made detailed drawings of the remains, including a reconstruction of two arches of which only the foundations now survive. In this century a few more travellers have been there, but on the whole the site is seldom visited.

15   124   Tacitus, *Annals*, VI 41, XII.55

16   125   Strabo, 14.5.2

17   126   *Ibid.*, 14.5.4

18   127   *Ibid.*, 14.5.10

19   127   Plutarch, *Pompey*, XXVII

20   128   The earliest Corinthian capital we know of was a column in the temple of Bassae, but it has not survived. There were Corinthian capitals in the interior of the 4th-century BC Tholos of Delphi, which have likewise perished. The 4th-century BC monument of Lysicrates in Athens has Corinthian capitals. But the temple of Zeus at Olba is the earliest Corinthian temple of which there is any record.

21   129   Magie, *The Roman Rule in Asia Minor*, p.269

22   129   Bent, *J.H.S.* XII, 1891–2; Heberdey and Wilhelm, *Reisen in Kilikien* (Berlin, 1896)

23   131   Frazer, *The Golden Bough*, Part IV: *Priestly Kings of Olba*

24   133   Pindar, Ode 4; Aeschylus, *Prometheus Bound*, 355–72; Ovid, *Metamorphoses*, V.321ff

25   133   Strabo, 14.5.5

26   133   Bent, *J.H.S.*XII, p.226

27   134   Strabo, 14.5.12–13–14 (C.673–5)

28   135   Strabo, 14.5.10 (C.672; Pliny, *Naturalis Historia*, V.93; Jones, *The Greek City*, pp. 40, 71, 72; Gough, 'Anazarbus', *A.S.* II, 1952

29   135   Kastabala-Hieropolis was first visited and described by J.Th.Bent in 1890 (*J.H.S.*XI) and more recently by M. Gough (*A.S.*IV, 1954).

30   135   Strabo, 12.2.7

31   135   *Iphigenia in Tauris*, 30

32   136   Strabo, 12.2.3

CHAPTER VI
NORTH OF THE TAUROS & THE MAEANDER

1   137   Strabo, 12.2.7 (C.537)
2   140   *Ibid.*, 12.6.1 (C.568)
3   140   Xenophon, 1.II.19
4   141   *Ibid.*
5   141   Strabo, 12.6.1 (C.568); Pliny, *Naturalis Historia*, V. 95
6   141   Strabo, 12.6.3 (C.569)

7   141   Zosimos, 5.29.3
8   142   Tertullian, *On Baptism*, 17
9   143   Strabo, 12.1.2. (C.533–4)
10 143   Jones, *The Greek City*, p.41
11 144   Strabo, 12.2.7
12 144   *Ibid.*, 12.2.3
13 145   Harper and Bayburtluoglu, 'Report on Excavations at Comana', *A.S.* XVIII, 1968
14 146   Pausanias, X.30.9. Apparently, according to Athenaeus XIV.627, in diplomatic negotiations as well as in military conflicts 'many of the barbarians', by which he meant the Phrygians and Lydians, 'would play the flute to soften the hearts of their opponents.'
15 147   Herodotus, I.17.2
16 147   Strabo, 12.3.31 (C.556)
17 147   Jones, *The Greek City*, p. 61. In Ramsay's *Historical Commentry on St Paul's Epistle to the Galatians* we have a detailed study he made in 1899 of Antioch's social structure during the centuries of its Roman colonial constitution. He argued that the *incolae*, or non-colonial inhabitants who formed the mass of the Greek-speaking people, whether of Magnesian or Phrygian origin including many hellenized Jews who preferred Greek, being the language of business, to Latin, became *coloni* in the course of time, namely fully-fledged citizens of the colony. As such they would assume Latin names, though Greek, according to Ramsay, had become the ordinary tongue by the middle or end of the 2nd century AD. More recently, however, Barbara Levick (*Roman Col-*

onies in Southern Asia Minor, Oxford, 1967) has been inclined to see romanization enduring at Antioch somewhat longer, which the persistence of Latin nomenclature, widely adopted, would seem to suggest. But Ramsay pointed out that even names relating to the city and city constitution tended to become hellenized in the course of the 3rd century AD, for instance the term *boule* coming to be used again, and the term *strategos* for the magistrate of that category instead of the Latin *duumvir*. Antioch would be referred to as the metropolis of the Antiochians and no longer as the *Colonia Antiocheia*.

It seems reasonable to conclude from the ever increasing number of inscriptions in Greek as against Latin, as time went on, that although the *coloni* continued to use Latin for official purposes it is unlikely that they went on speaking the language in the normal course of everyday life after the inevitable intermarriage and intermixture with the far more numerous Greek-speaking population had set in.

18 148   Xenophon, *Anabasis*, 1.2.7
19 149   Herodotus, VII. 30
20 149   Pliny, *Naturalis Historia*, V.106
21 149   Strabo, 12.8.15
22 149   Jones, *The Greek City*, p. 15
23 150   Herodotus, VII. 30
24 150   Strabo, 12.8.16
25 150   Xenophon, *Anabasis*, I.2.7
26 150   Pliny, *Naturalis Historia*, V.145
27 151   *Ibid.*, V.105
28 151   Strabo, 12.8.16
29 151   *Ibid.*, 12.8.20
30 153   Strabo, 13.4.14
31 156   Arundell, vol. 2, pp. 81–2; Hamilton, vol. 1, pp. 128f
32 157   'Bericht über eine Reise in Lidien', *Denkschriften der Österreichische Akademie der Wissenschaften in Wien*, Bände 53, 54
33 157   Pausanias, 7.17.9
34 158   Strabo, 12.5.3. The close political ties between the Pergamenian kings and the sacerdotal state of Pessinus is

reflected in a message king Attalus II sent to the high priest of the temple in the year 159 BC. The text of the message has survived inscribed, apparently at a later date, on blocks of marble (OGIS 3151 C VI). The communication, conveyed in very friendly terms, is about possible military action against their common enemy, the Galatians, though they are not mentioned by name, who were well entrenched immediately to the east of the territory ruled by Pessinus. King Attalus seems in favour of the plan, but urges caution and advocates no action without Roman participation or approval.

35 158 Livy, 38. 18. Both Pliny and Livy refer to Gordion as a small town, but Pliny adds that it was a busy market.

36 158 Strabo, 12.5.3. Subsequently in his account Strabo adds, however, that in his days Kleon, a chieftain of robbers, enlarged Gordion making it a city and calling it Juliopolis.

37 159 Herodotus, I.94
38 160 Strabo, 13.4.17
39 160 Herodotus, I.79
40 160 Klearchos of Soli, F.H.G. tII
41 160 Radet, *La Lydie*,
42 160 Herodotus, I.193
43 160 Athenaeus, XIV.634
44 160 Plato, *Republic*, 398
45 160 Herodotus, V.101
46 161 Sylloge inscriptium Graecorum, 548, 549
47 161 Pausanias, V.13.7
48 161 FGr H765; 90 144; FGr H767
49 163 Strabo, 12.4.7
50 164 Pliny, *Letters*, X. 39, 40
51 164 Acts 16:8–11; 20:9–12
52 165 Livy, 38.17–30
53 166 Strabo, 12.5.1
54 168 Jones, *The Greek City*, p. 70
55 168 Strabo, 12.3.39
56 169 *Ibid.*, 2.5.24
57 170 Lewis, *Greeks in Ptolemaic Egypt* (Oxford, 1986), *passim*
58 170 Aristotle, *Politics*, I.2.8

APPENDIX A

Some distinguished writers, philosophers, rhetoricians, orators, grammarians and artists who were natives of the hellenized cities of Anatolia. Included in the list are some whose city was a Seleucid or Attalid foundation, but inhabited predominantly by hellenized Anatolians.

Aemilianus of Nicaea – Epigrammatist, 2nd cent. AD

Agathinos of Bithynia – Physician, 1st cent. BC

Alexander of Antioch on the Maeander – Sculptor, made the Venus of Melos, 2nd cent. BC

Alexander of Aphrodisias – Aristotelian philosopher, *fl.* end 2nd cent. AD

Alexander of Tralles – Physician, 6th cent. AD

Alexander Philalethes of Laodikeia at the Lykos – Physician, 1st cent. BC

Anthemios of Tralles – Mathematician and architect, the main architect of St Sophia, b. *c.* AD 500

Antipatros of Tarsos – Stoic philosopher, 1st cent. BC

Apollonides of Nicaea – Grammarian, 1st cent AD

Apollonios Malakos of Alabanda – Grammarian and rhetorician, 2nd–1st cent. BC

Apollonios Molon of Alabanda – Grammarian and rhetorician, 2nd–1st cent. BC

Apollonios of Nysa – Stoic and grammarian, under whom Pompey studied, 2nd–1st cent. BC

Apollonios of Tyana – Neopythagorean, 1st cent. AD

Archedemos of Tarsos – Stoic philosopher, 1st cent. BC

Arrian of Nicomedia – Historian and philosopher, 2nd cent. AD

Artemidoros of Tarsos – Grammarian, 1st cent. BC

Artemidoros of Tralles – Sculptor, 1st cent. BC

Aschlepiades of Prusa – Physician, 1st cent. BC

Athenaios of Attalia – Physician, founder of the Pneumatic School, 1st cent. BC

Athenaios of Seleukeia on the Kalykadnos – Peripatetic philosopher, 1st cent. BC

Athenodoros of Kanana near Tarsos – Stoic philosopher, scientist and pupil of Posidonius, friend of Strabo, 1st cent. BC

Athenodoros of Tarsos, called Kordylion – Stoic philosopher, librarian of the Pergamon library, 1st cent. BC

Charinos of Laodikeia at the Lykos – Sculptor, 1st cent. BC

Chariton of Aphrodisias – Novelist, 1st cent. AD

Chrysanthios of Sardeis – Neoplatonist philosopher, 4th cent. AD

Daidolus of Bithynia – Sculptor, *fl.* 250 BC

Damasos Skombros of Tralles – Famous orator, 1st cent. BC

Demetrios of Apameia – Physician, *c.* 100 BC

Demosthenes of Bithynia – Poet, 1st cent. BC

Dio Cassius of Nicaea – Historian, 2nd cent. AD

Diodoros of Sardeis – Epigrammatist, 1st cent. AD

Diodoros of Sardeis – Rhetorician, *c.* 100 BC

Diodoros of Sardeis – Historian and poet, friend of Strabo, relation of above

Diodoros of Tarsos – Grammarian, 1st cent. BC

Diogenes of Oinoanda – Epicurean philosopher, 2nd cent. AD

Diogenes of Tarsos – Epicurean philosopher, *c.* 2nd cent. AD

Diogenes Laertius of Laerte in Rough Cilicia – Wrote lives of philosophers, 1st half of 3rd cent. AD

Dion Chrysostomos of Prusa – Orator and philosopher, 1st cent. AD

Dionysios of Philadelphia – Author of extant poems, Ornithakia, 1st cent. BC

Dioskourides Pedanios of Anazarba – Famous physician and chemist, 1st cent. AD

Donysokles of Tralles – Famous orator, 1st cent. BC

Epictetus of Hierapolis – Stoic philosopher, 1st–2nd cent. AD

Eunapios of Sardeis – Platonist philosopher and orator, 4th cent. AD

Eustathios of Cappadocia – Neoplatonist, 4th cent. AD

Eustathios of Caria – Rhetorician, 4th cent. AD

Hermogenes of Alabanda – Architect, 2nd cent. BC

Hermogenes of Tarsos – Rhetorician, 2nd cent. AD

Hierokles of Alabanda – Rhetorician, *c.* 100 BC

Hikesios of Laodikeia at the Lykos – Physician, 1st cent. BC

Hipparchos of Nicaea – Famous astronomer, 2nd cent. BC

Jason of Nysa – Philosopher, pupil of Posidonius, 1st cent. BC

Kratenas of Pontus – Pharmaceutical chemist, 1st cent. BC

Menandros of Laodikeia at the Lykos – Rhetorician, 3rd cent. AD

Menippos of Stratonikeia – Rhetorician under whom Cicero studied, 1st cent. BC

Menodotos of Nicomedia – Physician and sceptic philosopher, 2nd cent. AD

Menodotos of Nicomedia – Sculptor, 2nd cent. BC

Metrodoros of Stratonikeia – Epicurean philosopher and mathematician, 1st cent BC

Metrophanes of Eukarpia in Phrygia – Neoplatonist sophist, *c.* AD 300

Nestor of Laranda – Epic poet, *c.* AD 200

Nikolaos of Myra – Distinguished sophist, friend of Proclus, 5th cent. AD

Nikostratos of Prymnessos in Phrygia – Famous athlete, won contest in the 204th Olympiad AD 37

Oppian of Korykos (Rough Cilicia) – Wrote poems on hunting and fishing, 2nd cent. AD

Parthenios of Nicaea – Poet and writer of love stories, 1st cent. BC

Pausanias of Lydia, probably Sardeis – Author of 'Description of Greece', 2nd cent. AD

Peisander of Laranda – Epic poet, son of Nestor, *c.* AD 200

Polemon of Laudikeia at the Lykos – Celebrated sophist, 1st–2nd cent. AD

Prochairesios of Caesaria, Cappadocia – Sophist, follower of Julian the Apostate, 4th cent. AD

Proklos 'the Lycian' of Xanthus – Famous neoplatonist, 5th cent. AD

Protagenes of Kaunos – gifted painter, mentioned by Pliny, 4th cent. BC

Strabo of amaseia – Geographer and historian, 63 BC–AD23

Theodoktes of Phaselis – Rhetorician, philosopher and dramatist in 4th cent. BC

Theodosios of Bithynia – Mathematician and astronomer, 1st cent. BC

Tribonianus of Sida – councillor to the emperor Justinian, 6th cent. AD

Xanthos of Sardeis – Historian, writer of a history of the Lydians, 5th cent. BC

Xenarchos of Seleukeia on the Kalykadnos – Peripathetic philosopher, 1st cent. BC

Xenokrates of Aphrodisias – Physician, 1st cent. BC

Xenophilos of Sardeis – Historian, wrote a history of Lydia, 3rd cent. BC

Zeno of Aphrodisias – Sculptor: there were four sculptors of this name at Aphrodisias in the 1st and 2nd cent. AD

Zeno of Laodikeia at the Lykos – Rhetorician, 1st cent. BC

Zeno of Laodikeia at the Lykos – Pharmaceutical chemist, 1st cent. BC

Zeno of Tarsos – Stoic philosopher, follower of Chrysippos, 3rd cent. BC

Zeuxis of Laodikeia at the Lykos – Physician, 2nd–1st cent. BC

APPENDIX B

HELLENISTIC DYNASTIES
IN ASIA MINOR & THE MIDDLE EAST

Ptolemaic	Seleucid	Attalid	Bithynian	Cappadocian	Pontic
Ptolemy I Soter I, 306–285	Seleucos I Nikator, 306–280		Zipoites, 327–279	Ariarathes II, 301–280	Mithradates, 301–280
Ptolemy II Philadelphos, 285–246	Antiochos I Soter, 280–261	Philetairos, 283–263			
	Antiochos II Theos, 261–246	Eumenes I, 263–241	Nikomedes I, 279–250	Ariaramnes, 280–230	Ariobarzar, 260–249
Ptolemy III Euergetes, 246–221	Seleucos II Kalinikos, 246–226	Attalos I, 241–197	Ziailas, 250–229	Ariarathes III, 257–220	Mithradates
	(Antiochos Hierax, 227)		Prusias I, 229–182		
Ptolemy IV Philopator, 221–203	Seleucos III Soter, 226–223				
	Antiochos III, 223–187			Ariarathes IV	
Ptolemy V Epiphanes, 203–181					
	Seleucos IV Philopator, 187–175				Pharnakes, 190–169
Ptolemy VI Philometor, 181–145	Antiochos IV Epiphanes, 175–164		Prusias II, 182–149		
	Antiochos V Eupator, 164–162				Mithradates 169–121
	Demetrios I Soter, 162–150	Attalos II, 159–138		Ariarathes V, 163–130	
	Alexander Balas, 150–145		Nikomedes II, 149–95		
Ptolemy VII Eupator, 145	Demetrios II Nikator, 146–125				

Ptolemaic	Seleucid	Attalid	Bithynian	Cappadocian	Pontic
Ptolemy VIII Euergetes II, 145–116	Tryphon and Antiochos VI, 145–142				
	Antiochos VII Sidetes, 138–129	Attalos III, 138–129			
	Alexander II Zabinas, 128–123			Ariarathes VI, 130–112	
	Seleucos V, 125				Mithradates IV Eupator, 121–63
	Antiochos VIII Grypos, 125–95				
Ptolemy IX Soter II, 116–107	Antiochos IX the Cyzicene, 116–95			Ariarathes VII, 112–100	
Ptolemy X Alexander I, 107–88				Ariarathes VII, 100–96	
	Antiochos X, 94–83		Nikomedes III, 94–74		
	Seleucos VI, 96–95				
	Philip I, 92–83				
	Demetrios III, 95–88				
Ptolemy XI, 88–80	Antiochos XI, 89–84				
Berenice III, Ptolemy XII Alexander II, 80	Antiochos XII, 69–65				
Ptolemy XIII Sidetes, 80–51					
Cleopatra VI, 51–30					

GLOSSARY

Agora – Market place.

Analemmata (sing. analemma) – The supporting walls of the two projecting sides of a theatre.

Anta – Pilasters slightly projecting from the ends of the lateral wall of a cella or of a small temple.

Andron – Room reserved for men.

Apse – Curved recess.

Architrave – Lintel resting on the columns of a building, thus the lowest part of the entablature.

Ashlar masonry – Masonry consisting of finely cut rectangular blocks of stone closely fitted together without mortar.

Bouleuterion – Meeting place of the council.

Cavea – The auditorium of a theatre.

Cella – The inner chamber of a temple, sometimes also called the naos.

Cornice – The upper member of the entablature.

Dentil – Rectangular blocks in the entablature representing what had in earlier times been the ends of beams which carried the roof of a temple or temple-like structure.

Diazoma – Horizontal passage separating the rows of seats in a theatre.

Dipteros – Temple surrounded by two rows of columns.

Distyle-in-antis – Temple front with two columns between antae.

Entablature – Superstructure of a temple carried by columns.

Exedra – Rectangular or semicircular open recess for a seat or a statue.

Flutes – The vertical channels of columns.

Gymnasium – The building and name of the educational institution.

Heröon – Small shrine dedicated to a hero or a deified person.

Megaron – The principal hall of a house, originally of the Mycenaean palace.

Odeion – Roofed building for musical performances, rectangular or semi-circular.

Opisthodomos – Porch at the rear of a temple.

Palaestra – Training school; building for physical exercises.

Parodos – Lateral entrance to the theatre between the *cavea* and the stage building on either side.

Peripteros – Temple surrounded by a row of columns.

Peristasis – Row of columns surrounding a temple.

Peristyle – Same as peristasis; also a courtyard surrounded by columns.

Podium – Raised platform carrying a temple or any significant structure.

Portico – Colonnade or a colonnaded porch in front of a building.

Pronaos – Porch in front of a cella.

Propylon – Porch entrance to the temenos.

Proskenion – Raised platform in front of the *skene*: theatre stage.

Prostyle – Temple with a portico of columns in front.

Pseudo-dipteros – Dipteral temple of which the inner row of columns is omitted.

Pteron (wing) – The flank colonnade of a temple.

Skene – The structure in front of which the actors played in a theatre.

Stoa (portico) – Building with its roof supported by one or more rows of columns parallel to the rear wall, in many cases to provide shelter for rows of shops by the agora.

Stylobate – The platform above steps on which the columns of a temple rested.

Temenos – Sacred enclosure containing one or more temples.

Tholos – Circular building with or without a peristasis.

BIBLIOGRAPHY

AINSWORTH, W. P., *Travels and Researches in Asia Minor*, London, 1842

AKURGAL, E., *Ancient Civilizations and Ruins in Turkey*, Istanbul, 1983
—— *The Birth of Greek Art*, London, 1968
—— *Kunst Anatoliens*, Berlin, 1961

ANDERSON, J. G., 'Phrouria', *J.H.S.* XIX, 1899, pp.63, 31

ARUNDELL, F. V. J., *Discoveries in Asia Minor*, London, 1834

BEAN, G. E., *Aegean Turkey*, London, 1966
—— *Journey in Northern Lycia*, London, 1971
—— *Lycian Turkey*, London, 1938
—— *Turkey Beyond the Maeander*, London 1980
—— *Turkey's Southern Shore*, London, 1984
—— and MITFORD, T. B., *Journey in Rough Cilicia*, Vienna, 1965
—— 'Journeys in Rough Cilicia, 1962, 1964 and 1978', *Denkschriften der Österreichischen Akademie der Wissenschaften in Wien*, Bände 85, p. 44
—— 'Sites Old and New in Rough Cilicia', *A.S.* XII, 1962

BEAUFORT, SIR FRANCIS, *Karamania*, London, 1817

BENNDORF, O., and NIEMANN, G., *Das Heroon von Trysa*, Vienna, 1890
—— *Reisen in Lykien*, Vienna, 1884

BENT, J. TH., 'Castabala', *J.H.S.* XI, 1890
—— 'A Journey in Cilicia Tracheia', *J.H.S.* XII, 1891, p. 2171

BEVAN, E.R. *The House of Seleucus*, London, 1902

BIEBER, M., *The History of the Greek and Roman Theatre*, Princeton, 1934

BORCHHARDT, J., 'Das Heroon von Limyra', *AA*, 1970, pp. 353–90
—— 'Myra', *Ist Forsch.* Bd. 30, 1975

BROUGHTON, T. R. S., *Roman Asia Minor*, Baltimore, 1938

BROWN, PETER, *The Making of Late Antiquity*, Cambridge, Mass., 1978
—— *The World of Late Antiquity*, London, 1978

BRYCE, J. R., *The Lycians in Literary and Epigraphic Sources*, Copenhagen, 1987

BUTLER, A. C., *Sardis*, Leiden, 1925

CHANDLER, R., *Travels in Asia Minor*, London, 1764–5

CHOISEUL GOUFFIER, MARIE-GABRIEL, *Voyage pittoresque en Grèce*, Paris, 1782

CLARKE, E. D., and DANIEL, E., *Travels in Russia and Turkey*, London, 1848

COCKRELL, C. R., *Travels in Southern Europe . . .* (1810–17), London, 1903

COHEN, GATZEL M., *The Seleucid Colonies*, Wiesbaden, 1978

COOK, JOHN, *Ionia and the East*, London, 1962

COUPEL, P., and DEMARGNE, P., *Fouilles de Xanthos*, Vol. III, Paris 1969

CRAMER, J. A., *Discoveries in Asia Minor*, London, 1834
—— *Geographical Description of Asia Minor*, Oxford, 1832

DAVIS, EDWIN J., *Anatolica*, London, 1874
—— *Life in Asiatic Turkey*, London, 1879

DE BERNARDI-FERRERO, D., *Teatri classici in Asia Minore*, Milan, 1969

DELORME, JEAN, *Gymnasion*, Paris, 1860

DEMARGNE, P., *Fouilles de Xanthos*, Vol. I, Paris, 1958

VON DIEST, W., *Nysa*, Berlin, 1813

DINSMOOR, W. B., *The Architecture of Ancient Greece*, London, 1975

DUGGAN, ALFRED, *He Died Old: Mithradates, King of Pontus*, London

DUNBABIN, T. J., *The Greeks and their Eastern Neighbours*, London, 1957

EICHLER, F., *Die Reliefen des Heroon Von Trysa*, Vienna, 1950

ERIM, KENAN T., *Aphrodisias, City of Venus Aphrodite*, New York, 1986

FELD-WEBER, OTTO, 'Bericht über eine Reise durch Kilikien', *Istanbuler Mitteilungen* 13–14, 1963
—— 'Tempel und Kirche über der Korykische Grotte in Kilikeien', *Istanbuler Mitteilungen* 17, 1967

FELLOWS, CHARLES, *An Account of Discoveries in Lycia*, London, 1852 (second excursion in Asia Minor, 1840)
—— *Travels and Researches in Asia Minor*, London, 1839

FOX, R. L., *Pagans and Christians*, London, 1986

FRAZER, J. G., *The Golden Bough*, Part IV: *Priestly Kings of Olba*, reprinted in *Adonis*, 1932

FREELY, JOHN, *Turkey*, London, 1979

FUSTEL DE COULANGES, N. D., *La cité antique*, Paris, 1864

GLOTZ, G., *The Greek City*, London, 1929

GOUGH, M., 'Anazarbus', *A.S.*, II, 1952
—— 'Kastabala-Hierapolis', *A.S.* IV, 1954

GREEN, PETER, *Alexander to Actium*, London, 1990

HAMILTON, W. J., *Researches in Asia Minor*, London, 1842

HAMMOND, M., *City-State and World-State*, Cambridge, Mass., 1951

HANFMANN, G. M. A., *Archaeological Exploration of Sardis*, Leiden, 1971

HANSEN, E. V., *The Attalids of Pergamon*, New York, 1971

HARPER, R. P., and BAYBURTLUOGLU, 'Report on Excavations at Comana', *A.S.* XVIII, 1968

HAYNES, SYBIL, *The Land of the Chimaera*, London, 1974

HEBERDEY, R., and WILHELM, A., *Reisen in Kilikien*, Berlin, 1896

HOGARTH, D. G., 'Notes in Phrygia Paroreus and Lycia', *J.H.S.* XI, 1890, p. 151

—— *Accidents of an Antiquary's Life*, London, 1910

HOPKINS, K., 'Economic Growth and Towns', in Abrams and Wrigley (eds.), London, 1978

HORNBLOWER, S., *Mausolos*, Oxford, 1982

HOUWINK TEN CATE, CH. H. J., *The Luwian Population Groups of Lycia and Cilicia Aspera during the Hellenistic Period*, Leiden, 1961

JONES, A. H. M., *The Cities of the Eastern Roman Provinces*, Oxford, 1950

—— *The Decline of the Ancient World*, London, 1966

—— *The Greek City*, Oxford, 1940

—— *The Later Roman Empire*, Oxford, 1964

JONES, N.F., *Public Organisation in Ancient Greece*, Ch. 7 'Asia Minor', 1987

JOUGUET, PIERRE, *Macedonian Imperialism and the Hellenization of the East*, London, 1928

JÜTHNER, J., *Denkmäler aus Lycaonien, Pamphylien und Isaurien*, Prague, 1935

KEIL, J. K., 'Bericht über eine Reise in Lydien', *Denkschriften der Österreichisches Akademie der Wissenschaften in Wien*, Bände 53, 54

—— and WILHELM, A., 'Denkmäler aus Rauhen Kilikien, 1928', in *Monumenta Asiae Minoris Antiqua* III, p. 44, Manchester, 1936

KINNEIR, J. M., *Journey Through Asia Minor*, London, 1818

KRISCHEN, FRITZ, *Die Befestigungen von Herakleia an Latmos, Milet II*, Berlin, 1912

—— *Die Griechische Stadt*, Berlin, 1938

LABORDE, L. E., *Voyage en Asie Mineure*, Paris, 1835

LAMBRECHTS, PIERRE, *Les Fouilles de Pessinus*, De Brug, 1967, 1969

LANCKORONSKI, GRAF K., *Städte Pamphyliens und Pisidiens*, Vienna, 1890

LANGLOIS, V., *Voyage en Cilicie*, Paris, 1861

LAWRENCE, A. W., *Greek Architecture*, London, 1957

LEAKE, W. M., *Journal of a Tour in Asia Minor*, London, 1824

LEVICK, BARBARA, *Roman Colonies in Asia Minor*, Oxford, 1967

LEWIS, NAPHTALI, *Greeks in Ptolemaic Egypt*, Oxford, 1986

LITTELTON, M., *Baroque Architecture in Classical Antiquity*, London

LLOYD, S. *A Traveller's History of Anatolia*, London, 1989

LUCAS, PAUL, *Voyage en Grèce . . .* , Paris, 1712

VON LUSCHAN, F., *Reisen in Sudwest Kleinasien*, Vienna, 1889

MACDONALD, W. L., *The Architecture of the Roman Empire* Vols 1 & 2, New Haven, 1987

MACKAY, T. S., *Olba in Rough Cilicia*, Dissertation, Bryn Mawr, 1968

MAGIE, D., *The Roman Rule in Asia Minor*, Princeton, 1950

MAYER, L., *Views of the Ottoman Empire*, London, 1803

MCGING, *The Foreign Policy of Mithradates VI Eupator, King of Pontus*, Leiden, 1986

METZGER, H., *Fouilles de Xanthos* Vol. II, Paris, 1963

MEYER, ERNST, *Die Grenzen den Hellenistischen Staaten in Kleinasien*, Zurich, 1925

MURRAY, JOHN, *Handbook for Travellers in Asia Minor*, London, 1895

NEPPI-MODONA, A., *Edifici teatrali greci e romani*, Florence, 1961

ORMEROD, H. A., *Piracy in the Ancient World*, London, 1924

—— 'Campaigns of Servilius Isauricus against the pirates', *J.R.S.* 12, 1922, p. 35

OWENS, E.J., *The City in the Greek and Roman World*, London, 1991

PATON, R., and MYRES, J. L., 'Alinda', *J.H.S.* XVI, 1896, p. 23

PEDLEY, JOHN G., *Sardis*, Norman, Okla., 1968

PERROT, G., *Exploration archéologique de la Galatie etc. et de la Bithynie*, Paris, 1962

—— *Souvenirs d'un voyage en Asie Mineure*, Paris, 1864

PETERSEN, E., and VON LUSCHAN, F., *Reisen in Sudwest Kleinasien*, Vienna, 1888

POCOCKE, RICHARD, *A Description of the East*, London, 1745

PRICE, S., *Rituals and Power*, Cambridge, 1984

Princeton Encyclopedia of Classical Sites, Princeton, 1976

PUCHSTEIN, O., and HUMANN, K., *Reisen in Nord Syrien und Kleinasien*, Berlin, 1890

RADET, GEORGES, *La Lydie*, Paris, 1891

RAMSAY, W. M., 'Antiquities of Southern Phrygia', *A.J.A.*, 1887

—— *The Cities and Bishoprics of Phrygia*, Oxford, 1895

—— *Historical Geography of Asia Minor*, Oxford, 1890

—— 'Pisidia', *J.R.S.*, 1926

REINACH, TH., *Mithridate Eupator, roi de Pont*, Paris, 1890

—— *Trois Royaumes de l'Asie Mineure*, Paris, 1888

ROBERT, L., *A travers l'Asie Mineure*, Paris, 1980

—— *La Carie*, Paris, 1954

—— *Les gladiateurs dans l'orient grec*, Paris, 1940

—— *Villes dans l'Asie Mineure*, Paris, 1935

ROBERTS, D. S., *Greek and Roman Architecture*, Cambridge, 1945

ROSTOVTZOFF, M., *Social and Economic History of the Hellenistic Age*, Oxford, 1941

—— *Social and Economic History of the Roman Empire*, Oxford, 1957

ROTT, HANS, *Kleinasiatische Denkmäler*, Leipzig, 1902–8

RUGE, W., and BITTEL, K., 'Paphlagonia', *R.E.* XVIII, 1918, pp. 2486–550

SARTIAUX, F., *Villes mortes d'Asie Mineure*, Paris, 1911

SCHAFFER, F. X., 'Olba', *J.O.A.I.* V, 1902, p. 106

SCHÖNBORN, A., *Beiträge zur Geographie Kleinasiens*, Posen, 1849

SCHULTZE, V., *Alte Städte und Landschaften Kleinasiens*, Leipzig, 1913–30

SEAR, FRANK, *Roman Architecture*, London, 1983

SEWELL, BRIAN, *South from Ephesus*, London, 1988

SPRATT, T. A. B., and FORBES, E., *Travels in Lycia*, London, 1847

STARK, FREYA, *Alexander's Path*, London, 1958

—— *The Lycian Shores*, London, 1956

STERRETT, J. R. S., *The Wolfe Expedition in Asia Minor*, Boston, 1884–5

STONEMAN, RICHARD, *Across the Hellespont*, London, 1987

TARN, W. W., and GRIFFITH, G. T., *Hellenistic Civilization*, London, 1952

TEXIER, CHARLES, *Description de l'Asie Mineure*, Paris, 1849

TRÉMAUX, PIERRE, *Exploration archéologique de l'Asie Mineure*, Paris, 1863

TREUBER, O., *Geschichte der Lykier*, Stuttgart, 1887

TSCHERIKOVER, V., *Die hellenistische Städtegründungen . . .*, Berlin, 1927

VERMEULE, C. C., *Roman Imperial Art*, Harvard, 1968

VEYNE, P., *Le pain et le cirque*, Paris, 1976

VITUCCI, G., *Il regno di Bitinia*, Rome, 1953

WALBANK, F. W., *The Hellenistic World*, London, 1981

WESTHOLM, A., *Labraunda: The Architecture of the Hieron*, Lund, 1955

WIEGAND, TH., *Milet, Latmos III*, Berlin, 1925

WILAMOWITZ-MOELLENDORF, *Apollo*, Oxford, 1908

INDEX